Portland Community College

COACH AND COUCH

COACH AND COUCH

The psychology of making
better leaders

Manfred F. R. Kets de Vries
Konstantin Korotov
Elizabeth Florent-Treacy

First published 2007 by
PALGRAVE MACMILLAN
Houndmills, Basingstoke, Hampshire RG21 6XS and
175 Fifth Avenue, New York, N.Y. 10010
Companies and representatives throughout the world

PALGRAVE MACMILLAN is the global academic imprint of the Palgrave Macmillan division of St. Martin's Press, LLC and of Palgrave Macmillan Ltd. Macmillan® is a registered trademark in the United States, United Kingdom and other countries. Palgrave is a registered trademark in the European Union and other countries.

ISBN-13: 978–0–230–50638–1
ISBN-10: 0–230–50638–0

This book is printed on paper suitable for recycling and made from fully managed and sustained forest sources. Logging, pulping and manufacturing processes are expected to conform to the environmental regulations of the country of origin.

A catalogue record for this book is available from the British Library.

A catalog record for this book is available from the Library of Congress.

10   9   8   7   6   5   4
16   15   14   13   12   11   10   09   08

Printed and bound in Great Britain by
Cromwell Press Ltd, Trowbridge, Wiltshire

To Abraham Zaleznik,

who showed us the way

CONTENTS

CONTENTS

CONTENTS

CONTENTS

CONTENTS

LIST OF FIGURES AND TABLES

Figures

LIST OF FIGURES AND TABLES

Tables

LIST OF CONTRIBUTORS

EDITORS

Manfred F. R. Kets de Vries holds the Raoul de Vitry d'Avaucourt Chair of Leadership Development at INSEAD, France & Singapore. He is also the Director of INSEAD's Global Leadership Center. In addition, he is program director of INSEAD's top management seminar, The Challenge of Leadership: Creating Reflective Leaders, the program Consulting and Coaching for Change (CCC), and Leadership for Creativity. He is a graduate in economics (Econ. Drs.) from the University of Amsterdam), in management from the Harvard Business School (ITP, MBA, and DBA degrees), and in psychoanalysis (member of the Canadian Psychoanalytic Society and the International Psychoanalytic Association).

He has also held professorships at McGill University; the Ecole des Hautes Etudes Commerciales, Montreal; and the Harvard Business School, and he has lectured at management institutions around the world. He is a founding member of the International Society for the Psychoanalytic Study of Organizations. *The Financial Times*, *Le Capital*, *Wirtschaftswoche*, and *The Economist* have rated Manfred Kets de Vries among the world's top 50 thinkers on management and among the world's most influential people in human resource management.

Kets de Vries is the author, co-author, or editor of more than 24 books and over 250 scientific papers as chapters in books and as articles. He has also written approximately 100 case studies, including 8 that received the Best Case of the Year award from the ECCH. His books and articles have been translated into more than 25 languages. He is a member of 17 editorial boards and is one of the few Europeans elected a Fellow of the Academy of Management. He was also the first non-American recipient of the International Leadership Award for "his contributions to the classroom and the board room."

Kets de Vries is a consultant on organizational design/transformation and strategic human resource management to leading U.S., Canadian, European, African, Australian and Asian companies. As an educator and consultant he has worked in more than forty countries.

He was the first fly fisherman in Outer Mongolia and is a member of New York's Explorers Club. In his spare time he can be found in the rainforests or savannas of Central Africa, the Siberian taiga, Arnhemland, the Pamir mountains, or within the Arctic circle.

Konstantin Korotov is an Assistant Professor of Leadership and Organizational Behavior at ESMT (Berlin, Germany) and also an Executive Coach and Research Fellow with the INSEAD Global Leadership Centre, France. In addition to his academic work, he has over 12 years of practical international leadership development and coaching experience. He has designed and delivered executive programs for, among many others, Ernst & Young, Deutsche Bank, Johnson & Johnson, Deutsche Telekom, Deloitte, BAT, Mittal Steel, Elster Group, and KPMG, as well as taught executive- and MBA-level courses at ESMT and INSEAD. Konstantin Korotov conducts research and writes on leadership, identity dynamics, and career entrepreneurship.

Elizabeth Florent-Treacy is Research Project Manager at INSEAD. She has conducted research on global leadership; corporate culture in European and global organizations; American, French, and Russian business practices; family business issues; entrepreneurial leadership; cross-cultural management; women and global leadership; expatriate executives and families; and the psychodynamics of leadership. She has coauthored three books: The New Global Leaders (1999); *The New Russian Business Leaders* (2004); and *Family Business on the Couch* (2007). She has also written many case studies, six of which have won top case-writing awards.

CONTRIBUTING AUTHORS

Randel S. Carlock is INSEAD's first Berghmans Lhoist Chaired Professor in Entrepreneurial Leadership, and founding Director of the Wendel International Centre for Family Enterprises and the Family Enterprise Challenge Executive Program (INSEAD, France and Singapore). He has an MA in education and training, an MBA in strategic management (1983), and a PhD (1991) in organization development. He has also completed a postgraduate certification in family therapy at the Institute of Psychiatry, King's College, University of London (1998), and a certificate in psychodynamic counseling at Birkbeck College, University of London (1999). He was awarded a Certificate in Family Business Advising with Fellow Status in 2001 by the Family Firm Institute, Boston, MA (USA). Carlock has spent 25 years in business, serving first as an executive with Dayton-Hudson (now Target Corporation) and then as a CEO and chairman of a NASDAQ-listed corporation he founded. He serves as a consultant and adviser to several of the world's largest family businesses.

Theo Compernolle holds the Suez Chair on Leadership and Personal Development at the Solvay Business School of the Université Libre de Bruxelles, and is a medical doctor, neuropsychiatrist, and psychotherapist. He is an expert on individual and corporate stress management and the emotional and relational aspects of leadership. He consults, trains, teaches, and coaches executives and entrepreneurs in companies and business schools. He has published several books (three best sellers) and more than a hundred articles. He was a manager himself, as the director of inpatient and outpatient departments. He is associated with IGLC as a visiting professor and coach.

Elisabet Engellau is an Adjunct Clinical Professor of Management at INSEAD. As Program Director at IGLC, she focuses on leadership development and coaching in executive programs. In addition, she regularly serves as visiting faculty at the Stockholm School of Economics. She is a graduate of INSEAD's Consulting and Coaching for Change program (CCC). She has been an affiliate professor at the Faculty of Management, McGill University, and a teaching fellow at Harvard University and Concordia University, Montreal. She has also produced and directed a number of video films for management education and has recently been involved in developing two new feedback instruments. She is the coauthor of "'Doing an Alexander': Lessons on Leadership by a Master Conqueror" (2004) and contributing author to "Conversations in Leadership: South African Perspectives" (2004). She is a member of the Research Group on Leadership Practices, the International Society for the Psychoanalytic Study of Organizations (ISPSO), the American Psychological Association (APA), and Institut de Psychoanalyse & Management (IPM).

Engellau also works as an independent consultant, specializing in one-on-one executive coaching, leadership development, cross-cultural management, and team building. Her professional activities are focused on the dynamics of corporate transformation and change. In her work with individuals and teams in major multinational organizations she combines her long-term interest in creativity with a clinical approach to human resource management.

Ann Houston Kelley is a Managing Partner with Nomadic Life Management Consultants. She is American and Dutch, based in the Netherlands. During her stay in Europe for more than 17 years, she has developed a successful European consulting firm with a Dutch business partner. Nomadic Life assists international organizations in using differences to "get the job done." Her key area of expertise lies in coaching senior executives and their globally dispersed teams on effectiveness and change management issues. She is trained as an economist and family systems psychotherapist, and is a senior associate of the Centre for Creative Leadership, and a coach with IGLC. She is a member of the Worldwide Association of Business Coaches, the International Society for the Psychoanalytic Study of Organizations, the Society for Intercultural Education, Training and Research, and the American Psychological Association.

Roger Lehman is an Adjunct Clinical Professor of Management at INSEAD, where he designs and teaches in both open and company-specific programs, providing a focus on executive leadership, personal and professional development, and high-performance teams. As codesigner and Program Director of INSEAD's CCC program, he is deeply involved in supporting leadership transformational processes.

Dr. Lehman's clinical, teaching, and organizational consulting career spans over 25 years, during which time he has held a variety of staff and leadership positions in both public and private institutions. As managing partner of "insite GmbH" in Frankfurt, Germany (an organizational consulting company specializing in leadership development, executive coaching, change management, and post-merger integration) he offers consultancy services to a wide variety of multinational corporations in the USA, Europe, Africa, and Asia.

He is a licensed clinical psychologist (Indiana, USA) and a psychoanalyst with membership in the American Psychological Association, the German Psychoanalytic Society, and the International Psychoanalytic Association.

Jean-Claude Noel is an Adjunct Clinical Professor and Program Director at IGLC. He holds a MSc and Diploma from HEC-INSEAD's CCC program (2002). He also has a private Executive Coaching and Leadership Development practice in New York, Atrium Consulting LLC (affiliated to Executive Coaching Network Inc. in California), and is an operating executive with Global Leisure Partners in London. He has a global business background at the board level in various industries, including Christie's as Group Chief Operating Officer; Hilton International with responsibility for Western Europe and Africa based in Paris; and the Americas based in New York. He is also on the management board of TNT Express Worldwide heading the Americas, Asia/Pacific, Middle East, and Africa. He is a French-born American citizen living in New York since 1991.

Anton Obholzer is, by training, a medical doctor, psychiatrist, psychoanalyst, and group and organizational consultant. He was Director of the Tavistock Centre, London, from 1985 to 2002. He is currently a visiting professor at the Universities of Vienna, Graz, and Innsbruck, and a senior faculty member at the INSEAD Global Leadership Centre (IGLC).

Over his career he has increasingly moved into the application of psychological understanding in the management and leadership of organizations. His consultancy experience covers a wide range of commercial, banking, and public sector organizations. The main emphasis of his work and publications is on "under the surface" unconscious factors causing resistance to change. He has worked with chief executives and senior management as a mentor, coach, and organizational consultant in projects in the United Kingdom, Scandinavia, Germany, Austria, France, Italy, Spain, and South Africa.

Stanislav Shekshnia is an Affiliate Professor of Entrepreneurship and Family Enterprise at INSEAD. Dr. Shekshnia spent 10 years as a business executive and entrepreneur in France, USA, Russia and Central Europe. He has a master's (in Economics) and PhD from Moscow State University and an MBA from Northeastern University in Boston. During 1991–2002 Shekshnia held positions of Director of Human Resources, Central and Eastern Europe, for Otis Elevator; President and CEO, Millicom International Cellular, Russia, and CIS; Chief Operating Officer of VimpelCom; and CEO of Alfa-Telecom. He served as chairman of VimpelCom-R and board member of a number of Russian companies.

In 2002 Shekshnia cofounded Zest Leadership international consultancy. With Zest Leadership he concentrates on leadership, leadership development, organizational development, and intercultural management. Dr. Shekshnia is the author, coauthor, or editor of five books. He has published book chapters, articles, executive commentaries, interviews, and case studies on entrepreneurship, leadership, people management, intercultural management, and business and management in Russia.

Erik van de Loo is an Adjunct Clinical Professor of Management at INSEAD, where he is Program Co-Director of the CCC program. He is a partner and cofounder of Phyleon, Centre for Leadership and Change in The Hague, the Netherlands. Phyleon specializes in interrelated change processes on individual, group, and organizational levels.

Dr. van de Loo is a graduate in clinical psychology (cum laude) from the Catholic University, Nijmegen. He obtained a doctoral degree in social sciences from Leiden University in 1987 and holds a master's degree in Work and Organization in Occupational Health from SIOO (1997). He is a member of the

International Psychoanalytical Association and the Dutch Society of Psychoanalysis, and has a private psychoanalytic practice. He is a member of the International Society for Psychoanalytic Study of Organizations and cofounder and program director of European Psychodynamic Organizational Consulting (EPOC), a two-year training program to bridge the world of psychoanalysis and organizational consulting.

Martine Van den Poel is an Executive Coach and Program Director at IGLC, where, since 2004, she has developed programs and coached for leadership development in various INSEAD open-enrollment and company-specific programs. She is also a graduate of INSEAD's CCC program. Prior to joining IGLC, she held the positions of Associate Dean for External Relations and Director of Executive Education, managing INSEAD's portfolio of public and customized programs for over 5000 executives per year. From 1992 to 1995, she was Director of Company Specific Programs.

Cornelie van Wees was unitll recently the Director of Group Communications & Brand Management at Eureko/Achmea, the largest insurance and pension company in the Netherlands and mother company of Interpolis. At Interpolis she worked to position Interpolis as a leading brand in the Dutch market ("Advertiser of the Year 2004"), with brand campaigns, PR, and internal branding. Her main interest and focus has been to face the challenge of combining leadership with organizational and personal development to build a corporate identity and shared culture. Van Wees graduated from law school at the Erasmus University, Rotterdam. In 2004 she completed the year-long INSEAD CCC program (cum laude).

Pierre Vrignaud is a Professor of Work and Vocational Psychology at the University of Paris 10. His main topics of interest are differential psychology and psychometrics. He is the author of several papers on these topics as well as questionnaires and software. He is the representative of the Société Française de Psychologie to the International Test Commission and provides expertise in developing assessment surveys of adults' skills for French Ministries (Work and Education) and for international organizations (OECD, UNESCO). He is a research faculty member of IGLC and directs the psychometric design and testing of IGLC 360° survey instruments. He has published several papers with Manfred Kets de Vries about the validation of the questionnaires constructed and used at IGLC.

Graham Ward is the founder of Amandla AB and a Program Director at IGLC; he specializes in coaching executives at board level and managing change programs in London's financial centre. He spent 22 years in finance, working for Goldman Sachs. In 2000 he spearheaded an initiative to introduce a coaching and development office internally at Goldman. This effort culminated in the remit spreading over three continents and deepened to include diversity, mentoring, recruitment, and succession planning up to senior management level.

Ward received his MSc and Diploma in Consulting and Coaching for Change, which focuses on the psychodynamics within organizations, from HEC-INSEAD's CCC program in 2002. In 1994 he received a Diploma in Investment Management from London Business School. He has undertaken individual training at the Tavistock Centre in London from a specialist in group dynamics and is coaches regularly in a number of executive programs. He has also worked as visiting faculty at ESMT (European School of Management and Technology) in Berlin.

Abraham Zaleznik is the Konosuke Matsushita Professor of Leadership, Emeritus, at the Harvard Business School. In recognition of his 43 years on the Faculty, the Harvard Business School Alumni Association awarded him the Distinguished Service Award in 1996.

In 1971, Professor Zaleznik received certification for the practice of psychoanalysis from the American Psychoanalytic Association. His objective in undertaking psychoanalytic training was to prepare himself for specialized research and teaching in the psychodynamics of leadership and group psychology. During his career at the Harvard Business School, he authored or coauthored 14 books and numerous articles. His *Harvard Business Review* article entitled "Managers and Leaders: Are They Different?" received the McKinsey Award for the best Harvard Business Review article in 1977 and was republished as a classic in 1992. Earlier and later articles received the same recognition. He has published articles in academic journals such as *Behavioral Science* and *Psychiatry,* as well as in business journals such as the *Harvard Business Review.*

Extending his clinical practice of psychoanalysis, Professor Zaleznik has engaged in consulting work on organizational planning, succession, and in the resolution of conflict in organizations.

PREFACE

There is no doubt about it: executive coaching has become *the* business buzzword of the new century. In an increasingly stressful environment, across all industries and at all organizational levels, executives are turning to coaches for support, advice, and feedback. Executive coaching is discussed in management literature, and world-renowned business schools include coaching in their leadership development programs. Human resources and other development professionals are seeing the advantages of working with coaches to help good executives become excellent ones. The supply of coaches is growing to meet the demand; in October 2006, a casual Internet search turned up 670,000 websites using the term "executive coach." To date, executive coaching is still something of a Wild West with no restrictions, other than common sense, on the *who* and the *how*, a point we will return to later in the introduction.

What is the real reason behind this staggering interest in executive coaching, aside from its trendy cachet? A major contributing factor is the pace of change in our global world. There is an ever-increasing pressure on executives to transform their way of thinking to accommodate present-day realities. Competencies that were once highly effective quickly become outdated. There is a relentless pressure for bottom-line results. Young, results-hungry executives are to be found in offices everywhere, particularly in areas of the world–China, India, Russia–which have never before been considered sources of great management talent. Organizations themselves are undergoing metamorphosis; even companies with hundreds of thousands of employees are tending toward flatter, networking structures; boundary-less teamwork; and temporary, or virtual, partnerships.

At the same time, legal and corporate governance responsibilities have been growing. After recent corporate scandals throughout the world, any board or executive misstep triggers a reaction from legal advisors, shareholders, journalists, and the general public. The result is often serious financial consequences and damaged reputations for the organization, executives, and shareholders.

Diversity is another challenge faced by modern organizations. While many have become more sensitive to local minorities in the workforce – involving issues such as gender, disability, sexual orientation, and so on – we now know that many other diversity factors also impact the behavior of people in organizations, including national culture differences, religious or spiritual orientation, unresolved psychological consequences of international conflicts, variety in educational systems, differences in employees' socio-economic and political background, and various expectations in terms of the socialization of people into the world of work. This diversity occurs at all levels, from the shop floor or front line to the very top executive level. For a leader to reframe these diversities as strengths, he or she must have a high level of openness, attention to detail, readiness to experiment, sensitivity, assertiveness, and other competencies.

In sum, it is *human capital* that differentiates good organizations from excellent ones. The "three Cs" organizational structure of the past – command, control, and compartmentalization – is being superseded by a new focus on "three Is" – innovation, interaction, and information – at all levels. The top performers in these organizations want challenges, excitement, continuous learning opportunities, and excellent pay and benefits. They expect to be listened to, and to be treated as multifaceted human beings. All these factors put much higher demands on the emotional intelligence of executives, necessitating an ever-greater emphasis on effective interpersonal relationships.

There are multiple pressures on executives who reach the top. Many star performers are promoted to senior executive positions at a young age, with responsibilities often incommensurate with their level of life experience. Becoming a member of an executive board, at any age, is a highly stressful move for many people. Adjusting to this type of responsibility may generate strong feelings of insecurity and loneliness. Relatively few top executives will be able to turn to trusted work colleagues, or friends and family members, who can help them resolve these issues.

Facing increasing pressure from all sides, high achievement-oriented executives are eager to acquire competencies, skills, and experiences that will help them deal with present-day realities. They have come to realize that, without continuous learning and development, they risk being left behind. They need a chance to reinvent and revitalize themselves to prevent burn out. Practically speaking, though, it is no simple matter for an executive–with limited time and energy for the task–to explore the multitude of learning opportunities available and choose the right one.

All this argues for a targeted intervention that goes far beyond providing tools and techniques. People need to be able to take the time to reflect on their own career and life trajectories, how their organization or team functions, and explore new possibilities in all these arenas.

THE INSEAD GLOBAL LEADERSHIP CENTRE

The INSEAD Global Leadership Centre (IGLC), located in Fontainebleau (France) and Singapore, was set up by Professor Manfred Kets de Vries and his associates to help people in organizations face the challenges outlined above. We saw a need for research-based global executive leadership development courses with a practical, applied orientation. Our goal is to help executives create results-driven, sustainable organizations by putting people first.

IGLC brings together faculty and thought leaders on leadership from around the world. It continually researches and observes leadership practices in public and private organizations in many different countries. IGLC research focuses on exemplary leadership in high performance organizations, dysfunctional leadership practices, and leadership development approaches. By sharing research methodologies, and describing intervention and change techniques used in leadership development and the education of executive coaches, we hope to contribute to a better understanding of how people become extraordinary leaders, and equip practitioners with ideas and tools for developing executive coaches and working with business leaders.

In our work at IGLC, we have seen that executive coaching can be one of the most powerful strategic and tactical weapons in the executive development repertoire. In our executive programs, we minimize traditional methods of delivering one-size-fits-all content from a lectern. Participants use their own organizational challenges and leadership dilemmas as "live" case studies, and work in groups with IGLC faculty, coaches, and fellow executive education participants to explore issues and support one another during the implementation of real-life organizational change efforts.

KNOWLEDGE BASE AND DATA COLLECTION

Every year, IGLC faculty, researchers, and coaches work with thousands of executives in programs and leadership modules at INSEAD. Faculty from other innovative business schools with a strong emphasis on leadership development around the world, as well as the participating executives themselves, contribute to the development of our knowledge base on leadership development—an on-going process through which IGLC programs and tools are continually improved.

In putting this book together, we have involved various IGLC associates: academics who conduct research, teach, and consult; leadership development coaches; change consultants; and executives who adopted IGLC methods. We also included people who have experienced IGLC methods in the process of their developmental journeys; they have dug into their research and practice notes, analyzed data from inquiry projects, and shared their personal experiences in individual essays.

INTENDED AUDIENCE

The purpose of this book is to share IGLC research findings and practical methods with interested academics, executives, leadership coaches, and consultants working with organizational leaders who are faced with the daily task of setting and meeting their own and their followers' expectations for achievement.

We have written this book for executives concerned with maximizing their own potential as leaders of organizations; leaders in charge of succession planning in their companies; human resource management and training professionals interested in effective and efficient leadership development efforts; leadership development consultants and executive coaches; families who own or control businesses and the advisors who work with them; faculty who teach leadership courses; academics doing research on leadership topics; and MBA students and graduate students in the fields of organizational behavior, human resource management, organization development, entrepreneurship, and strategy.

BOOK OUTLINE

Introduction: A psychodynamic approach to leadership development

Manfred F. R. Kets de Vries, Konstantin Korotov, and Elizabeth Florent-Treacy

The introductory chapter outlines the leadership development challenges faced by human resources and development professionals in helping executives in the journey of personal and organizational change. The authors also provide an overview of their data collection methods and introduce the IGLC approaches, methods and, instruments described in subsequent chapters.

PART ONE: CONCEPTUAL FRAMEWORKS

Chapter 1   The clinical paradigm: A primer for personal change

Manfred F. R. Kets de Vries and Konstantin Korotov

The goal of this chapter is to introduce the four premises of the clinical paradigm. The themes presented in this chapter will appear again in greater depth in subsequent chapters both in theoretical discussions and in practical applications of some of the ideas and methods described.

Chapter 2 Group dynamics: What coaches and consultants need to watch out for

Anton Obholzer

Anton Obholzer provides readers with the necessary understanding of psychodynamic patterns in group processes. Readers will learn how and why people in groups act in functional and dysfunctional ways. The findings will be helpful to all managers working with and/or in teams, as well as for executive coaches and leadership development specialists using team settings.

Chapter 3 Developmental coaching from a systems point of view

Theo Compernolle

The functioning of an executive team cannot be predicted only on the basis of information and hypotheses about the individual executives; the whole is not the sum of the parts, it is something totally different. The consequence for coaches is that it is impossible to know how an executive team functions based only on information about and from individual executives. In this chapter, the author explores qualities of the whole system by taking into account the relationships between the interacting units.

Chapter 4 Leadership coaching in family businesses

Randel S. Carlock

This chapter, written by a former CEO and current professor of Family Enterprise and Entrepreneurship at INSEAD who also has training as a family therapist, focuses on psychological processes in family firms and coaching in family-firm environments. Carlock provides insights into opportunities and challenges in these complex organizations, which will be of particular interest to families who own or control a business, and family business service providers and advisors.

Chapter 5   Goodbye, sweet Narcissus: Using 360° feedback for self-reflection

Manfred F. R. Kets de Vries, Elizabeth Florent-Treacy, Pierre Vrignaud, and Konstantin Korotov

This chapter describes the IGLC 360° instruments used as a basis for discussion in the leadership development process. Coaches and HR practitioners, as well as executive teaching faculty and consultants, will learn about the methodologies used to develop survey instruments. The chapter includes a general discussion on the purpose, use, and misuse of survey instruments in coaching and leadership development.

PART TWO: COACHING PROGRAM DESIGN

Chapter 6   Executive development and leadership coaching

Martine Van den Poel

The author, a program director at INSEAD, shares her experience as a director of executive education programs. She talks about building coaching elements into executive education. Faculty, consultants, coaches, and HR people will find numerous examples of how to make programs with coaching elements really work for participants and organizations.

Chapter 7   Executive education from the participant's point of view

Konstantin Korotov

This is a chapter on research and practice in identity laboratories – special environments in which participants can stage identity "experiments" to help them consider new directions for their lives; get feedback from mentors and fellow experimenters; and develop transitional objects or tools that allow them to make a bridge between experimentation in the "laboratory" and the real world. The chapter discusses the use of identity laboratories in education, leadership development, and in coaching situations.

Chapter 8   Transformational executive programs: An owner's manual

Manfred F. R. Kets de Vries and Konstantin Korotov

Specific needs of executives have to be taken into consideration in the design and delivery of executive development programs and coaching interventions. This chapter presents a conceptual framework to guide program directors, teachers, facilitators, and coaches in creating courses that allow participants to work on personal and professional issues while simultaneously helping other executives learn from their own experience.

PART THREE: BECOMING A COACH

Chapter 9   From the boardroom to the classroom: A personal journey

Jean-Claude Noel

Jean-Claude Noel, a former high-level executive at Christie's and now a program director and professor at INSEAD, shares his journey from executive at Christie's to executive coach for Christie's top management. His story will interest managers who want to improve their own leadership skills and/or change occupations, and inform people studying identity and identity dynamics. It will also be of use to career coaches and counselors seeking to better understand professional identity changes in successful people.

Chapter 10   Coaching within and without

Graham Ward

Graham Ward, a program director at INSEAD, shares his personal experience of building a coaching practice. He tells the story of how he switched from investment banking to coaching, with detours into experimenting with internal coaching practices in a well-known global financial institution. This chapter will give insights into the challenges of building internal and external coaching practices.

Chapter 11   Coaching executives across cultures

Ann Houston Kelley

The ability to coach effectively across cultures is a key competency for today's international executives. These executives must understand the cultural complexities of the global marketplace and steer their organizations in a rapidly changing world. Through case examples, the author illustrates that doing this well is both a science and an art.

PART FOUR: THE PROCESS OF COACHING

Chapter 12   The art of listening

Erik van de Loo

Erik van de Loo shares his research and practice on the role of listening and talking in helping people identify their strengths and weaknesses. He also shares his techniques for evaluating the personality traits that contribute to leadership success or failure. The chapter presents both concepts and techniques for constructive dialogue in leadership development.

Chapter 13   The dos and don'ts of coaching: Key lessons I learned as an executive coach

Elisabet Engellau

Elisabet Engellau, an INSEAD adjunct professor, IGLC program director, and executive coach, shares her professional insights with aspiring leadership coaches. Lessons for coaches and coaches in training are drawn from her many years of experience working with individual executives, teams of young potential top executives, and existing executive teams and company boards. This chapter will also be helpful for "consumers" of coaching services as a guide for structuring their relationships with an executive coach.

Chapter 14   Reflections on teaching leaders to coach: Using the self as a tool in developing others

Roger Lehman and Konstantin Korotov

In this chapter, the authors discuss how executives and professionals become clinically oriented coaches. The authors' discussion of designing and running programs for coaches-in-training and coaching-oriented executives will be of value to people looking to create an in-depth coaching experience.

PART FIVE: COACHING IN ORGANIZATIONS

Chapter 15   Coaching: A chairman's point of view

Stanislav Shekshnia

The author, an adjunct professor at INSEAD and an IGLC program director, discusses the challenges of coaching board members. He describes the journey he made with the members of the board of a Russian power and coal generation company as they worked together to become more effective in their roles.

Chapter 16   Cracking the code of change: How one organization transformed itself through the transformation of its people

Cornelie Van Wees

The author talks about her role of "leader as coach" and her personal experience of learning to use coaching as a leadership style. Her contribution will also explore the effects of introducing a coaching style in the workplace.

Chapter 17   The case for not interpreting unconscious mental life in consulting to organizations

Abraham Zaleznik

In this chapter, Abraham Zaleznik describes the boundaries between psychoanalysis and coaching. He argues that the main use of psychoanalytic psychology in consulting work is for observation and understanding on the part of the consultant who as an advisor has to be extremely discrete in making unconscious processes conscious.

Conclusion: Toward authentizotic organizations

Manfred F. R. Kets de Vries

This concluding chapter takes us beyond the "leader on the couch" to apply lessons learned. We discuss humane and effective leaders who make their organizations *authentizotic* places to work, where people feel at their best and are prepared to make an extraordinary contribution. It explores ways to create effective, humane, and sustainable organizations.

ACKNOWLEDGMENTS

This book owes its existence to generous contributions from a vast number of people. First and foremost are the executives in our executive education programs, research studies, and consulting work who with honesty and perspicacity have examined their own "inner theater" and shared their insights with us and one another. Through their feedback, they have made it possible for us to develop new and better programs and tools. We particularly appreciate those who have kept in touch over the years, telling the stories of their progress. *Sine qua non*–without them, nothing.

The chapter authors are more than fellow writers, they are our respected colleagues at IGLC, each of whom brings expertise, and more importantly wisdom, to the work they do. We were very pleased that they accepted our invitations to contribute to this book, despite the imposition on their already full lives.

We gratefully acknowledge the institutional support of the INSEAD Faculty Affairs department. Landis Gabel, Alison James, Isabel Assureira, and Veronique Pereira are always kind, patient, and ready to help us work out a way to make our ideas possible. We are also indebted to Anil Gaba and the INSEAD Research and Development Committee who are always generous with funds.

Our work is nurtured and grounded by the IGLC administrative team. In alphabetical order, we warmly thank Silke Bequet, Fabienne Chemin, Sheila Loxham, Nadine Theallier, as well as IGLC Executive Director Agata Halczewska-Figuet. We are equally grateful for the responsiveness and technical competence of our IT partners at INSEAD, in particular Vasanth Raju and Laurent Viel.

ACKNOWLEDGMENTS

We would like to acknowledge the tremendous job accomplished by our editors at the Cambridge Editorial Partnership. Kate Kirk, Sally Simmons, and Rosalind Horton grasped a rough work with over a dozen different writing styles and wrestled it into shape. We have also benefited greatly from the patient, watchful eye of Stephen Rutt at Palgrave.

Last but not least, the contributors to this book would like to acknowledge the leadership of Manfred Kets de Vries. Guided by his original vision, be it in executive programs; research endeavors; interactions with business practitioners, coaches and educators; consulting activities; or within the IGLC team, we are surrounded by motivated, autonomous people who are excited about what they do, together creating a sense of community that makes our working lives more fun and more meaningful.

MANFRED F. R. KETS DE VRIES,
KONSTANTIN KOROTOV, AND
ELIZABETH FLORENT-TREACY

Fontainebleau, March 2007

INTRODUCTION: A PSYCHODYNAMIC APPROACH TO LEADERSHIP DEVELOPMENT

MANFRED F. R. KETS DE VRIES, KONSTANTIN KOROTOV, AND ELIZABETH FLORENT-TREACY

A man made an appointment to see a psychologist. When he arrived at the doctor's office, the man said, "Doctor, I always feel depressed. What should I do?"

The psychologist looked at him and said, "Come with me to the window."

The man followed. The psychologist pointed outside and said, "Do you see that tent over there in the distance? Well, there is a circus in town and it is really good. There are lots of acts to watch, especially the clowns. And there is one clown in particular who is extremely funny. He will make you rock with laughter over and over again. Go and see that clown and I guarantee that you will not have reason to be depressed again!"

The man turned to the psychologist with sad eyes and said, "Doctor, I am that clown!"

COACHING AND LEADERSHIP DEVELOPMENT: THE EVOLUTION OF CLIENTS

Coaching is certainly not a new phenomenon, despite the recent interest it has generated. Throughout most of human history, the vast majority of people lived out their lives in small communities, with their work and personal life experiences constricted and interwoven. Every passage in human experience was guided by elders. Babies were born, grew up (and sometimes died) watched over from their first breath by a circle of grandmothers, aunts, cousins, and sisters. The destiny of a child, male or female, was predetermined by ancestry and birth order. Religious obligations set the rhythm of daily life and measured the seasons. Nobility protected and exploited the peasants on their lands. Even queens were not exempt; in 1712 the poet Alexander Pope wrote of Queen Anne, "[she] dost sometimes counsel take–and sometimes tea."

As economies and populations transitioned from an agricultural to an industrial context, social and moral conventions strictly sanctioned deviation; it was made obvious at just about every moment of a person's life what his or her role would be. Many societies were paternalistic, socialist, or communist, freeing individuals from the need or desire to think for themselves. Post–World War II, many people in Western cultures fervently pursued individual happiness, funded by a job for life and a steady progression in salary that would enable the working man to provide a home and comfortable life for his wife and children.

Then suddenly (from a historical point of view) the rules of the game were thrown out altogether in many parts of the world. The information age brought change at the speed of light. Matrix structures in organizations flattened hierarchies. Organizations went global. Meritocracy, particularly in the United States, shook the foundations of bureaucracy. The result was huge increases in productivity, efficiency, and size of markets, with a correlated mobility of employment and reduction in workforces. And in the midst of this downsizing, outsourcing, networking, rationalizing, and general moving around, who had time, or even any good reason, to look out for anyone but himself?

The demand for executive coaching is one natural outcome of this unprecedented upheaval in the basic structures of society. Many people, like the clown in our opening story, feel a profound sense of disconnection from their colleagues, their superiors, their subordinates, and unfortunately, even from their families. They do not feel there is much meaning or purpose to their work. The most entrepreneurial among them have succeeded in managing their own career development path, changing jobs or companies in a manner reminiscent of the children's game of Chutes and Ladders, where luck might provide you with a ladder to the top, but on the other hand, with one misstep you could slide all the way back to the bottom.

Realizing that many potentially excellent executives were not reaching their full potential for lack of feedback, training, and mentoring, organizations and human resource directors began to design programs to help their people develop specific skills, or gain industry knowledge. These one-size-fits all programs were and are useful, but could not replace individual mentoring, particularly for women and minorities. Occasionally, consultants were brought in to work individually with particularly irascible but valuable executives. But in the boomtown atmosphere of the late 1990s, it became apparent that something more had to be done to develop and retain executives with the requisite portfolio of skills, knowledge, and emotional intelligence.

In addition, changes in the workplace greatly increased the psychological costs of leadership, which were, and still are, often underestimated. These costs are difficult or impossible to measure, and therefore they do not show up on any balance sheets. And yet they can prove disastrous to the bottom line. Even the most successful executive will probably face the following challenges at some point in his or her career:

- *Loneliness of command.* When an executive reaches a senior position in an organization, stress and frustration often develop, as old relationships and support networks change. Job pressures require developing multiple new relationships quickly, many based on functional needs rather than on trust, adding to the leader's feeling of being isolated.
- *Fear of envy.* Some people find being the subject of envy very disturbing. That fear can reach the point where dysfunctional self-destructive behavior "snatches defeat out of the jaws of victory."
- *"What now?"* After achieving a lifetime's ambition, executives sometimes suffer from a sense of depression, feeling that they have little left to strive for, finding it difficult to maintain the excitement of a personally important "project" or goal that kept them going for quite some time.
- *Feeling constantly watched.* Sometimes, it seems that no matter what an executive does in work or non-work life, it attracts attention from various constituencies in society (from paparazzi to governmental officials, and from the general public and journalists to business analysts and business school professors). It requires a lot of courage and effort to remain authentic and avoid constantly

looking over one's shoulder and checking every statement with the public relations or legal advisors.
- *Addiction to power.* The fear of losing what has been so difficult to gain – a top leadership position – sometimes encourages people to engage in malevolent acts.
- *Feeling of personal guilt.* Many executives at certain moments start to feel that some of the important people around them, and in particular members of their families, have invested their personal energy and time, and perhaps ignored their own needs and preferences, to advance the career of the executive. The executive in this situation feels an increasing sense of guilt about the cost of his or her own success.
- *An ever-steeper learning curve.* Executive competencies quickly become obsolete. Accepting that one must learn continually is a challenge. Executives must identify areas in which their skills are weakening, decide what to concentrate on, then find the courage, energy, and time for training or new experiences.

All these psychological processes may cause discomfort, stress, anxiety, and/or depression, which if left unaddressed may provoke irresponsible and irrational behavior that affect the organization's culture and patterns of decision making. But it is very difficult indeed for an individual to admit to these fears or concerns, let alone change his or her behavior to create a new and better reality.

Executive coaching can address these issues by supporting executives as they seek to capitalize on their strengths, mitigate their weaknesses, create supportive and well-balanced teams, and determine their own career goals.[1] Often, this creates a virtuous cycle, fostering loyalty to the organization as the executives reduce the psychological pressure on themselves and their subordinates. Coaches work with clients to encourage entrepreneurship, effective team behavior, accountability, and commitment. They help leaders to enjoy being more responsible corporate citizens. These are tasks that could arguably be carried out by any consultant, but a good executive coach will go deeper, creating a safe, transitional space in which an executive can deal with personal and organizational transformation anxiety. Through the coaching relationship, executives learn not only to face their own issues, but in addition, they become better able to coach their employees.

Recent trends in coaching and executive education confirm that executive development has changed. People are no longer sent to expensive executive education programs for a remedial course in whatever skill they appear to be lacking. Similarly, coaching is no longer seen as a way to save a manager who is about to derail. Contrary to other forms of intervention, the basic intent of most coaching is *not* about dealing with dysfunctional behavior. As a matter of fact, in our experience "last chance" coaching is usually an attempt by a conflict-avoiding senior executive to delegate a problem case to someone else.

Once a professional embarrassment–an indication that something was wrong with the person–coaching is now a perk, or a signal that an executive is on the fast track. Some cynics say that coaching can be seen as a contemporary form of psychotherapy, neatly packaged for the office. However it is defined, the purpose of executive coaching is to develop a targeted strategy to help individuals, teams, and organizations become more productive, especially when success depends on personal commitment and engaging people at a deep emotional level.

Although the "fatal flaw" executive–the one who, despite excellent professional skills, will not make it to the next level unless he or she deals with issues of micromanagement, mistrust, low emotional intelligence, and so on–may benefit from working with a leadership coach, ideal coaching clients are already quite effective. They have not got where they are by accident: they read practitioner business journals, attend top leadership conferences, and take executive education courses. They have shown that they want to develop their leadership skills, and that they are willing to take advice to heart.

The problem, for many of them, is that they recognize their weaker areas, but do not really know what they can do about them. They may be aware of their specific strengths, but hesitate to capitalize on them. To design strategies for further personal growth in these areas, they look for advisors (usually outside their organization) who can help them shape half-developed ideas, discuss critical decisions, evaluate options, and support them in their commitment to change. Executive coaches can provide the additional perspective clients need to put decisions and action plans about their careers into a larger, longer-term context.

GOING BEYOND RATIONALITY: DECODING DEEP STRUCTURE

Coaching as a leadership development and executive education intervention has great potential at both individual and organizational levels. But, as the story of the sad clown illustrates, too many leadership coaches and executive education providers only see the obvious. They are too quick to jump to conclusions that lead to superficial solutions. They restrict themselves to a very mechanical view of life in the workplace and fail to realize that real, lasting change can only take place if they can shed light on the deep structure underlying the surface phenomena, in their own minds as well as in their clients'.

Many leadership coaches, business practitioners, and scholars still subscribe to the myth that it is only what we see clearly (in other words, what is conscious) that matters. Assumptions made by economists about human rationality, and the models of learning and behavior modification developed by behavioral psychologists, have evolved into elegant, parsimonious, and measurable explanations for the way people act. For far too many people, the spirit of the economic machine seems to be chugging away in organizations–although the existing repertoire of "rational" concepts has proven time and again to be insufficient to untangle really knotty individual and organizational dilemmas.

Consequently, organizational behavior concepts used to describe processes such as individual perception and motivation, decision making, interpersonal relationships, group and intergroup processes, conflict dynamics, leadership, corporate culture, organizational structure, change, and development are often based on economic or behaviorist models, with an occasional dose of humanistic psychology thrown into the equation for good measure. Such an approach (with the irrepressible ghost of scientific management advocate Frederick Taylor hovering about) sets the stage for a rather two-dimensional way of looking at people and the world of work. Until recently, this approach was also perpetuated in traditional academia, ironically opening many doors to consultants called in by executives who, faced with the real-life complexities of organizations and relationships, could not find answers in their notes from their "hard" Strategy or Finance MBA courses. Convinced that behavior in organizations concerns only conscious, mechanistic, predictable, easy-to-understand phenomena, executives are often frustrated and disillusioned when they try to apply formulae to change human behavior. Executives frequently say to us, "I wish I had paid more attention to what the professor was saying in my organizational behavior class!"

Ignoring deep phenomena is actually quite costly for a practicing executive, both in terms of leadership capacity and personal development. But without guidance and experience, it is not easy to accept that employees and leaders are not just rational, highly focused machines; they are also subject to many (often contradictory) wishes, fantasies, conflicts, defensive behaviors, and anxieties–some conscious, others beyond consciousness. It is also difficult to understand how concepts taken from fields such as psychoanalysis, psychodynamic psychotherapy, dynamic psychiatry, cognitive theory, developmental psychology, anthropology, group psychotherapy, and family systems theory can be applied to the world of work.[2] To the uninitiated, these concepts often appear irrelevant: they are too individually based; too focused, at least in their original form, on abnormal behavior; and (in the case of the psychoanalytic method of investigation) too reliant on self-reported case studies.

The fact remains, however, that any meaningful explanation of humanity requires multiple lenses for investigation, and a variety of means of verification. In spite of what philosophers of science like to say about this subject, no causal claim in clinical psychology (or history and economics, for that matter) can be verified empirically. When we enter the realm of someone's inner world–seeking to understand that individual's desires, hopes, and fears–efforts at falsification (in an attempt to discover an exception that falsifies a hypothesis) are meaningless.

Though the notion that there is more to organizational behavior than meets the eye is antithetical to some management scholars, educators, and practicing coaches who deny the reality of unconscious phenomena–who refuse to bring them to consciousness and take them into consideration–for most, experience often proves the contrary. Take a very common example: an executive rejects a rational proposition for no obvious reason, and in fact is unable to explain his decision. Or, another common example, a CEO decides to change the name and identity of the company and then embarks on disastrous acquisition spree. Our natural reaction would be, "That just doesn't make sense." When our illusions of *homo economicus* prevail over the reality of *homo sapiens,* we have a vague awareness that strange things are occurring. This is why most people, when faced with organizational situations such as dysfunctional leadership, distorted perceptions, interpersonal conflicts, collusive relationships, self-inflicted career destruction, ineffective team processes, resistance to change, and similar disturbing organizational phenomena, are left feeling ineffective and helpless.

Management scholars, business practitioners, consultants, executive educators, and leadership coaches need to rethink their answers to the following questions. Is the typical executive really a stable, logically minded human being? Is management really just a series of predictable tasks, performed by rational executives and stakeholders? After all, it is individuals, with all their talents and idiosyncrasies, with all their past history and future dreams, who make up organizations. Like it or not, irrational behavior is more "normal" than most people are prepared to admit. All of us have a neurotic side. Mental health and illness are not dichotomous phenomena but opposing positions on a continuum: whether a person is labeled normal or abnormal, exactly the same dynamics apply. Much of what really goes on in organizations and societies takes place in the intrapsychic and interpersonal world of the key players, below the surface of easily observable day-to-day behaviors. Rational organizational processes may hide underlying conflicts, defensive behaviors, tensions, fantasies, and anxieties, something like the impermeable black crust that forms, temporarily, over a lake of molten lava.

BRINGING IN THE "COUCH": TAKING A CLINICAL ORIENTATION IN LEADERSHIP COACHING AND EXECUTIVE DEVELOPMENT

The clinically informed executive coach, trained to explore causes that lie below surface "symptoms" both at the individual and organizational level, will be more effective in these situations. An integrative, clinically oriented psychodynamic perspective helps the coach understand the hidden dynamics associated with individual perception, motivation, leadership, interpersonal relationships, team behavior, collusive situations, social defenses, corporate culture, "neurotic" toxic organizations (that is, organizations dominated by the particular neurosis of top executives), and the extent to which individuals, groups and teams, organizations, and even societies can be prisoners of their past. To help executives understand the whole picture, the executive coach can work with them to decipher their organization's internal and social dynamics, revisit the playing fields where leaders and followers engage, and explore the various unconscious and invisible psychodynamic processes and structures that influence the behavior of individuals, dyads, and groups in organizations.

In organizations as in individual life, therefore, psychological awareness is the first step toward psychological health. Organizations cannot perform successfully if the quirks and irrational processes that are part and parcel of the organizational participants' inner world are not taken into consideration. Because unconscious dynamics have a significant impact on life in organizations, organizational leaders (and followers) must recognize and plan for those dynamics, using tools and processes similar to those used with individuals in various forms of personal growth interventions or psychotherapy, but on a bigger, more systemic scale.

There are many ways in which clinically informed leadership development professionals can help an executive identify areas of psychological pressure or dysfunctional leadership and help him or her come up with alternatives:

- A leadership style that may have been effective under one set of circumstances may no longer be working. A coach may be able to help the executive recognize the need to change, and create a process that supports change. In addition, the support of a leadership coach may help a leader in a new position–newly promoted, hired, beginning to work with a new team, or taking over a cross-functional project, for example–to avoid suffering from the psychological costs that these transitions may impose.
- The coach can assist with the challenge of creating and managing effective executive role constellations. Recently there has been

academic debate about whether a group of top executives can really work as a team; can a group of ambitious achievers subjugate their own wishes to the greater good of the team? Leadership coaches can help otherwise incompatible individuals see the logic of working with one another. Similarly, a clinical orientation may provide essential clues to an executive coach working to resolve interpersonal or intergroup conflict, or various forms of collusive relationships in organizations (such as *folie à deux*, the type of insular relationship in which two individuals mutually, though often subconsciously, facilitate one another's irrational thinking and behavior).

- Executive coaches understand how complex any change process can be. If system-wide change is going to happen, leaders need to explore the "pain" in the system, link past to present through a new vision, buy into the change effort, and then reconfigure systems, structures, cultural elements, and behavior patterns, while simultaneously providing support to others going through the change process. Executive coaches can help executives create a shared mind-set, encourage an attitude that contributes to changing behavior, train for a new set of competencies, identify small "wins," and reward people who support the intended changes.

- On the other hand, when change efforts *fail* to work, a clinical orientation can help the coach disentangle social defenses within organizations, teams, or leaders themselves in order to reassess the approach to change and come up with new types of change interventions. In the process it is often necessary to assess organizational cultures and see what elements of the culture may be promoting or hindering change efforts.

- In healthy organizations, clinically oriented leadership development professionals can facilitate knowledge sharing and help leaders stimulate creativity and experimentation. Coaches can help identify and develop a new generation of leaders, or help with the selection process for a new leader from outside the organization. In family businesses, they can also help untangle knotty problems stemming from the potential conflict between business family systems.

- Work-life balance is another important area in which a clinically oriented coach can provide insights. Here again the challenge is complex: How can the executive explain, and then change, inefficient working patterns? What are the current professional and personal priorities, and what are the alternatives? Leadership development consultants can also provide the necessary support as the executive experiments with new ways of structuring his or her work and non-work time, and help the individual make a transition to a healthier and more balanced life.

THERAPEUTIC, BUT NOT THERAPY

Given the relative newness of leadership coaching in leadership development practice and executive education, it is important to clarify the similarities and differences between coaching and clinically oriented executive development, and more short-term oriented forms of psychotherapy. We have already indicated that clinical coaching and leadership development borrows from academic fields and clinical protocols. To start with the obvious, unregulated as the field may have been at the time of its inception, psychotherapy is now subject to strict regulation and oversight. One cannot call oneself a psychotherapist without the proper education, training, and supervision. In contrast, the coaching and executive development field is still relatively unregulated and fragmented.[3] Just about anybody can be a coach, and any business school professor, human resource director, or consultant can provide leadership development activities. Coaching websites exist where an individual can list his or her coaching services after a perfunctory interview and payment of a hefty "membership" fee. However, as the field matures, professional executive coaches are working to establish standardized educational credentials, structures for supervising one another's work, and codes of ethics and deontology.

Executive coaching and clinically oriented leadership education draw heavily on psychotherapeutic frameworks and skills. After all, both coaching and psychotherapy deal with behavior, emotion, and cognition, and both depend on meaningful discussions between the client and the therapist or coach. Depending on the psychological background and orientation of the coach, coaching can take on many different forms, at times making it very hard to differentiate it from short-term psychotherapy.[4] To illustrate, in the interpersonal field between coach and clients, we see how many coaches go from mere confrontation–helping the clients recognize that there may be a problem, to clarification–the gaining of a new understanding of the problem, to interpretation–the examination of unconscious conflicts and wishes, and finally to working through–acquiring an increased capacity for self-understanding. In coaching, as in psychotherapy, there may be an exploration (depending on how deep the coach and the client are prepared and willing to go) of blind spots, defensive reactions, forms of distorted thinking, and irrational thoughts.

However, executive coaches need to have a broader perspective than psychotherapists. To be effective, coaches need to take a more systemic approach to working with a client. The coach must also have a deep understanding of the overall organizational context. The coach needs to take a holistic, rather than reductionist, approach to framing the problem, gathering information not only from the executive, but also from his or her colleagues, and possibly friends and family. In contrast, in most forms of psychotherapy, information is principally obtained from the client. This leads us to another essential difference between psychotherapy and executive coaching: the need to establish who the client is. Is it the human resource director in the organization who is paying the bill, the chairman of the board, or the individual executive? In order to respect confidentiality and create a relationship of trust, the boundaries of the interaction with an executive must be clear to all.

Ideally, a coaching intervention should lead to organizational benefits. Sometimes that requires a transformation in the way executive teams operate, with one individual having the potential, or position, to be a catalyst. In this situation, both the organization *and* the individual are clients, and all the people involved–human resource directors, colleagues, the executive coach, and the target individual–should work together to identify and address a specific set of issues. In other situations, the benefit to the organization comes not from an intervention in one area, but rather (for example) by helping an executive deal with psychological pressure, or from hedging the future, in a sense, by ensuring that a pool of leadership talent is continually being strengthened. In this case, the executive coach should work only with an individual, and their consultations should remain private.

Executive education programs are a different case. New forms of executive education now target whole layers of executives in companies, thus becoming a real catalyst for change efforts in organizations, but once again, it should be made clear from the outset who the client is, or who the clients are.

In coaching the setting is also much more flexible than it is in a psychotherapeutic situation. Coaching can take place in many different environments: face-to-face meetings, e-mail, telephone conversations, dedicated sessions of executive development programs, or specially convened group coaching meetings or teleconferences. In psychotherapy, the conventions are well defined. Therapy takes place in the therapist's office, usually in the form of regular 45–50 minute sessions. With coaching, the time spent with the client can be as long as two, three, or even more hours.

Finally, there is the question of boundaries. Therapists generally avoid having social relationships with their patients. They feel such contact will contaminate future interactions. In coaching and leadership education, the situation is significantly blurred. Coaches and faculty may interact with executives in company or executive program events outside their coaching or class sessions, and these occasions can be a great opportunity to observe the manager in a different context.

An executive coach, therefore, must be familiar with the essentials of the psychotherapeutic approach, and also with the ins and outs of management. This kind of organizational expertise is not really necessary to be effective as a psychotherapist. Most psychotherapists, although they may have a great deal of clinical experience, do not have the kind of training to diagnose problems of executive leadership, team dysfunctional behavior, corporate culture, and organizational strategy. Furthermore, psychotherapy, particularly psychotherapy with a psychodynamic orientation, tends to be past, present, and future oriented, while coaching has a more present and future orientation. (As a caveat we would like to mention here that psychodynamically informed therapies emphasize the importance of early development, unconscious aspects of behavior, the therapeutic relationship between therapist and client, defensive reactions, and the presence of repetitive behavior.) In coaching and coaching-based executive education interventions, we find more of a goal and action orientation, while in psychotherapy, the interaction is of a more passive and reflective nature. Finally, in coaching the focus is on leadership and personal growth, problem-solving, and skill development, while in therapy, the question of symptom reduction and character problems becomes more the area of interest.

GOING FORWARD: A CRITICAL COMMENTARY

Effective and constructive organizational intervention, therefore, is built on a solid base of psychological understanding and business experience. But the coach's responsibility goes beyond knowing what to know; the best, and least dangerous, executive coach will also recognize what he or she does not know, and respect that limit.[5] Because the leadership coaching process often awakens deep-seated psychological problems of a characterological nature, raising issues that need much more than a simple intervention, those "coaches" who lack training and experience in these two fundamental areas are likely to do more harm than good. What may start as a simple attempt to bring about desired changes in specific cognitive skills may turn into something far more complicated. Too often, issues that executives present require more than simple, surface interventions. Many organizational interventionist coaches do not have the expertise to recognize the deeply rooted nature of specific problems. Also, they probably would not recognize transferential issues (which will be discussed in greater detail in Chapter One), a critical dimension of the bi-personal field (and a natural occurrence in any meaningful interpersonal relationship). The same applies to often well-meaning business school and consulting professionals who want to bring coaching to the repertoire of methods that they offer to an ever more demanding and sophisticated executive education market. A clinically trained executive coach will recognize problems that are beyond his or her scope of experience, and will refer the client to another professional.

1

It should also be noted that many business leaders have become more emotionally astute in recent years. Having seen organizational fads come and go, they now realize that most organizational problems are deeply ingrained, and as such are not susceptible to quick-fix formulas. Experienced leaders have become wary of fakes and their simplistic (but costly) interventions. Leadership coaches and educators can bring a dose of realism to organizational intervention, although this should not be seen as a cure-all and certainly does not herald the coming of a new messiah. Still, it makes sense that in-depth approaches to organizational interventions have a greater chance of addressing the deeply entrenched causes of organizational problems than superficial solutions. Organizational life is like a mirror, and what we see reflected there, we must examine inside ourselves. For executive educators, the consequence is that a single, off-the-shelf program, sprinkled with "coaching-like" interaction over a two- or three-day session with executives, will not work. Business schools, if they really want to make a difference, now offer multi-modular programs where faculty and coaches have the space to help executives stage experiments and then transform themselves and their behavior.

The transformation process is key. Clinically informed leadership coaches and faculty members, unlike many traditional coaches, educators, or consultants, do not simply make a diagnosis and provide a set of recommendations, leaving it to the client to implement their suggestions. Rather, they help the client to make their recommendations a reality. The aim of clinically informed leadership coaching is not a temporary high, but lasting change. They want to move beyond reductionistic formulas to sustainable transformation. This can mean that some client-coach relationships are long-lasting. Though the aim of every intervention is greater self-efficacy for the client (rather than continued dependency), the coach's services may be asked for repeatedly, on an as-needed basis, over a period of years. The aim of the leadership coach, however, is to help clients engage in self-analytic activities so that they can learn how to engage in interventions on their own. The ultimate goal of the leadership coach is to create self-aware individuals and a healthy, effective organization.

NOTES

1. Fitzgerald, C. and J. Garvey Berger, Eds. (2002). *Executive Coaching*. New York, Consulting Psychologist Press; Flaherty, J. (1999). *Coaching: Evoking Excellence in Others*. Boston, MA, Butterworth Heinemann; Goldsmith, M., A. Freas et al., Eds. (2000). *Coaching for Leadership*. New York, John Wiley & Sons; Hudson, F.M. (1999). *The Handbook of Coaching*. San Francisco, CA, Jossey-Bass; Kilberg, R.R. (2000). *Executive Coaching*. Washington, DC, American Psychological Association; Peltier, B. (2001). *The Psychology of Executive Coaching*. New York, Brunner-Routledge; Whitmore, J. (1996). *Coaching for Performance*. New York, Atrium.
2. Czander, W.M. (1993). *The Psychodynamics of Work and Organizations*. New York, Guilford Press; Gabriel, Y. (1999). *Organizations in Depth*. London, Sage; Hirschhorn, L. (1990). *The Workplace Within: Psychodynamics of Organizational Life*. Boston, MA, MIT Press; Jaques, E. (1965). *Glacier Project Papers*. London, Heineman Educational Books; Jaques, E. (1974). "Social Systems as Defense Against Persecutory and Depressive Anxiety" in *Analysis of Groups*, G.S. Gibbard, J.J. Hartmann and R.D. Mann (Eds.). San Francisco, CA, Jossey-Bass; Kets de Vries, M.F.R. (1993). *Leaders, Fools, and Impostors*. San Francisco, CA, Jossey-Bass; Kets de Vries, M.F.R. (2001). *The Leadership Mystique*. London, Financial Times/Prentice Hall; Kets de Vries, M.F.R. (2001). *Struggling with the Demon: Essays in Individual and Organizational Irrationality*. Madison, CT, Psychosocial Press; Kets de Vries, M.F.R. (2006). *The Leader on the Couch*. London: Wiley; Kets de Vries, M.F.R. and D. Miller (1984). *The Neurotic Organization*. San Francisco, CA, Jossey-Bass; Levinson, H. (1972). *Organizational Diagnosis*. Cambridge, MA, Harvard University Press; Levinson, H. (1996). "Executive Coaching." *Consulting Psychology Journal: Practice and Research* 48 (2): 115–123; Menzies, I.E. (1960). "A Case Study of the Functioning of Social Systems as a Defense against Anxiety: A Report on a Study of the Nursing System in a General Hospital." *Human Relations* 13: 95–121; Obholzer, A. (1994). *The Unconscious at Work: Individual and Organizational Stress in Human Services*. London, Routledge; Schwartz, H. (1990). *Narcissistic Process and Corporate Decay: The Theory of the Organization Ideal*. New York: New York University Press; Zaleznik, A. (1966). *Human Dilemmas of Leadership*. New York, HarperCollins; Zaleznik, A. (1989). *The Managerial Mystique*. New York, Harper & Row; Zaleznik, A. and M.F.R. Kets de Vries (1975). *Power and the Corporate Mind*. Boston, MA, Houghton Mifflin.
3. Brotman, L.E., W.P. Liberi et al. (1998). "Executive Coaching: The Need for Standards of Competence." *Consulting Psychology Journal: Practice and Research* 50 (1): 40–46.
4. Levenson, H., S. F. Butler et al. (1997). *Concise Guide to Brief Dynamic Psychotherapy*. Washington, DC, American Psychiatric Press; Malan, D. and F. Osimo (1992). *Psychodynamics, Training, and Outcome in Brief Psychotherapy*. Oxford, Butterworth Heinemann; Mander, G. (2001). *A Psychodynamic Approach to Brief Therapy*. London, Sage Publications; Rawson, P. (2002). *Short-Term Psychodynamic Psychotherapy: An Analysis of the Key Principals*. London, Karnac; Sperry, L. (1996). *Corporate Therapy and Consulting*. New York, Brunner/Mazel.
5. Berglas, S. (2002). "The Very Real Dangers of Executive Coaching." *Harvard Business Review* 80 (6): 86–92.

PART ONE: CONCEPTUAL FRAMEWORKS

1

THE CLINICAL PARADIGM: A PRIMER FOR PERSONAL CHANGE

MANFRED F. R. KETS DE VRIES AND KONSTANTIN KOROTOV

Many philosophers, poets, and other thinkers have posited throughout the ages that the key to growth and happiness lies in knowing and accepting oneself. A variation on this theme–that leadership development starts with an exploration of, and by, the leader himself or herself–will reappear in many chapters in this book. In undertaking this kind of human adventure, we use a concise but robust framework: the clinical paradigm.[1] The clinical paradigm is based on several premises. The first premise is that **all human behavior, even in its most odd or deviant forms, has a rational explanation**. Although deceptively simple, this premise poses a huge challenge to a business school professor, an executive coach, or other professionals working with leaders; it means they will have to use the tools and methods of a "psychological detective" to uncover explanatory factors underlying the behavior they perceive. Fortunately, the leader as an executive education or coaching client can become a detective as well; the clinical paradigm, when explained, offers the coach or educator a tremendous opportunity to use the leader's own behavior as a real-life case study, with the added advantage that *this* particular text is sure to be of interest to the executive concerned.

The second premise of the clinical paradigm tells us that **our unconscious plays a tremendous role in determining our actions, thoughts, fantasies, hopes, and fears**. The areas outside our direct rational observation and understanding are enormous, although they directly impact what happens in the so-called rational domain of our actions. Obviously, until we grasp at least some of the content of our irrational domain, it is unlikely that we can do anything with it. Moreover, the unconscious can hold executives as prisoners of their own past, not letting them get rid of things that become a hindrance to their development and growth as leaders and as human beings. Plenty of executives refuse to consider the possibility that there may be issues in their work and life that originate in the area beyond their comprehension or their immediate awareness. Faculty members and executive coaches may do well to begin by helping these individuals understand that being afraid of looking into the unconscious may be counterproductive to one's development. Looking into this domain may require courage, though, and this is where the leadership development professional can provide help and support. As an example, in one of our executive programs, we take participants to an exhibition about the life and work of Sigmund Freud. This visit comes as a surprise at the end of a long class day and before a good dinner, and many of the executives initially try to avoid the visit, or reveal their anxiety through complaints or negative comments. However, once in the museum, hearing about Freud's cases and seeing examples of how the unconscious may affect their lives, they start to realize how making the effort to look into oneself may significantly boost career and life success.

The third premise of the clinical paradigm is that **our emotions contribute to our identity and behavior**. Throughout life, we acquire different ways of expressing and regulating emotion, and in parallel, our cognitive, thinking side becomes more sophisticated. Cognition and emotion together eventually determine what we do and what we don't do. By exploring our emotions, we can access the more hidden parts of our identity: the type of emotion we express when doing certain things, imagining certain events, or dealing with certain people explains in part who we are. Emotional awareness also allows us to predict what kind of situations we naturally seek or avoid, and what kind of people we prefer or loathe; these insights therefore help explain our behavioral preferences and relationship patterns. Executive educators, coaches, and consultants may find the concept of the role of emotions important when working with people who have difficulties expressing their emotions. By helping individuals acknowledge how they feel, and how their feelings affect their behavior, leadership development professionals give their clients another lens for perceiving behavior and another key to changing it.

4

The fourth premise of the clinical paradigm states that **human development is an *inter*personal and *intra*personal process**. Our past determines who we are throughout our lives. Our earliest life experiences, over which we obviously had no control, have a deep, lasting impact on our personality and the patterns of our behavior and relationships. Through early interactions with significant people in our lives, primarily our care-takers, we develop a pattern of responses to the actions, desires, and emotions of others. These responses become engrained because they work in those early situations. Later in life, the same responses may no longer be adequate or appropriate.

THE INNER THEATER

The clinical paradigm can be described metaphorically as a way of exploring a person's "inner theater."[2] Behind the curtain, we all have a rich tragi-comedy playing out on our inner stage, with key actors representing the people we have loved, hated, feared, and admired. Early experiences are re-enacted over and over again. Some are extremely painful, and others fill us with a sense of well-being. These unconscious forces affect not only love, friendship, and artistic expression, but also patterns of relationships with bosses, colleagues, and subordinates; deci-sion making; management styles; and many other aspects of the work-related parts of life. Every executive and every employee brings their inner theater, with all its dramas and comedies, to the workplace. Dysfunctional behavior arises when we try to keep the curtain closed; ultimately, the show must go on.

Our physical bodies are ruled by motivational need systems, with varying levels of sophistication.[3] One need system regu-lates our basic physiological needs, another regulates the need for sensual enjoyment and sexual excitement. Yet another system causes us to respond to certain situations through antagonism or withdrawal (fight or flight). Higher-level systems deal with the need for attachment and affiliation, and the need for exploration and assertion. A product of nature and nurture, each of the need systems increases or decreases in importance on our inner stage theater in response to innate and learned response patterns. These motivational need systems are among

5

the rational forces behind actions, words, and behaviors that may initially seem irrational.

Another important notion in our understanding of how the inner theater operates is the "core conflictual relationship theme," or CCRT.[4] Our CCRT develops over time as a theme, or combination of themes, within our motivational needs systems, and takes a prominent position inside us, making a fundamental contribution to who we are, and the way we behave toward others. To put it another way, we can say that our basic wishes are reflected in our life-scripts. CCRT adds the nuances and shading that makes each of us unique. We bring our CCRT-colored behaviors and expectations to work and society, and sometimes the expectations are different from reality.

CONFUSION IN TIME AND PLACE: THE T-FACTOR

The four premises of the clinical paradigm provide important keys to understanding behavior and relational patterns. By exploring an individual's inner theater, not only do we revisit their past, but we can also draw parallels between past relationships and current behavior.[5] All of us are subject to a relational "confusion" in time and place, which gives rise to what are called transferential patterns, the act of using behavior patterns from the past to deal with situations in the present. Looking at transferential reactions can provide important insight into why executives behave in certain ways in certain situations. Consultants and faculty in executive programs need to realize and accept that executives may well have a seemingly irrational reaction to some of the people they work with. In addition, it is quite likely that the executive will experience some form of transferential response to the professor or coach; these responses should be discussed as they arise.

The concept of transference is grounded in observations of how human beings develop and mature. Through interactions with parents, family members, teachers, and other authority figures we encounter, we develop behavior patterns that become the basis for specific cognitive and affective "software." These patterns can be activated by particular cues without our awareness; we meet someone who subconsciously reminds us of a nagging older

6

sister, and we react as if she really were that older sister. This kind of transferential trigger may occur several times a day.

To put it more precisely, transference is the process by which one person displaces onto another thoughts, ideas, or fantasies that originated with figures of authority encountered very early in an individual's life. It is a revival or reliving of issues from the past directed toward persons in the present. Executives need to understand that the phenomenon of transference is natural and ubiquitous, although we are not always capable of noticing and recognizing it.

Transference can erase the psychological boundary between past and present, causing people–employees and executives alike–to replay the "scripts" that they have lived in the past. Followers may attribute unusual, almost mystical, powers or qualities to their leaders; thus charismatic leaders are born in organizations. It may also happen that, unwittingly, villains are created in a similar fashion, when issues from a dark past become attributed to the organizational leader. In all cases, a subjective reality materializes. This may happen even if people attempt to resist it. Leadership development professionals need to help executives see that the tendency to modify and distort the whole context of relationships is present in all meaningful interactions, including work-related ones. In addition, a clinically informed coach or consultant may use the phenomenon of transference as a source of clues about how the leader acts toward other significant people in his or her organization, and how he or she reacts to important events.

Obviously, leadership development professionals, faculty, and coaches are also human beings, and all of the above applies to them as well. When forming a relationship with an executive, they need to be aware of *counter-transference*–a phenomenon in which the executive becomes an outlet for the transferential reactions of the helping professional.[6] Coaches and educators need not only to recognize such reactions in themselves, but also to find ways of using the information about their own feelings and reactions to help the leader become more aware of the types of cues he or she provides to others, and the possible responses of people to those cues. A coach or educator attuned to his or her inner theater may recognize situations when his or her own transferential reactions may serve as sources of important insights in coaching or developmental relationships.

No discussion of transference in the leadership development context can be complete without a special emphasis on two subtypes of the phenomenon that are especially common in organizational settings. They are mirroring and idealizing.[7] Mirroring and idealizing have their roots in our very early interactions with other people. Most would probably agree that the first mirror a baby looks into is its mother's face. The quality of an individual's early relationship with his or her mother (or other primary caretaker replacing the mother) significantly contributes to the shaping of identity and mind. Through mirroring, from individuals around us we learn who we are and how we should behave. We internalize signals from significant others, in turn dealing with the world on the basis of these behavioral "suggestions." As children, we cope with our sense of fragility and insignificance by idealizing adults as sources of protection. We imagine them as strong and infallible. In the normal course of psychological development, we internalize the idealized parental figure, recreating an internal sense of power and security.

As authority figures, leaders fit easily into the subconscious imagery of a parental role. Followers very commonly manifest transference reactions through the idealization of their leader. This creates an equivalent to the sense of security and importance that they experienced in their early years through idealizing other significant adults. Subordinates following the unconscious psychological temptation of associating omnipotence with the leader may relinquish all responsibility and autonomy. Just as fears of fairy tale characters or of a big dog in the neighborhood could be overcome with the help of a parent, employees often hope leaders will protect them from the threats of downsizing, change, delocalization of jobs, and other such fears that modern workers face.

Obviously, leadership development professionals also have to be aware of the mirroring and idealizing processes taking place in their interactions with executives. The latter may also feel vulnerable and insecure in the illusory world of leadership described in popular books. The psychological challenges and pressure faced by today's leaders (mentioned in the introduction to this book) make this leadership world confusing and frightening to many. As leaders look for support from coaches and executive development professionals, it should not be difficult to imagine that the latter may also become idealized protective figures for a leader dealing with his or her fears and anxieties. As it is not uncommon in today's coaching world to see people who facilitate clients' dependency on their services (albeit unconsciously), it is really important for a leadership development professional to assess from time to time if he or she is not turning into a similar object of idealization for the leader.

THE PSYCHOLOGICAL PAINKILLERS: DEFENSE MECHANISMS

Pain and suffering are unlikely motivators for most people. Psychological pain may be as difficult to tolerate as physical pain, and sometimes it is even stronger. To survive, we develop defense mechanisms, ways of protecting our sense of self when we feel under attack. Our psychological defense mechanisms range from the primitive to the sophisticated, and allow us to remain relatively functional even when we are suffering. Like physical painkillers, psychological defense mechanisms provide a temporary relief from suffering and discomfort. But if the underlying cause is left untreated, the pain will return.

Any painkiller has a list of precautions with regard to its use. You should refrain from driving a car while taking codeine, for example. Then there is the risk of becoming too dependent on the medication. Likewise, leadership is one of those areas where "painkillers" have to be taken with caution. A leader who constantly resorts to psychological defense mechanisms to avoid facing painful situations may lose touch with reality, distort it, or create his or her private, illusionary world, often at the cost of shareholders, employees, and clients.

Descriptions of psychological defenses are included in the *Diagnostic and Statistical Manual of Mental Disorders* published by the American Psychiatric Association,[8] which makes it seem as though anybody who resorts to these types of defense must be truly crazy. But this is false; healthy people, leaders included, use them. What is important is to watch out for defenses that are primitive, misplaced, and potentially costly to the career of the executive and the health of his or her organization. Among such potentially costly defenses are denial, repression, rationalization, intellectualization, and projection.

Denial is a way of pretending unconsciously that important and significant things have *not* happened. It is about ignoring reality, despite the obviousness of the situation or facts to everybody else. *Repression*, an extreme version of denial, is about making a particular issue psychologically non-existent. In *rationalization*, people come up with internally acceptable excuses and explanations for what has happened, twisting reality in the process. *Intellectualization* is another reality twisting mechanism, through which people make the emotional side of an issue psychologically invisible, and concentrate their energy on the intellectual side of the topic. *Projection* is a way of making peace with an internal desire that, paradoxically, the individual believes is unacceptable, by attributing that desire to others.

Lower-level defense mechanisms also include passive-aggressive behavior, reaction formation, conversion, regression, acting out, and displacement. Higher-level mechanisms include positive identification, affiliation, constructive rituals, overcompensation, sublimation, humor, and altruism. Executive development professionals need to learn to recognize the signs of these various defenses and to inform executives about them. An important point is that even higher-level defense mechanisms sometimes hide important issues that may need to be explored for an executive to move forward in his or her behavior.

Importantly, leadership coaches, consultants, and faculty members also need to learn to deal with their *own* defense mechanisms. Working with today's executives is not for the faint of heart. Helping leaders become better equipped psychologically for the challenges they face often requires the qualities of a "good-enough" caretaker: someone who provides a safe environment, able to absorb the executive's anxiety while simultaneously challenging the individual to move forward. This role is not always comfortable, and executive development professionals may need to see if, by chance, they themselves are clinging to psychological defense mechanisms that prevent them from being effective in helping the leader in question.

ADDRESSING THE PHENOMENON OF NARCISSISM IN LEADERSHIP DEVELOPMENT

From developmental psychology we know that the healthy process of human growth is necessarily accompanied by a degree of frustration. During a baby's intrauterine existence, any needs that exist are taken care of immediately and automatically. This situation changes the moment an infant makes its entry into the world. In dealing with the frustrations of trying to make his or her needs and wants known, and as a way of coping with feelings of helplessness, the infant tries to retain the original impression of the perfection and bliss of intrauterine life by creating both a grandiose, exhibitionistic image of the self and an all-powerful, idealized image of the parents.[9]

Over time, and with "good enough" care, these two configurations are tamed by the forces of reality–especially by parents, siblings, other caretakers, and teachers, who modify the infant's exhibitionism and channel the grandiose fantasies. How the major caretakers react to the child's struggle to deal with the paradoxical quandary of infancy–how to resolve the tension between childhood helplessness and the grandiose sense of self found in almost all children–is paramount to the child's psychological health. The resolution of that tension is what determines a person's feelings of potency versus impotence. Inadequate resolution often produces feelings of rage, a desire for vengeance, and a hunger for personal power. If that hunger is not properly resolved in the various stages of childhood, it may be acted out in highly destructive ways in adulthood. A lot hangs on the good enough parenting mentioned earlier. Children exposed to extremes of dysfunctional parenting often believe that they cannot rely on anybody's love or loyalty. As adults, they remain deeply troubled by a sense of deprivation, anger, and emptiness, and they cope with this by resorting to narcissistic excess.

From a conceptual point of view, coaches and educators, as well as their clients, need to make a distinction between two varieties of narcissism: *constructive* and *reactive*.[10] Constructive narcissists are those who were fortunate enough to have caretakers who knew how to provide age-appropriate frustration–in other words, enough frustration to challenge, but not so much as to overwhelm. These caretakers were able to provide a supportive environment that led to feelings of basic trust and to a sense of control over one's actions. People exposed to such parenting tend to be relatively well-balanced, have a positive sense of self-esteem, a capacity for introspection, an empathetic outlook, and radiate a sense of positive vitality.

Reactive narcissists, on the other hand, were not as fortunate as children. Instead of receiving age-appropriate frustration, they received over- or under-stimulation, or chaotic, inconsistent stimulation, and thus were left with a legacy of feelings of inadequacy and deprivation. As a way of mastering their feelings of inadequacy, such individuals often develop an exaggerated sense of self-importance and self-grandiosity, and a concomitant need for admiration. As a way of mastering their sense of deprivation, they develop feelings of entitlement, believing that they deserve special treatment and that rules and regulations apply only to others. Furthermore, having not had empathic experiences, these people lack empathy; they are unable to experience how others feel. Typically, they become fixated on issues of power, status, prestige, and superiority. They may also suffer from what has been called the "Monte Cristo Complex" (after the protagonist in Alexandre Dumas' *The Count of Monte Cristo*), becoming preoccupied by feelings of envy, spite, revenge, and/or vindictive triumph over others; in short, they become haunted by the need to get even for real or imagined hurts.[11]

Undoubtedly, faculty and executive coaches will see narcissistic behavior of both types among those with whom they work. Failure to pay attention to a factor such as narcissism in the executive may lead to frustration for both the executive and the helping professional in the short term, and to confusion and dissatisfaction in the longer term. Moreover, by not paying attention to the issue, intentionally or unintentionally, the leadership development professional may fail to engage the leader in the change process. The outcome of such an incomplete intervention (whether through coaching or a leadership development executive program) is often seen in all-mighty executives who are totally convinced that everybody around them must change, and who are ready to work hard on changing *others* but who forgets that the change in an organization starts with *themselves*.

KNOW THYSELF

These descriptions of the premises of the clinical paradigm and concepts are by no means comprehensive or complete. The goal of this chapter is simply to introduce the practicing leadership development professional to some areas of knowledge that may be helpful in working with leaders who aspire to be more effective in creating healthier organizations. The themes presented in this chapter will appear again in greater depth in subsequent chapters, both in theoretical discussions, and practical applications of some of the ideas and methods described. The concepts outlined in this chapter can also serve as an introduction to sophisticated executives interested in using the principles of the clinical paradigm in their own leadership development process.

By exploring present realities and fantasies in the light of past experiences, people whose personality characteristics have been largely formed (this includes most people over 30) can still make significant changes in their behavior. The clinical paradigm supports learning from past mistakes in a new way, through examining repetitive behavior patterns that have become dysfunctional and a liability. In short, this kind of self-exploration in an organizational context can help executives with one of the most difficult leadership tasks they may ever face: changing themselves.

NOTES

1. Kets de Vries, M. (2006). *The Leader on the Couch: A Clinical Approach to Changing People and Organizations*. San Francisco, CA: Jossey-Bass; Kets de Vries, M. (2006). *The Leadership Mystique: Leading Behavior in Human Enterprise*, 2nd edition, London: Financial Times Prentice Hall.
2. McDougal, J. (1985). *Theaters of the Mind: Illusion and Truth on the Psychoanalytic Stage*. New York: Basic Books.
3. Lichtenberg, J.D. (1983). *Psycho-Analysis and Infant Research*. Mahwah, NJ: The Analytic Press.
4. Luborsky, L., and Crits-Christoph, P. (1998). *Understanding Transference: The Core Conflictual Relationship Theme Method*. Washington, DC: American Psychological Association.
5. Breuer, J., and Freud, S. (1895). *Studies on Hysteria. The Standard Edition of the Complete Psychological Works of Sigmund Freud*. Vol. 2, J. Strachey (Editor and translator). London: Hogarth Press and the Institute of Psychoanalysis; Etchegoyen, R.H. (1991). *The Fundamentals of Psychoanalytic Technique*. London: Karnac Books.

6. Racker, E. (1968). *Transference and Countertransference.* New York: International Universities Press.
7. Kohut, H. (1971). *The Analysis of the Self.* New York: International Universities Press.
8. *Diagnostic and Statistical Manual of Mental Disorders DSM-IV-TR,* 4th edition, Arlington, VA: American Psychiatric Association.
9. Kohut, H. (1971). *The Analysis of the Self.* New York: International Universities Press; Kernberg, O. (1975). *Borderline Conditions and Pathological Narcissism,* New York: Aronson.
10. Kets de Vries, M. (1993). *Leaders, Fools, and Impostors: Essays on the Psychology of Leadership.* San Francisco, CA: Jossey-Bass.
11. Kets de Vries, M. (2006). "'Complex' Executives I Have 'Met' in Coaching and Consulting." INSEAD Working Paper 2006/57/EFE.

2

GROUP DYNAMICS: WHAT COACHES AND CONSULTANTS NEED TO WATCH OUT FOR

ANTON OBHOLZER

INTRODUCTION

Attempting to lead without any knowledge of group and institutional process is, in my view, equivalent to attempting to cross the Sahara without a compass or a map. With great luck it is possible, but definitely not the best way of going about things. Yet it is not uncommon for leaders to have very little training or awareness about group and institutional forces in everyday working life, but nevertheless to be at the helm of vast and influential organizations.

This is something of a puzzle when group processes clearly have enormous influence over work outcomes. With awareness, they can be harnessed to drive excellent organizational results, but when they are ignored, the results can be disastrous for both the individual and the workplace.

The answer to this blindness probably lies in our early roots as individuals. From birth, we negotiate the psychological and social pathways of kindergarten, school, further education and work as individuals. In a way this makes complete sense, and so it should. But it ignores one crucial fact–that from the moment we are born, and for that matter even when we are *in utero*, we are and always will be members of a group. Being a group member is not a conscious, voluntary activity or decision, it is a given. Even a hermit is a member of a group, albeit the member that rejects the group–you cannot be a hermit if the group does not exist. We may consciously opt in or out of a variety of groups, social clubs, political parties and so on, but there are other groupings of which we are an inevitable and constant member, for example, family, neighborhood and, in

15

the context of this book, workplace. There is no opting out of the group process inherent in the workplace. To a limited degree, individuals have a conscious capacity to decide how and whether they relate to others at work, but at an unconscious group level, they will inevitably have an effect on, and be affected by, the group psychology and ecology in which they operate.

This perspective goes against the grain of our usual thinking, namely that we function principally as individuals and that the group or workplace is nothing more than a collection of individuals. It is reassuring, however, to believe that a group is only a collection of individuals and that we, as individuals, are wholly and competently in charge of ourselves. Therefore there is no risk of loss of self-control, or of falling into states of mind that we do not understand. We can reassure ourselves that everything is under control–but in fact very often the opposite is true, as anyone reflecting on their behavior at a Saturday night party might realize the morning after the night before. The same dynamic can also occur when we review our behavior following, say, a conflicted-ridden board meeting.

Turning a blind eye to group processes and our own behavior when caught up in such processes is understandable if we do not want to face the anxiety of a new group dynamic in our personal lives, but when it comes to group dynamic processes in the workplace, it is quite a different matter. Here, awareness of group processes, whatever role we play in the organization, can be a matter of life and death. Succumbing to psychologically toxic processes, at work can lead to burnout, illness, and, in extreme cases, suicide or early death. Group processes writ large across the organization can seriously damage the morale, well-being, success and profitability of the organization.

This chapter addresses a number of conscious and unconscious group processes, how they influence and endanger individual and group effectiveness and, most importantly, what can be done to minimize their negative effect, and maximize the possibility of harnessing them in a constructive way. It explores the position of the executive coach, educator or consultant to recognize group processes for what they are, while at the same time remaining adequately detached to be able to observe, to think and to link the observations with experience drawn from

16

other fields. This in turn enables the coach, educator or consultant to provide feedback aimed at encouraging insight and growth in the client, and development in the organization.

THE INDIVIDUAL AND THE GROUP

The basic question is not whether there is such a phenomenon as a group process, but more accurately, whether there is such a thing as an individual process? Within hours, a newborn child will relate to its parents or caregivers through smell, touch and sight. The child comes into the world with a certain genetic makeup, which influences its personality; intrauterine and birth experiences may leave an emotional trace, and after that the child builds up a picture of the world through its interactions with its external environment. This leads to a state of mind in which new events are viewed through the lens of past experience, both negative and positive.

Many of our inner world experiences are not consciously available, but they are constantly present, in that they affect our interpretation of events as they happen (most people do not have conscious memories from before the age of five or six yet we accept that it is the first few years of life that have most influence on our personality). All interpersonal and group experiences are interpreted at least in part against this background of unconscious experience. Those who argue that we are capable of interpreting any present-day event completely free from past experiences or influences, and solely on the basis of conscious logic are, in my view, more at risk of being sandbagged by unconscious processes than those that acknowledge that past experiences influence present-day perception, and that learning from past experience might be of benefit in future planning and behavior. An executive coach or consultant can be helpful in sorting present-day reality from misinterpretation due to past experience.

All human activity therefore takes place in both a concrete (outer world) and symbolic (inner world) group setting. Group processes depend on past experience and can have a positive, negative or ambivalent influence on the interpretation and management of current situations. An awareness of one's own pattern of behavior and of the basic principles of such behavior in human beings is absolutely essential if we are to manage our-selves competently in our various roles. And when it comes to the leadership function in organizations, it is hard to see what could be more important than an understanding of this web of processes in which individuals constantly operate. This fact is recognized nowadays by the importance given to the concept of emotional intelligence (EI), which focuses fundamentally on one's capacity to manage in a social and emotional climate.

A framework that helps executives to understand individual and group processes, as leadership and followership roles are enacted in the workplace, is essential. The development and servicing of such a framework is a crucial part of the leader-ship role, and outside input from colleagues, a coach, a faculty member, a consultant and others ensures a sound perspective. In developing this framework, it is helpful to approach the matter in a systematic way, as there are identical psychologi-cal mechanisms at play at each level of complexity–the best analogy of this is the Russian *matryoshka*, where every doll is the same but a different size, and the largest doll contains all the smaller dolls. And so it is in human institutions. Even the largest corporation needs to realize that it is also a collection of individuals, and the individuals bring with them their inner worlds and their past.

The layers in an institution are the individual, the pair, the trio or threesome, the very small group (3–5 people), the small group (8+), the medium group (15) and the large group (24+), after which there are groupings of increasing size until we get to national, religious and other configurations. Young children have cottoned on to this effect when they give their address starting with the house and ending with the universe. It is therefore helpful to understand the innate dynamics of human psychology as manifested in different magnifications. It is also helpful to understand that certain dynamics are inherent in each specific configuration. This understanding then allows one to differentiate between normal behavior, in other words, what is expected, and abnormal behavior in specific individual or work processes. So, for example, if one sets up a management or committee group consisting of three individuals and then finds a dynamic of two-against-one at play in the threesome, it is helpful to understand that this is at least in part due to the intrinsic design of a threesome, rather than entirely to do with the psychopathology of one, or all, of the three group members. The management implications of this illustration are that one should look at the overall system design first, and see whether it is appropriate for the task, before looking at alternative courses of action such as counseling, coaching, retraining or even firing one or all of the supposedly fractious members of the group. The problem could be a systemic one, so addressing individual members would be ineffective and might cause further turbulence elsewhere in the organization.

In terms of the position of an individual in a pair, it is essential to understand that how one perceives oneself is by no means how one is perceived by someone else. And so in any human interaction it is essential to ask oneself how the "other" perceives one, and what misperceptions are at play on both sides of the equation. For example, one might see oneself as a benevolent, helpful, facilitating leader, yet an individual with bad experiences of authority figures in the past might very well perceive you as a crafty, mean leader who hides his hostility under a mask of pleasantness. In addressing one another, whether verbally or in writing, thought needs to be given not only to what must be communicated and, in a work situation, whether it is within the role boundaries, but also how it might be misinterpreted or misperceived, and how it might be phrased to minimize the chances of this occurring. In such a situation, it is also important to look at not only what is said but also at what is not said, for it is often the latter that surfaces at a later time and creates problems. If a pair relationship is to work, it needs time, place and, if appropriate, confidentiality.

Conversations in corridors or concepts like the permanently open office door might grease the wheels of social nicety but are no substitute for setting clear time and space aside to address matters of importance, and particularly so in leadership matters in the workplace. An individual who takes telephone calls during meetings, looks at the computer screen, or has people popping in and out of the office while conducting a meeting is giving a clear message—you are not important enough to merit my full attention. This might of course suit two parties who prefer to simulate a discussion rather than to really address issues, but avoidance can have adverse effects on the relationship and the future of the organization. Managing the pair group is thus the cornerstone of good working relationships. In this configuration, it is easy to see how poor or inadequate experiences of paired relationships in earlier life can be unconsciously re-enacted in later adult life, both personally and at work, and be a handicap.

In groups of three, particularly if the members are of equal status (for example, production director, sales director and director of finance), the dynamic process changes. In such a configuration, the dynamic is often that of a pair and a third. If the person left out changes from time to time, then the situation is manageable. But if two of the group constantly gang up on the other, then basic primitive processes can be evoked. This can be highly problematic: decisions might be taken not on sound, conscious work-related principles, but on the basis of hurt and retaliation, especially if the work element of a meeting is mishandled, leaving space for personal issues to surface. Who is in and who is out will rotate in some conscious or unconscious way, but the essential dynamic of a threesome will always be present and influence the group's capacity to work.

Groups of four, five or six often unconsciously recreate aspects of family dynamics and, although they have the capacity to work well, the echoes of family pecking order are not far away. Work groups of eight to ten are the ideal size, and if handled with an eye to the task in hand, they can achieve a great deal. Once a group contains fifteen or more, it becomes increasingly difficult to hold the entire group simultaneously in your mind and to grasp what each member stands for. In such groups, work can really only be carried out in subgroups that operate separately from the group of fifteen, which then serves the function of agreeing, or not, with what has been decided outside that setting. If invited into such a group, you are unlikely to be asked to do specific work: you are more likely to have been asked as a symbol, representing one or other point of view or faction. Equally, your presence often has less to do with constructive work than ensuring that your or your group's position is not disadvantaged. This is an understandable position, but not likely to further constructive decision making or creativity and growth in the organization. Once we get into largish (25 or more) or large (50+) groups, there is the risk of losing one's personal identity and becoming a group particle–witness, for example, the dynamics at work in lynch mobs or the Nuremberg rallies. The chances of such dynamics occurring, say, in an employees' meeting are obviously lessened if the purpose of the meeting is clearly stated and the meeting is managed both concretely and psychologically to perform a clear work-related task.

In summary, there are certain innate dynamics related to the size of a group and whether you are setting up a group, a group member or managing or leading one, these dynamics will always be there and affect the group's functioning. It is essential that these factors are taken into account when designing systems, or when asked to participate in them. The risk attached to these group processes is that the participants get caught up in the dynamics and lose sight of the real issues. An outside view, such as that provided by a coach or a consultant, can help restore a sound perspective. (The systemic approach will be discussed further in Chapters Three and Four.)

CONTEXTUAL ISSUES IN GROUP DYNAMICS

Size matters, but so does setting. If you seat individuals in serried rows you will evoke memories of school or church and, in all likelihood, end up with a passive dependent group. Put them in a circle and you will get maximum discussion and minimum control of topic. A horseshoe format is halfway between the two. Different sizes of chairs create issues of status; having a table in the middle emphasizes work. Do you set out the correct number of chairs for the number of people expected or not? If not, the message you are giving is that you do not really care how many people attend, nor indeed have thought much about them at all. Is there an expected arrangement of seating, for example for different people in the organization's hierarchy or not? A phalanx of senior executives seated together might suggest "them and us." Then again, the absence of any order might undermine people in their roles by implying "we're all equals here" when that is not the case.

A meeting should have clear guidelines about time, attendance, disruption, mobile phone calls etc. The more *laissez-faire* the attitude, the more unconscious dynamics take over and participants start to feel that the meeting does not really matter, that they are there only to rubber-stamp a *fait accompli*, a way of thinking that, once established, can create a climate of detachment and cynicism that will seriously undermine morale, creativity and the effectiveness of the organization.

Another dynamic of importance is the question of whether substitutes are allowed. The more this happens, the less effective the group is in its working capacity and the more likely that members attend to protect the particular interests of the group that they represent rather than to further the task in hand. Substitutes rarely know the full history and so slow down and hinder work. In fact, they are often sent for that very purpose–to be the barnacles that slow down the ship. Attendance is also a vexing question. Excuses like urgent business elsewhere may be true, but failure to attend can be a most effective way of expressing opposition to a project without having to spell out and deal with your objections. Setting out the correct number of chairs for people expected to attend and then leaving chairs empty is a powerful suggestion that there may be another contingent or view that is not represented.

And then there are the thorny issues of scheduling and agendas and whether these are fixed in advance or not. The sloppier the approach, the more likely that issues will creep in that interfere with the effective running of the organization. It is important to construct an agenda so that key contentious items are not at the top, running the meeting, but also so that they are not at the bottom and subject to the "ran out of time" defense.

THE UNCONSCIOUS AT WORK IN BOARD MEETINGS: ROLES EXECUTIVES PLAY

It is a common belief that decisions can be reached by consensus, particularly in well-run organizations. My experience is that only matters of no consequence can be decided by consensus. Matters of consequence are by definition contentious and, if agreed by consensus, the negative views of individuals and groups will have been swept under the carpet, only to resurface at a later and usually particularly inconvenient time. It is therefore especially important to focus not only on what is being said but also on what is not being said. Letting sleeping dogs lie is not a good policy because they always wake up and create havoc. The same applies to silent group members. If invited to speak, they often make an important contribution to the debate. If they do not contribute, the risk of the debate being skewed is greater. Ambivalence is normal and it is part of the leadership task to cope with it. As a consultant or as a coach to these kinds of situations, it is essential to keep an eye open for such processes and to see that they are brought to the attention of the group.

Management by and large is about managing the status quo. But the environment is constantly changing and merely managing the status quo can mean managing oneself out of existence. Leadership is about having passion, a longer time horizon than the membership, and the capacity to cope with the anxiety associated with an uncertain future. There is pressure on leaders to shorten their time horizon and vision and to busy themselves with more domestic, short-term issues. The role of the coach, executive educator or consultant is to watch out for such regressive moves and help focus the discussion in assisting the executives in dealing with the various "undiscussables."

Within the group itself, a variety of conscious and unconscious processes are at play. There will be a variety of people on the board with recognizable roles and titles – among them: CEO, COO, CFO, VP sales – depending on the nature of the organization. All these roles are relevant and, when performed competently, contribute to the effective functioning of the board and of the company. But at another level, there are unspoken roles: bully, victim, buffoon, valiant supporter, font of negativity and so on. These roles are delegated unconsciously according to the needs of the company and its work process: for example, a funeral parlor must have a member who helps protect the staff by being a constant source of gallows humor. Who auditions for and gets these roles depends partly on personality, and partly on talent or vulnerability.

Individuals who perform certain tasks psychically necessary to a system present complex issues. Mr. X, who is a pain in the backside in meetings, does not necessarily behave like this because he has an aggressive, undermining personality disorder and should be fired. The chairman of the meeting should understand that Mr. X may be acting as the unconscious mouthpiece of resistance to the change being discussed and, rather than being seen as a pain (or as well as being seen as a pain), he should be seen as a warning signal that should be heard, acknowledged and acted upon. Firing Mr. X will only delay addressing the problem. Many of us will have had the experience of getting rid of a troublemaker only to find that the troublemaking role appears elsewhere. In contrast to Mr. X, a devoted supporter of the chairman might be equally problematic, interfering with the judgment of the chief executive who becomes emotionally overloaded with ill-thought-through enthusiasm.

In a board meeting, for example, two concentric circles of activity and thought are at play, the conscious and the unconscious. It is an essential part of the coach or consultant's role to keep a watch on these processes since they comprise an integral component of leadership. Leaders must be aware of both and manage meetings in a task-oriented way that enables them to navigate through them. The independent perspective that a third party brings, whether a professor, coach or consultant, can make an enormous difference to the capacity of the leader and the group to see what lies beneath the surface, and to deal with what they find in a constructive way. (See Chapter Fifteen for a case study of a board intervention.)

TASK AND ANTI-TASK IN THE WORKPLACE

In looking at any particular intervention in the workplace, it is important to ask whether this event furthers the task, the direction of travel toward the intended goal or outcome, or not. If the answer is yes, it obviously needs to be supported; if the answer is no, then thought must be given to how to curtail its negative effects. Leaders must pay constant attention to the heuristic task of thinking, "What am I here to do in my role and how do I further the work of the organization?" This process is a core requirement of survival. The debate about who determines the task and different views on how the outcome might be achieved is par for the course and an essential part of creativity.

So where do undermining, sabotage, negativity, burnout, toxicity and so on fit this picture? There is often little debate in organizations about what the organization is really there for, and what task it is to perform: to make a profit for the shareholders? To be responsible employers in the community? To satisfy customers? All of the above? Or none? It is not surprising that this debate is often avoided.

What if the task seems impossible? For instance, rehabilitating drug addicts, turning them into responsible citizens: is it good enough to salvage the occasional individual and keep some of the rest from undue destructiveness by helping them get by on pharmaceutical substitutes? And what about jobs that are emotionally painful, such as nursing premature babies, caring for the ill and dying, being a police officer or firefighter? The same thinking can be applied to an executive who must close a plant and make people redundant, blighting them and their families, perhaps for life.

These situations, and many others, cause anxiety and stress. We all want to avoid anxiety and stress, so we turn a blind eye to it, deny it, see it in others but not in ourselves. So the painful questions need to be asked – what stress is inherent in my job, my workplace, my industry? How am I dealing with it and do I need outside help? The underlying processes that are inherent in all individuals and all organizations are inclined to seep out into institutional life and fuel the negative, defensive and toxic processes mentioned above. Coaches and consultants need to monitor these dynamics, and business school professors need to teach executives about these phenomena.

ON CREATIVE, SANE AND SOBER LEADERSHIP

It is axiomatic that a leader will to some extent be a role model for all members of staff and, however fancy and enlightened the mission statement and HR policies, if the leader does not walk the talk, the whole caboodle is no more than a public relations exercise. So how does one walk the talk in a way that encompasses the emotional intelligence component of work, with its emphasis on individual and group, conscious and unconscious, psychological processes?

For a start, leaders who are not in touch with themselves are unlikely to have much success in being in touch with others. Many of the 360° feedback elements described elsewhere in this book (and introduced in Chapter Five) are very helpful for getting a workplace perspective on how one functions, but there is also a lot to learn from parents, grandparents, siblings, friends, family and others. In my work at INSEAD, I have been consistently impressed by the astuteness and effectiveness of feedback that we obtain from children about their high-flying executive parents.

Next, the leader needs to ask himself or herself about the particular stresses and anxieties inherent in the industry they are in and their particular organization. The CEO who proudly proclaims that there is no stress and no problem in his organization is not running a perfect organization (far from it). He is fundamentally out of touch with the reality of everyday life and is setting a role model example of denial that could cost him, his staff and his workplace dearly. Without stress or problems, there is no requirement to learn from mistakes, to build on experience and to adapt to changing circumstances.

Leadership is obviously a complex business. Leaders must have vision and a time horizon that exceeds the time horizons of most, if not all, of their colleagues, and certainly of most of their employees. They must have the capacity to bear the anxieties that go with facing the uncertainties inherent in a long time horizon. And with that goes the need to be able to change or modify direction as determined by events. Leadership also requires an acute awareness of the importance of followership– an active process of cooperating on joint tasks rather than being sucked along in a passive, dependent slipstream behind the leader. Leaders must not only manage followership in their staff, but also be able to adopt a followership role when certain times or tasks demand it.

Delegation, and how it is managed, are important leadership tasks. Only practice makes for effective leadership development. Delegation, however, requires that the leader has the capacity to bear the anxiety over the effectiveness of delegation, and is able to contain the anxiety of the person to whom the work is delegated.

Another important leadership function is communicating external matters relevant to the workforce in such a way that staff are informed but not overwhelmed, and, conversely, communicating internal issues to the outside world to ensure that the organization is firmly placed in its industry and society. In a way, the leader influences and manages a symbolic, semi-permeable boundary between the organization and the outside world, with flow in both directions.

Commitment to the task, and vision, are obviously essential aspects of the leader who walks the talk. But it is also very helpful if the leader can develop a "visiting anthropologist" role. By this I mean the capacity to be grounded in an organization, and have the feel of it, while simultaneously able to observe what is going on within it, and to query whether what is going on is actually in the service of the task and the organization, like an anthropologist observing a strange tribe. Many leaders are unable to take on their role alone. Here is where coaches and consultants can play an important role.

THE ROLE OF THE COACH

Leaders, however, are at risk when employing a coach or consultant. The coach or consultant may fall into the trap of hubris, thinking "I know better than them"; that he or she is inspired, wise, worth the fee. Another risk is that the coach or consultant might move out of the coaching or consulting role and fall into a managerial role. The risk for the institution is that existing leadership/management structures might be undermined and leaders/managers and staff could adopt a passive-dependent role in the coach or consultant's wake. But with a competent coach or consultant and a well-run organization, such risks will be minimal.

In the case of coaches or consultants, and even more so in the case of business school professors, it is central to their role that they are not part of the organization. This gives them a very specific advantage in that they have an independent position, perspective and state of mind. They are therefore in a much better position to keep an eye open for the various group

27

processes like those described in this chapter and the next. They are able to craft their interventions in such a way that they can be heard and acted upon at the optimal moment. The coach or consultant has the dual function of being a safety net on the one hand, and a seasoned lookout able to spot risks and opportunities on the other. As an observer, the coach or consultant can introduce interventions so that they have the best chance of being taken up. To do this, they need not only good timing but also the ability to ensure that their additional perspective becomes part of the everyday life and thinking of the institution, rather than being rejected (or for that matter, mindlessly incorporated) as a foreign idea.

Awareness of group dynamics, and acting upon them as appropriate, will make a substantial difference to morale, well-being and effective functioning in an organization. A coaching or consulting relationship with someone outside the organization who promotes this awareness can make an enormous difference to the capacity of the organization and its leaders to deal with these difficult and complex matters.

3

DEVELOPMENTAL COACHING FROM A SYSTEMS POINT OF VIEW

THEO COMPERNOLLE

As we have seen, clinical coaching is an approach that borrows from developments in the fields of psychology and psychotherapy. Because the word "clinical" for some people implies the treatment of pathology, in talking to executives I prefer to use the term *developmental* coaching. The primary goal of coaching is to enhance the leadership skills of those who are basically healthy. Developmental coaching looks for health and the strength to overcome challenges, rather than for pathology to cure. It aims to prevent, rather than treat, personal and relational disturbances. A developmental coach must, however, be sufficiently trained to detect personal pathology where it occurs, address it if possible, or refer the client to a therapist or to a coach with clinical expertise. Coaches who are inspired by psychoanalytical thinking address the sometimes very irrational behavior of their coaching clients based on theories of *unconscious intrapersonal influences,* such as intrapsychic conflicts, defensive behaviors, tensions and anxieties.[1] This is only part of the picture. The developmental coach must also consider the very influential *interpersonal influences* that codetermine the behavior of executives, even when the executive is unaware of them.

WARNING: THE MAP IS NOT THE TERRITORY

Before describing the benefits of systems theories and various practices for understanding complex patterns of interaction, an important warning is called for. Theories help us to understand the complex reality around us. They focus us. However, too often practitioners and researchers in psychotherapy and clinical coaching think and behave as if their theories and metaphors are the one and only reality. They treat the map as if it is the territory.

Freud developed some beautiful metaphors. The Oedipus triangle is certainly fascinating and inspiring for many. Problems arise when such metaphors are treated as if they really exist, and even more so when they are taken as universal "truths." The same is true for family therapists who think boundaries between people really exist, or with behaviorists who think that positive reinforcement is real. Indeed, when clinicians fight their turf wars, they actually forget that they are looking at very different maps.

However, first and foremost: theories are not reality. They are only a simplified representation of reality, like maps we use to find our way in unknown territory.[2] The systems point of view acknowledges that theories are extreme simplifications of reality, and that is what they should be. If a map were a true representation of reality, it would actually lose its usefulness, to the point where a simpler map would be needed to understand it.

Second, one can make very different maps that refer to the same territory, depending on the goal or interests. To get as quickly as possible from Amsterdam to Fontainebleau, France, a very simple map showing only highways is sufficient. To visit the beautiful little villages around Fontainebleau, a detailed tourist map is required. To the engineer responsible for checking the pipelines buried under the INSEAD campus in Fontainebleau, all these maps are useless: he needs a custom-made map for his specific purposes.

Scientific research helps find support for a particular map by providing evidence that the map is a correct representation of reality. All theories about why people behave as they do should certainly not be formulated as truths, but as hypotheses to be tested in single coaching cases or in research projects that produce more generic conclusions.

A third problem with theory is that therapists and coaches often think that the success of interventions based on a particular theoretical approach proves the theory. This is a common error. Homeopathic healers, for example, believe that water has a memory, and that a solution of one in a billion is therefore still effective. There are about 40 scientific ways to prove that this theory is completely wrong. In practice, however, homeopaths cure people with their solutions regardless of the theory being wrong because of the placebo effect. Therefore, the success of homeopathic methods does not prove that water has a memory and that a solution of one in a billion can have an impact. Prayer can help people to overcome major difficulties, but that does not prove the existence of God. Exorcism is a very effective method of treating major disturbances, but that does not prove the existence of the Devil.

In brief: clinical theories are helpful and necessary tools for a better understanding of a very complex reality, and as subsequent guides to our interventions. But we must keep in mind that, like other theories, they are only simplified representations of reality, that we need to test different theories in scientific ways and that the success of interventions is no proof of the validity of the theory behind them.

WHAT IS A SYSTEM?

A system is a set of interacting units with relationships among them. The word "set" implies that the units have some common properties. These common properties are essential if the units are to interact or have relationships.[3] The state of each unit is constrained by, conditioned by or dependent on the state of other units. In human systems, these relations make the system self-organize into characteristic patterns of interaction.

It is impossible to predict the behavior of the whole system with only knowledge about the individual units, because we also need to understand the interactions, or the relationships, between the units. In other words, the system is something altogether different from the sum of the parts. For example, one cannot predict the quality of a couple based on knowledge about the individual partners from before they were married. Eccentric individuals can together form a well-functioning couple. People who are considered individually excellent can form a totally dysfunctional couple. The behavior of couples and individuals is governed by different rules.

The same is true for executives in an executive team. The functioning of an executive team cannot be predicted only on the basis of information and hypotheses about the individual executives. Again and again executives are hired who, when screened individually, seem excellent choices, but who do not function well in a particular team. Even with the best of assessments this cannot be avoided, because the whole is not the sum of the parts, it is something totally different. The consequence for coaches is that it is impossible to know how an executive team functions based only on information about and from individual executives.

The other side of "the whole is different from the sum of the parts" is that "the part derives properties from the whole that it does not have itself in any other context." These properties are sometimes called "positional value" and "extrinsic quality."

Imagine you want to study the value of the white knight in a game of chess. You may study thousands of individual knights, and learn a lot about wood, plastic, ivory, realistic and abstract representations, but you will learn nothing about the value of the knight in a chess game. You can move one systems level up and study the knight in an actual game, but only looking at the knight. You will discover the interesting fact that knights jump over other pieces and that they always go two steps ahead and one to the side or the other way around. Very interesting, but you still know nothing about the value of the knight in a game. It is only when you study the knight in an actual game, all the time taking into account its relationship with all the other pieces on the board, that you will learn something about the value of that knight in that game. You will also discover that the value of the knight changes with every move by the other pieces. The executive being coached is like the knight in a game of chess.

Nobody, not even using the most sophisticated psychological tests, can determine my qualities as a teacher for large audiences in any other way than by observing me while teaching. As a teacher, I derive properties from the teaching situation that I do not have in any other situation, and certainly not in a one-on-one test situation. In the same way, some of the main properties of a CFO in a team are extrinsic qualities that she derives from being a member of that team. It is impossible to discover these in a one-on-one conversation. It is only possible to guess how she will function in a particular team based on information about how she functioned in other teams, but there will always be unexpected extrinsic qualities that only apply in the particular team under investigation.

The only way to discover the qualities of the whole system as well as some of the most important extrinsic properties of the parts is by studying it as a whole, taking into account the relationships between the interacting units. Because in healthy, flexible teams, the relationships and roles of team members change according to the subject being discussed, one needs to observe the executive team while it is doing its job as an executive team, not while involved in outward-bound or leisure activities. Therefore, systems coaching integrates very well with task-focused coaching. While a task-focused coach focuses on the content (what, how, when, who) of the discussion, the systems coach keeps an eye on and intervenes in the interactions and relationships.

Finally, the useful concept of "unpredictable change," introduced to systems thinking by the Nobel Prize winner Ilya Prigogine in 1977,[4] refers to what happens when systems diverge far from equilibrium. Dynamic systems models about chaos, complexity and change show that systems develop and grow when they are pushed away from equilibrium. Trapped at equilibrium, they do not survive. When pushed away from equilibrium, human systems are forced to explore new paths and to discover new patterns of interactions, leading to spontaneous self-reorganization. These new patterns are not predictable. Hence, to realize real change a coach must be able to push executives or teams to the limits of their equilibrium, keeping in mind that the direction the change will take is never 100% certain.

SYSTEMS AT DIFFERENT LEVELS WITH DIFFERENT RULES

When professionals moved from looking for causes of behavior in individuals to observing actual interactions between people in real time in groups and families, they ran into conceptual and pragmatic problems. A group or a family turned out to be something totally different from the sum of the people involved. It was not possible to deduce the rules governing the interactions in the family from what was known about the individuals. Moreover, behavior changed a lot and in unexpected ways when the family, its composition or the subject of the discussion changed. It was not helpful to try and explain or predict interactions at the group level based on theories about the individual level, or vice versa. Each level seemed to have its own rules. Attempts to understand groups as a whole, without dividing them in parts, led to the ideas of systems thinkers and cyberneticians such as Ackoff, Ashby, Emery, Maruyama, Prigogine, Rapoport, Miller and von Bertalanffy.[5]

The systems view is like a zoom lens allowing us to zoom in and out to different levels of an organization, where each level is a subsystem of the next level above and a suprasystem for the next level below. For example, one can zoom out from the biological level of the brain cell, to the brain, to the human individual, to the team (or family),to the company ... and then reverse the process, zooming in (see Figure 3.1). With a systems orientation, one is continually aware that different observations at each level lead to different theories, different hypotheses and different interventions. Going from one level to another does not imply an increase or reduction in complexity; each level has its own complexity.

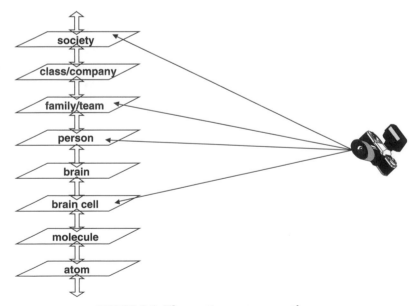

FIGURE 3.1 **The systems perspective**

The systems lens keeps us aware of the fact that one can study a phenomenon, such as leadership, on many different levels, making observations on a particular level leading to a hypothesis valuable for that level only and interventions specific for that level.[6] The level you choose to study and to intervene in depends on your interest, training, goal, knowledge, tools, capacities, power etc.

The reckless behavior of a CEO can be studied and addressed at the level of the brain cell, the brain, the individual organism, the individual psyche, the executive team, the company and society. One can understand his behavior on these different levels as, for example, a disorder in the production of a neurotransmitter in individual brain cells, a disorder in the processing of signals between brain cells, the manic phase of a bipolar disorder, the result of the emotional impact of his relationships with his parents, one aspect of a pattern of interactions between the team members, or the interplay between a man, his team and a company culture and so on. On all these levels, theories, methods and techniques can be developed to understand and change the ongoing patterns.

A theory about human behavior at the brain level will be different from a theory at the interpersonal or group level. The two theories do not invalidate each other, they complement each other. From a systems point of view, a well-trained developmental coach should at least be able to develop hypotheses and interventions at the individual level for the executive and at the group level of the executive team. A coach who is limited to one level only, and on that level to one method only, is like someone who uses a hammer to drive nails, fasten screws and bolts and even to paint. Of course one should not expect all coaches to be knowledgeable in the fields of neurology, psychiatry and group and organizational psychology, but they should have a minimal knowledge about different levels and methods, so that they understand their own limitations and can make the right referral if necessary.

In the clinical profession, there are often claims about the dominance of one level over others, for example the primacy of the psychodynamic/psychoanalytical or the interpersonal. From a systems point of view, however, this does not make any sense at all. Many very good hypotheses and explanations about issues such as leadership co-exist on different levels at the same time. Observations, research and hypotheses about, for example, the derailing of leadership at the company or executive team level, do not exclude very different observations and hypotheses at the level of the individual CEO, or his brain.

Not everybody sees the same relationships within the same level. In a museum, an inexperienced viewer might see nothing interesting in a heap of sheets of felt, pieces of metal, wood, fat and wax, while an art lover will see the relationships between the parts providing the perfect balance of form and colors that many works of the artist Joseph Beuys represent. On another level of abstraction, a more knowledgeable art lover might see the relationship of this work with other artworks in the past and the present. On still another level, he might know that there is a strong link between this art and a life-threatening experience the artist had as a young man.

Hence, personal, intellectual, ethical and esthetic considerations, as well as cultural and subcultural factors, influence our choice of a particular level in an organization, and the choice of a particular system at that level. Let's take as an example a case that will be developed later in this chapter. *A chairman has requested coaching for his executive team because the CEO is having problems getting along with the CFO.* As a developmentally oriented systems coach, I could choose to work:

- with the individual CFO, as the chairman suggested, without having any first-hand knowledge about the context he is working in,
    - solely based on information gathered from the transference between the CFO and the leadership coach, to generate a deeper insight into what drives his decisions,
    - using behavioral or cognitive methods, both to influence the behavior of the CFO in the session and as a tool to enable the CFO to have a more positive influence on others,
    - using a medical model, to treat his clinical depression or bipolar disorder;
- with the individual CFO, having information from others in the company through formal or informal feedback methods;

■ with the CFO and his spouse (in rare situations I include children too), not only to address tensions between family and work, but also to get a more multi-dimensional picture or to find a kind of "co-coach";

■ with the entire executive team,

  □ to improve the interactions between members without any individual coaching of team members,

  □ to improve the interactions between members in team sessions, in combination with individual coaching sessions with team members to address their personal goals of development;

■ or several other equally valid approaches.

A developmental systems coach applies Ockham's razor, "the simplest theory is usually the correct one," and uses the simplest model and the simplest intervention that is adequate to describe, and above all to change, a given process. Following Einstein's rule, "As simple as possible, but no simpler," I sometimes call this the "onion peel approach": very pragmatically going for the simplest superficial interventions possible to achieve change and development, peeling deeper and deeper only if necessary. (We will revisit this caveat in Chapter Seventeen.)

In this particular case, I chose team sessions together with individual sessions until it became evident that the board would have to be included if the problem was to be resolved.

FROM LINEAR CAUSALITY TO MULTI-CAUSALITY AND HISTORICAL HETEROGENEITY

One of the concepts that guides the behavior of coaches is causality. When a person behaves extremely cautiously or very aggressively, a clinical coach automatically looks for a historical cause for this behavior. We are so used to thinking in terms of cause and effect that we forget that causality is only a concept. We think that it is self-evident that an event now causes another event later, or that the problem we observe now must have a cause in the past (Figure 3.2.1).

In addition, from a reductionistic view of the cause-effect relationship, one tends to look for the one and only cause that explains the effect in a straightforward, linear way.

The CEO in our example repeatedly makes very bold, if not risky, entrepreneurial moves, causing conflict in the executive team, and especially with the CFO. Going back to his childhood, we traced this pattern of behavior to a very young age, when a father who never recognized his achievements made his young son try to impress him with ever greater feats.

Theories of linear causality underlie approaches such as psychoanalysis and traditional behaviorism. In a clinical approach, one would address this unresolved childhood experience to treat the risky behavior, the idea being that a particular dysfunction has only one cause and that the therapist, or the clinical coach, should address that cause. Thinking in a linear, causal model, the effect will be found if the cause is discovered and the cause will be detected if a particular effect is manifest. This leads to a model of chronological homogeneity or linear causality, where A (cause) leads to B (effect) directly and in one way only.

In single case studies, for example, one may repeatedly find a distant, punishing father in the history of narcissistic leaders. Within a linear causal model, coaches will therefore tend to see this type of father-child relationship as a cause of behavior in adult life (Figure 3.2.1). When they do not find any trace

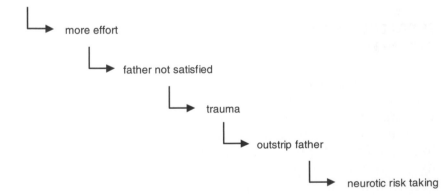

FIGURE 3.2.1 **Linear causality**

of such a father-child relationship, they will still keep to their cause-effect theory and conclude that this relationship has been pushed away into unconsciousness.

The linear causal model is nevertheless very useful as long as one is aware of its limitations and never forgets that this kind of linear cause-and-effect relationship does not actually exist, but is our way of simplifying a much more complex reality.

In the first half of the twentieth century, scholars and therapists realized that human behaviors and interactions cannot be fully understood, nor adequately changed, if they are seen as a link in a linear chain of events. It was recognized that, at any point in time, the actual situation is the result of many concurring influences. This is the notion of "multi-causality" (Figure 3.2.2). Each of these concurring influences has a different and changing impact, because it is also in its turn influenced by many other factors. At every step in the chain, multiple directions can be taken, leading to a stochastic process, wherein randomness and chance play a major role (Figure 3.2.3).

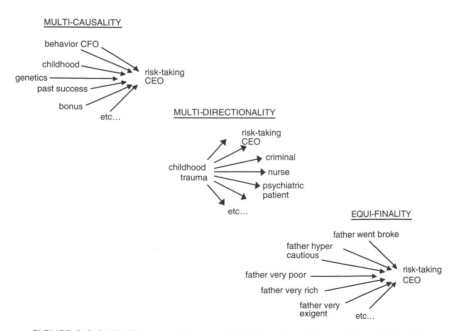

FIGURE 3.2.2 **Multi-causality, multi-directionality and equi-finality**

exigent father

risk taking
CEO

FIGURE 3.2.3 **Unique stochastic process**

Multi-causality leads to the notion of multi-directionality, in other words, any given starting point can lead to very different pathways (Figure 3.2.2). Bifurcations appear all the time. All branches are possible, but only one of them will be taken, depending on the influences at that point. From this point of view, history is also a succession of bifurcations.[7]

For example, in the history of many physically or mentally disordered people, one finds a traumatic childbirth. Hence, following a linear thinking model, doctors and psychologists tended to see birth trauma as a cause of these disorders. Prospective studies, however, following up on children with birth trauma, showed that most lead perfectly normal lives as adults. Moreover, the same psychologically traumatic childhood can lead to many different outcomes, varying from being an inmate in prison, a psychiatric patient, a househusband living an inconspicuous happy family life, a reckless CEO or a well-balanced Nobel Prize laureate. Prospective studies demonstrate that causality found in retrospective studies does not reflect causes but probabilities at most.

On the other hand, in different people the same behavior and attitudes are the result of totally different histories. For example, epileptic seizures in different people, which often look like carbon copies of one another, can be the result of totally different events, such as a childbirth trauma, an infection, a car accident or a drug. In the same way, the reckless behavior of a CEO can be the result of an extremely demanding father, a risk-averse father seen as a loser, a culmination of very gradual increases in risk-taking reinforced by positive results obtained throughout the CEO's life, an all-or-nothing attitude in a situation of being cornered, boredom in the job etc. This is called *equi-finality* (Figure 3.2.2) or to put it more simply, many roads lead to Rome. In the context of such chronological heterogeneity, looking back for the "real" cause in a chain of events does not make any sense at all.

Ascribing a cause that starts a chain of events becomes totally random: this is sometimes called "making an arbitrary interpunction." When, for example, two children fight, parents sometimes try to find out who started the fight. When one analyzes a video of an actual fight, it becomes clear that every behavior seen as the "cause" of the fight by one child is preceded by more or less subtle behaviors by the other child that caused this cause, sometimes even influenced or caused by (not so) subtle behavior by the parents themselves.

> *Returning to our sample case, in executive team meetings, we observed that each time the CEO wanted to make a very bold move, the CFO would warn about the risks. This would then escalate. The more cautious the CFO was, the more the CEO pushed for very daring initiatives, and the more risks the CEO wanted to take, the harder the CFO hit the brakes. In separate conversations, it became clear that these two people were blaming each other for the stalemate that often occurred in their discussions. The more the CFO emphasized the risks, the more the CEO became convinced that the CFO did not understand the opportunities represented by the acquisitions he wanted to make, which compelled him to ridicule the downside and exaggerate the upside, which of course proved to the CFO that the CEO did not understand the risks, and so on. This process resulted in a polarization between these two very intelligent and competent men.*

CIRCULAR CAUSALITY, FEEDBACK, ESCALATION AND HOMEOSTASIS

Who causes whose behavior? Does the CFO's extreme caution trigger the CEO's bravura, or is it the other way around? Struggling with similar observations, in the 1950s, therapists discovered cybernetics and started applying the notions of positive and negative feedback loops, escalation, runaway processes and others to human interactions. Here the traditional notion of cause and effect completely loses its meaning. In cases like the one described above, the term *circular causality* is used, indicating that in interactions between people, while a source may trigger an effect, this in turn has an impact on the source (Figure 3.3.1). In positive feedback loops, where every behavior by one person elicits an ever stronger reaction from the other, this will result in escalation (Figure 3.3.2). In negative feedback loops, where the behavior of one person elicits a correction in the behavior of the other, the process will result in equilibrium, or homeostasis (Figure 3.3.3), where a system oscillates within its boundaries.

In our case, when the conflict between the CFO and the CEO went too far, the chairman intervened and calmed things down ... until it started all over again.

Clearly, the question, "Who started this escalating interaction between the CEO and the CFO?" does not make sense and is not useful. The developmental systems coach no longer deals primarily with hypotheses about possible causes in the past, but with patterns of interaction in the present, in which the search for *the* cause is no longer relevant. Instead of just talking about them, the developmental coach prefers to observe such patterns himself and to be present in meetings where the issues are being

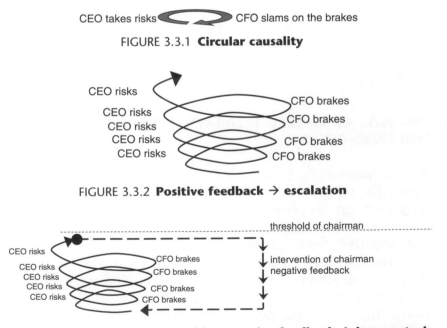

CEO takes risks ⟨⟨ ⟩⟩ CFO slams on the brakes

FIGURE 3.3.1 **Circular causality**

CEO risks
CEO risks   CFO brakes
CEO risks   CFO brakes
CEO risks   CFO brakes
CEO risks   CFO brakes

FIGURE 3.3.2 **Positive feedback → escalation**

threshold of chairman

CEO risks
CEO risks   CFO brakes   intervention of chairman
CEO risks   CFO brakes   negative feedback
CEO risks   CFO brakes
CEO risks   CFO brakes

FIGURE 3.3.3 **Escalation corrected by negative feedback → homeostasis**

discussed, to observe the actual interactions and relationships in real time. The focus is subsequently on possible interventions to change these interactions, also in real time.

The people involved in these relationships are usually not aware of the way their behavior is influenced, if not determined, by these circular, interpersonal patterns. They use a linear causal model unconsciously, usually ascribing the cause of the problem, the blame, to the other person.

GUILT, BLAME AND PATHOLOGY

Linear cause-effect theories, when dealing with people, unavoidably introduce guilt and blame in the discourse. When parents are seen as the cause of disturbance in their children, they get the blame, to the extent that the most terrible things have been written, for example, about the mothers of children with autism or anorexia nervosa.

In our example, it was the chairman who initially asked me to mediate in the conflict between the CFO and the CEO. He greatly appreciated both and thought they were excellent at their jobs, but he thought that the conservative, anxious attitude of the CFO was preventing the CEO from going after the big deals.

When the chairman sees the behavior of the CFO as the sole cause of the dysfunctional relationship with the CEO and the problems in the team, the CFO is "guilty" and gets the blame. However, when one looks at patterns of interactions, the concept of cause-effect and the notions of guilt and blame lose their meanings. The mere description by a coach of problem behavior or problematic relations in terms of cause-free, blame-free and guilt-free patterns of interactions can provoke a deep relief and free people to behave differently.

Moreover, when the coach does not use a linear causal model, he manifestly does not blame anybody himself. This has a very fundamental impact on his relationships with his clients. Coaches who think linearly and reductionistically in terms of cause and effect cannot avoid looking for culprits. A coach using a linear model will try not to blame anybody, but merely by thinking in terms of cause and effect, he *is* blaming. Analysis of videotapes of therapists who use a linear model when working with families clearly showed that the blaming often happened in subtle, almost subliminal, nonverbal and verbal ways, of which the therapists were unaware. So the best result a linearly thinking coach can hope for is not to *appear* to be blaming. In reality this is very difficult, if not impossible. The client will leave the session with a feeling of being blamed even if not a single blaming word has been spoken.

The blame of clinicians is often wrapped in the notion of pathology. However, from a systems point of view, whether behavior can be labeled pathologic or pathogenic depends on the social space in which it takes place and the arbitrary choice of the systems level and boundaries. A particular behavior can be considered constructive or positive within the realm of one system or one level, but at the same time destructive and negative in the context of another system or at another level of organization.

Being a scapegoat, for example, can be very destructive for the individual executive concerned, but at the same time it can be positive for the survival of the executive team or the company. Becoming indifferent can be a life-saving psychological flight behavior for an individual in a disturbing, stressful work situation, preferable to suffering from a heart attack. On the level of the team or the company, however, it is a big problem if too many people become indifferent.

Many different pathologies are possible, independent of human intention or psychological pathology. Individually perfectly healthy people together can become a dysfunctional team, while dysfunctional people together can be surprisingly successful. Processes at levels other than the individual, for example, the biological and the cultural, can provoke unintended dysfunction in the individual. In the same way, a group of individuals (such as an executive team) can be dysfunctional without pathology or intention from any of the individuals that make up the team.

Once a coach stops thinking in terms of cause and effect and begins to think in terms of interpersonal relationships, he no longer ascribes blame. From a systems point of view, nobody is to blame, but everybody is responsible for the necessary change in the pattern of interactions. When the relationships between a CEO and his team or between a CEO and his chairman have become dysfunctional, a systems-oriented coach will look for agencies for change, rather than look for causes within the person of the CEO or his executives. Dynamic systems theory is not a theory of single causes; it is a way of thinking about multiple possible levels of change.

MOVING FROM INDIVIDUALS TO SYSTEMS, VIA DYADS AND TRIADS

Dyads

We define a system, such as a family or an executive team, as a set of interacting units with relationships among them. The simplest way to describe relationships is to see them as dyads in mutual interaction, and to avoid linear causality by using a circular model to describe what happens between them. This leads to descriptions like the one represented in Figure 3.3.2: *The more cautious the CFO was, the more the CEO pushed for very daring initiatives, and the more risks the CEO wanted to take, the harder the CFO hit the brakes.*

This is an example of a positive feedback loop, leading to an escalation, a runaway process that will explode unless the CEO, the CFO or an outsider to the process breaks the cycle. Figure 3.3.3 illustrates: *When the conflict between the CEO and the CFO risked becoming destructive, the chairman stepped in and both calmed down, until a little later the fight started again.*

This is an example of a negative feedback loop. Each time the conflict reaches a particular level, in our case the threshold of the chairman, a correction occurs that brings the system back to its original state. Negative feedback leads to homeostasis, to stability within the limits of the system. It is what happens with the thermostat controlling the heating in your home.

Merely describing the problem in terms of feedback loops can be a very useful intervention to defuse the problem, especially as it eliminates guilt and blame. The question is no longer, "Who is wrong?" but, "How are we going to get out of this destructive loop?"

The perpetual third party

The intervention of the chairman in our example brings us to the rule of the perpetual third party: "When between two human systems (individuals or groups) the stress becomes too high, a third one gets involved."[8] A dyad under tension becomes a triad, unless one has killed or fired the other before the third one arrives.

The third party is dragged in by others or interferes on his own initiative. Often none of the three parties is really aware of this process. In companies, the third party is often a manager, but coaches can also be dragged, unaware, into such a triangle. It is important for a coach to see through this phenomenon, otherwise she might be tempted to seek the cause of the problem in the individual characters or groups, and lose the overview of the underlying relationships and interactions.

The third party can become involved in many ways. I shall call the principal characters here A, B and C (Figure 3.4.1, below). They could be individuals, teams, whole departments, companies or even countries at war. The roles of the third party could be as follows.

The heating transformer
A and B have a conflict: C goes in to mediate. C runs the risk that A and B will fight out their conflict through her. As a result, C comes under stress herself. C also runs the risk of being dragged into subsequent fights.

The scapegoat
A and B, in conflict, blame C for causing the problem. All their aggression is directed at C. After C is kicked out, the conflict flares up again – until a new scapegoat is found. However, exceptionally the scapegoat may attract so much shared feeling from

FIGURE 3.4.1 **Law of the eternal triad**

A and B that this joining of forces between A and B continues, regardless of C being there or not.

The lightning rod
If the conflict between A and B intensifies, C draws attention to herself, perhaps through deviant or annoying behavior. From now on, A and B focus on C, forgetting their original conflict. This is a phenomenon that often occurs in families, with a child in the role of C and parents in the role of A and B.

The dummy stallion
If A decides on a direct attack in the conflict with B, he runs the risk of becoming the loser because B might be much stronger. A therefore sets up C to attack B. When C and B are exhausted, A only has to deliver the death blow to B.

The coalition partner
C takes sides with B in a conflict between A and B. C can expect protection from B, but also runs the risk of catching A's blows even though they are intended for B rather than for her.

The loser
A says white so B says black. Whatever C, who depends on both of them, says or does is wrong: she is always going to be the loser. This situation often occurs in matrix organizations where one person reports to two or more bosses.

The Machiavellian
C is not passively subjected to the conflict between A and B. Although below them in the hierarchical pecking order, C knows how to play A and B off against each other in a divide-and-rule strategy. C can continue to dominate and get her own way as long as A and B continue their row. Thus C becomes Machiavellian and constantly intrigues. She sets A and B against each other and fans the flames of their conflict.

The explicit analysis of such triangular situations is critical, because:

- The coach may be the third party. If this is a deliberate policy, for example because you have assumed the role of mediator or adviser, that is fine, though even a mediator often unknowingly ends up in one of the other roles of C. The coach then becomes part of the problem rather than part of the solution. *In our example, the chairman was C. He was unaware of the fact that by intervening as a mediator, without addressing the conflict itself, he was part of the problem. His interference helped the CEO and CFO to avoid resolving their problem.*

- The third party may display stress signals before the two conflicting parties do. The third party then becomes, as it were, an alarm bell for what is happening between the two other parties.
- A coach must realize that any intervention directed against the third party (for example a scapegoat) will not solve the problem.
- The only fundamental solution lies in resolving the conflict between A and B.

Predicting relations in stable triads

The complexity of the relationships grows exponentially with every member added to a group. In a group of two, only one two-way relationship is possible, in a group of three there are three, with six people there are 15 with eight people there are 28. The number of possible two-way relationships is $[n\,(n-3)/2] + n$. Therefore, simple maps are essential for finding your way in these complex webs of relationships. Describing the complex relationships in an executive team in terms of triads is a very useful method, especially if there is conflict or tension among team members. A developmental systems coach must know how to handle triads in conflict, not only because his coaching client will often be caught in these, but also because the coach will be part of triads himself, even before the very first meeting with his client(s).

Let's return to our case.

The CEO invites **you** *to coach the executive team at the suggestion of the chairman, who knows you from a successful intervention in another company where he is on the board. The CEO calls you, saying that he thinks the chairman's suggestion is a good way to find out why the CFO is so risk-averse. He also asks you to talk with the COO too, because, "I do not understand why this very*

experienced man resists the obvious changes that have to be implemented."
You do not know the CEO; you have only had this one telephone conversation.
With only this information, there is plenty for a coach to consider. What kind
of a relationship do you think the CFO has with the chairman? How do you
think the CFO will react to your very first interventions, even a simple one like
inviting him for a one-on-one meeting? What is your guess about the relation-
ship between the COO and the CFO, the CEO and the chairman? How will the
COO most likely react to your interventions?

Imagine what you would do in this situation. If you think it makes no sense to start with so little information and without knowing the people personally, you are wedded too closely to the intrapersonal level of observation. Open up your systems lens and move to the interpersonal level.

The crux of the matter is that, from that first telephone call onwards, you
became part of the system and you now have a relationship with the CFO, the
COO, the chairman and the rest of the team, whether you want it or not and
even though you have never met them.

Such very complex relationships can be represented in simple triads. Just as in trigonometry, where you can calculate the third angle of a triangle when you know the other two, you can predict how two people will react toward each other when you know how they relate to a third person. Even when there is conflict in a triad, the triad can still be stable in the sense that it will tend to go on forever.

The two-way relationships in a triad can be predicted with three simple rules.[9] Cutting away the jargon, these are: "the friends of my friends are my friends," "the friends of my enemies are my enemies," and "the enemies of my enemies are my friends." A triad with a conflict is unstable when a relationship goes against one of these rules. Unstable triads tend to evolve into stable ones that obey these rules.

Following these simple rules, you can predict the relationships and reactions among people in a triad or a larger group without ever having met them. You can also predict how people will react to an internal or external mediator or coach without having met either the warring parties or the mediator. It is the system that determines their behavior rather than intrapersonal motives.

Now, before you read on, with these rules try to map the relationships of the CEO, the CFO, the chairman and yourself in the case we described above. Actually draw the triangles.

The same goes for the remainder of the executive team. Imagine you plan your first session with the team. While doing this, you learn that the COO does not get along very well with the young, bright, very dynamic CIO they just hired. Moreover, the CEO tells you that he has had long conversations with the HR director, who tried very hard to resolve the tension before, but failed. He adds, "You should certainly start with a conversation with the HR guy because he has an excellent insight into what's going on."

With only this additional information, draw a hypothetical map of the relationships in this team of CEO, CIO, COO and HR director. This will also help you understand better how conflict between two people in a team easily turns into coalitions and conflicts between subgroups.

Next, imagine what will happen when you first meet the team. In what direction will the system pull you? In what camp will you end up if you do not deliberately act against the pull of the system? Draw yourself into these triangles before you look at Figure 3.4.2.

Following the triad rules, you can predict that you risk having the CFO see you as being in collusion with the CEO and the chairman (Figure 3.4.2). There is no need to know anything

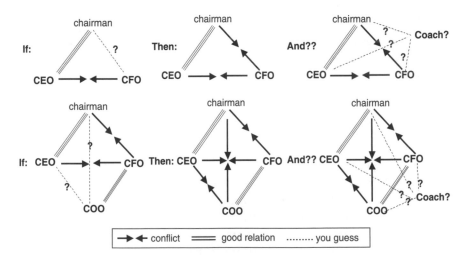

FIGURE 3.4.2 **Hypothetical relationship maps**

about these individuals to predict that when you meet the CEO and CFO together, the tendency of the system will be to develop collusion between you and the CEO. The CFO will resent this and spontaneously, but unconsciously, be rather guarded toward you, if not suspicious or unfriendly. The most important thing to remember is that this is not due to his intrapersonal makeup. It is what the system dictates, independent of the properties of the players. It is this kind of behavior (friends of my enemies are my enemy) that creates a stable triad. If you go against the pull of the system and try hard to develop a positive relationship with the CFO as well, the CEO will at once become more distant, if not less friendly, or will try to keep you on his side. If you try to keep both on your side, which is one of the things you could do to resolve the conflict, you create an unstable triad (where friends of enemies can be friends). You will feel the pull of the system toward stability, until the conflict is resolved, which creates a new stable triad ... or you could get stuck in a stable conflicted triad, where you now have become part of the problem.

When people and coaches get stuck in these kinds of triads, they are often unaware that it is the system that dictates their relationships and behavior, more than the characteristics of the individuals. As a result, they start looking for the cause of the conflict inside the people, declaring that it happens this way because "he is paranoid," "the CFO lacks courage," "the chairman is spellbound by the CEO," "the CEO is a neurotic risk taker," "the COO is afraid of change" and so on. These interpretations then further reinforce the behavior and relationships in the direction the system already pulls them.

It is much easier, practical and telling to literally draw these maps of interactions than to describe them in words. Drawing maps not only helps us to find our way in complex territory, but it also makes the last bit of causal thinking disappear and with it the last bit of blaming. Once the map is drawn, there is no beginning and no end, no cause and no effect, but only patterns of interaction, which inspire many possible interventions, in the system and in subsystems and suprasystems as well. With the map in mind, you can even try to change a relationship, when the two main actors are not present, by changing the other interactions in the team. More sophisticated maps and hypotheses are possible,[10] using concepts borrowed from dynamic systems theory, from chaos theory and about systems far-from-equilibrium,[11] but that goes beyond the scope of this chapter. (In Chapter Four, we will look at family business genograms, another way of mapping interactions.)

With these maps in mind, a systems-oriented coach can intervene in different ways. For example: by presenting his diagnosis in map form and tasking the team to look for solutions; by provoking an enactment of the conflict in the session and dealing with it in real time; by relabeling the scapegoating of a person as a healthy team process; by asking a series of questions in such a way that the team members themselves discover what is going on; by separately mediating in different conflicts; by giving homework to team members individually, in dyads or in triads; by addressing the individual needs of one member in individual clinical coaching sessions; by telling a story or presenting a powerful metaphor to change their view on the issues at hand and so on. Following the ideas of Prigogine about systems far-from-equilibrium, a systems coach might try to push the team to the point where change happens rather suddenly, but always in more or less unpredictable ways.

Interactions are most difficult to change when only one executive is being coached, because the coach is cut off from the other parts of the problem, that is, other team members and their relationships with the client and one another. Therefore, team coaching is much more efficient than individual coaching at changing the behavior of individual executives.

Nevertheless, when conducting individual executive coaching, a systems view will help the coach to predict what will happen in the team when his coaching client starts changing his behavior. He will then better understand that a lack of change or recidivism of the old behavior is not only due to intrapsychic resistances, but at least as much due to the pull of the larger system and its unspoken rules.

If as a coach you do not have much experience dealing with conflicts in real time, it is often better to start with shuttle diplomacy between the warring parties, seeing them separately. You can bring them together when you are comfortable yourself with the degree of conflict, and when you think there is enough mutual understanding to start a direct discussion between them. But never forget that while you have meetings with any single member alone, from a systems point of view your relationships with the others will play a role in that conversation, and in turn the conversation will affect these relationships as well.

CONCLUSION

A systems point of view gives a developmental coach a framework that integrates his thinking and inspires possible interventions at many different levels, from a single brain cell to society as a whole. One possible level is the individual executive, where an intervention might be individual clinical coaching with an intrapsychic orientation. Another level is that of an executive team, which is the most useful point at which to understand better, predict and change what is going on between people.

Key insights from systems thinking are that an executive team is something totally different from the sum of the individual executives that make up the team; that an executive has characteristics that he only has in that particular team; that one cannot predict the functioning of a team by knowing its members separately and that therefore it is necessary to observe the team as a whole while it is doing its job. To describe and change these interpersonal relationships, one can use cybernetic concepts like positive and negative feedback, runaway processes and homeostasis.

Since a system consists of a set of interacting units together with their relationships, a coach should try to map these relationships to understand better the functioning of the team. An important side effect of a systems view is that it makes the search for single cause-effect relations irrelevant and that it totally eliminates guilt and blame, while emphasizing everybody's responsibility for change. This viewpoint, together with the use of maps, will help coaches to understand, predict and handle how the system determines the reactions toward any intervention. The systems coach will be aware that these reactions are often independent from the intrapsychic makeup of the members, but part of the interpersonal composition of the team.

NOTES

1. Kets de Vries, M.F.R. (2005). "Executive leadership group coaching in action: The Zen of creating high performance teams." *The Academy of Management Executive* 19 (1), 61–76.
2. Korzybski, A. (1933). *Science and Sanity: An introduction to non-Aristotelian systems and general semantics.* New York: International Society for General Semantics.
3. Miller, J.G., & Miller, J.L. (1995). "Applications of living systems theory." *Systemic Practice and Action Research* 8 (1), 19–45.
4. Prigogine, I., & Stengers, I. (1979). *La nouvelle alliance, métamorphose de la science.* Paris: Gallimard.
5. Ackoff, R.L. (1974). *Redesigning the Future: A systems approach to societal problems.* New York: Wiley; Ashby, R. (1956). *An Introduction to Cybernetics.* London: Chapman & Hall; Emery, F.E. (1970). *Systems Thinking.* Harmondsworth: Penguin Books; Maruyama, M. (Ed.) (1997). *Context and Complexity: Cultivating contextual understanding.* New York: Springer-Verlag; Rapoport, A. (1984). *General Systems Theory: Essential concepts and applications.* Cambridge: Abacus; Miller, J.G. (1978). *Living Systems.* New York: McGraw-Hill; von Bertalanffy, L. (1969). *General System Theory: Foundations, development, applications.* New York: George Brazillier.
6. Compernolle, T.H. (1987). *Stress op de middelbare school.* Leuven: ACCO.
7. Prigogine, I. (1999). *Letters to future generations. The die is not cast.* http://www.unesco.org/opi2/lettres/TextAnglais/PrigogineE.html. Accessed in September 2006.
8. Compernolle, T.H. (1993). *Stress: Friend and Foe.* 1999. Synergo BV.
9. Cartwright, D., & Harsary, F. (1956). "Structural balance: A generalization of Heider's theory." *Psychological Review* 63 (5), 277–93.
10. Spronck, W.E., & Compernolle, T.H. (1997). "Systems theory and family therapy: From a critique on systems theory to a theory on system change." *Contemporary Family Therapy* 19 (2), 147–75.
11. Prigogine, I. (1999).

4

LEADERSHIP COACHING IN FAMILY BUSINESSES

RANDEL S. CARLOCK

Consultants and coaches brought in to help resolve a family business dilemma are often faced with an enigma wrapped in a riddle. As advisers, do we privilege the family perspective, and concern ourselves first with emotional issues and the well-being of family members? Or should we focus on the organizational context, putting the highest priority on strategic planning and financial concerns for the business? There are no easy answers. Working with families who own or control businesses is more of an art than a science, requiring skills that each coach or adviser must develop for himself or herself through study, experience, and reflection.

Family businesses present unique challenges to coaches and consultants because they represent the overlap of two interdependent and interrelated systems with often-conflicting values and behaviors. What makes the family business context so unique is that coaching family businesses requires intervention at the individual *and* group level, within the family *and* the business. To paraphrase Freud, in dealing with a business family system, we must concern ourselves with both work and love.

This chapter attempts to make some sense of the family business conundrum and provides a road map to help coaches and consultants to understand better the needs of family business clients, the special competencies required, and how to apply coaching and other leadership development strategies within the family business context.

FAMILY AND BUSINESS PARADIGMS

Conceptually, family businesses are different because the business and the family operate on two very different paradigms. Families are driven by emotions and by individuals' need for affiliation and self-fulfillment. Businesses, on the other hand, are driven by performance, results, and accomplishment (see Table 4.1). Non-family businesses, as we know from applying the clinical paradigm, are often driven by hidden forces while outwardly claiming to be rational. It is clear that a business with multiple family members involved experiences even more intense emotional responses, whether they admit to them or not, than an organization where employees have no other connection but their workplace.

The overlap of the two systems in a family business means that performance and outcomes are constantly measured against two, often-conflicting, sets of criteria. For example, appointing the current CEO's son to replace his father is a wonderful family move, but is only sound for the business if the son is the most capable candidate. This conflict in roles and motivations as a father or mother with those of a business leader and board member is often what creates the conflicts and challenges that make coaching and advising family businesses both interesting and difficult.

These family business issues are becoming more important to coaches and consultants because, although family business is the oldest form of economic organization, the contribution of this kind of organization to global economic output has only recently been recognized. The vast majority of the world's businesses are owned by families, from corner shops and small factories serving local communities, to middle-sized companies that are the backbone of regional economies, to global corporations with hundreds of thousands of employees. More important than prevalence is a considerable amount of research data reporting that family influenced firms often outperform more widely traded and owned

TABLE 4.1 **The values and behaviors of family and business systems**

Topic	Family system	Business system
Goals	Self-esteem, harmony	Profit, market share, growth
Authority	Seniority	Merit, formal position
Evaluation	Unconditional love/support	Performance against goals
Loyalty	Life-time commitment	Employment and rewards
Rules	Informal, traditions, flexible	Formal rigid policies
Fairness	Need-based and equal	Equity, effort, contribution

firms on the stock markets.[1] These findings demonstrate that despite the emotional complexity of family firms, there are other phenomena at play that may contribute to impressive financial results. This creates a great learning opportunity for coaches and consultants to develop new insights on how their family business clients organize and manage to create higher levels of financial return – with the added benefit that these lessons may very well apply to non-family business organizations.

Before we proceed further, we should address an essential question: What is a family business? Academics and others with a professional interest define a family business in different ways. The anthropologist sees it as a function of family culture and values, the economist in terms of control and ownership, and the management professor in terms of leadership and strategy. We define family business as a commercial organization in which decision making is influenced by the participation of multiple generations of a family related by blood or marriage or closely identified with the firm through leadership or ownership.[2] The key factors in our definition are decision making and family participation. A family firm can be a large publicly traded multinational in which a family trust is the reference (or largest) shareholder and the family takes no executive role, or it can be a completely privately held firm with multiple generations of family executives and shareholders. In both cases, it is important to consider the family's influence because family relationships, communications, and dynamics all affect the decision-making processes, strategy, and leadership of the business. In either of the situations described above, if the family relationships and interactions are conflicted, the business will eventually experience consequences.

COACHING AND CONSULTING COMPETENCIES IN THE FAMILY BUSINESS CONTEXT

It is the family business context, therefore, with its overlapping systems and complexities, that makes the adviser's role in this type of organization particularly challenging. For example, coaching the son or daughter of a well-known and highly successful entrepreneur may require a focus on the father-child relationship rather than business issues related to improving performance. Figure 4.1 illustrates that the coach or consultant needs to appreciate the wide range of advisory roles that a coaching or consulting relationship with a family includes.

There are significant opportunities for coaching and advising in family businesses. Advisers interested in working in this environment need to evaluate carefully their own personal readiness and professional capabilities, because a family business is not as forgiving as other types of organizational intervention. The dilemma confronting family business clients and their coaches and consultants is: what competencies are necessary to be an effective family business coach or consultant? Most of the professionals a family might turn to for advice–lawyer, accountant, architect, medical doctor–have degrees and affiliations that reflect standards of education, experience, testing, and professional qualification. Many of them work in professional partnerships that provide another level of peer review and support a shared interest in maintaining high professional standards and a strong reputation.

Unfortunately, with the exception of the US-based Family Firms Institute's Certificate in Family Business Advising, there

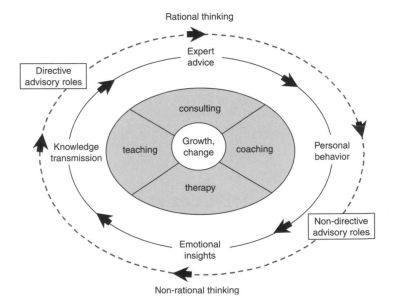

FIGURE 4.1 **Overlapping advisory roles in the family business context**

are no internationally recognized criteria for advisers working with family businesses.[3] There are, however, a wide range of academic and professional disciplines that offer training for some aspects of advising and consulting on family business issues–for example, psychology, family therapy, and so on. Having credentials and experience in one of these areas is essential, but not enough. The family business coach also needs to consider: how does my personal experience and training prepare me for work in the family business setting? And: do I have the psychological self-awareness to be effective in this context? As in many other helping professions, the family business adviser's self-awareness may be as important as his or her academic and professional experience.

Understanding what you know and how you know it is a powerful position for any social science professional. Figure 4.2 is a good framework for thinking about your unique capabilities and what you can bring as a coach or adviser to family businesses. It illustrates the two components in each individual's coaching and consulting toolkit, *technical competencies* and *emotional capability*. In most consulting or advising relationships, the criteria that the client would use to judge your competency would be the technical competencies labeled in the diagram, and which of these can be measured, certified, or demonstrated.

Equally important both for successful outcomes and for winning and maintaining clients are your emotional capabilities. The persona you present to the client is based on your personal style, emotional maturity, values, and spirituality, and this image

FIGURE 4.2 **Exploring your coaching toolkit**

influences the development of effective relationships with individuals and families. The coach's self-awareness, demonstrated in the way he or she interacts across generations and genders, is a critical factor for success in working with families.

It is beyond the scope of this chapter to develop a detailed competency model for family business coaches and consultants, but I will identify here some areas of technical knowledge that are generally accepted as important to work effectively with business families. I will not expand on other coaching skills or knowledge because those are topics that are thoroughly addressed in other chapters in this book.

Psychological foundations. A coach or adviser needs a strong psychological foundation upon which to anchor their work (as various authors suggest throughout this book). It is essential that they understand conflict, change, and human motivation. In the family setting, almost all coaching or consulting will address conflict and managing change. A psychological framework such as life cycle is important for understanding how family and businesses mature and develop. Many of the conflicts faced by family businesses are directly related to life transitions that require renegotiation of personal and professional relationships.

Consider the following example involving a coaching assignment with a next-generation adult son or daughter who wants to devote his or her career to the family business. In a non-family firm, coaching an executive in preparation for a promotion to CEO is a relatively straightforward assignment. But when the potential CEO is the son or daughter of a father who is used to being in charge, and loves it, the situation is even more complex. What usually happens? A few years after passing retirement age (and often after a few health scares) the father agrees that the son or daughter is ready to take his place as chief executive. The unforeseen (to him) result is a dramatic reduction in the father's day-to-day business role. He may be the chairman but that is not enough for him because he wants to be in the thick of the action. So one day, out of the blue, dad notifies the board of his intention to acquire a competitor; he is going to take personal responsibility for the new operation, so his son, the new CEO, won't be overburdened. There are now, in effect, two CEOs because there was no renegotiation of the father's role when his son became CEO. Great efforts were made to prepare the son, but little or no thought was given to coaching the father who was losing the thing he loved most–being in charge. Many of the difficulties confronting business families are the conflicts that result from failed family business transitions, and this happens most often in the psychological rather than the managerial domain.

Management and financial literacy. Advising a family business is a very personal experience. Owners expect a family coach or adviser to have a working knowledge of management and finance. In a large corporate setting, professional expertise and process skills are critical, but it is difficult, without sufficient business knowledge, to work as a coach for a family board member who will be facing major financial and strategic decisions.

Coaching and consulting scope. Perhaps a better way to describe coaching scope would be appreciating your personal limits as a coach and adviser. One of the dilemmas that coaches and advisers face is that family businesses have informal organization structures, so family members often play many roles (executive, board member, owner) and are involved across a range of business activities, including strategy, philanthropy, investments, and governance. By its nature, family business is a multidisciplinary field and coaches and consultants need to appreciate the limits of their training and experience and be willing to work with other professionals to complement their skills set and help the client with a well-rounded and complete solution to their issues.

Knowledge creation and teaching. Knowledge creation and teaching serves a double purpose. Coaches and advisers learn when they teach by working on their own skills set, expanding their own personal understanding and gaining insights to share with clients. A key skill that most clients need to develop is learning how to learn: teaching clients how to develop their skills set and how to explore new issues and problems and come to solutions on their own is another important part of the coaching and consulting process. The development of new exercises, case studies, and written publications such as books or articles, all serve to give the coach or consultant a broader knowledge base and a deeper understanding of the issues that clients face.

Values and worldview. Values are important to business families who are very sensitive to relationships and dealings with outsiders. The key success factor in family business coaching and consulting involves developing a therapeutic relationship with the client or the family. The coach's ability to develop supportive relationships that enable the client to learn new behaviors, and also help the client see new possibilities, is fundamental. It is also important for the coach or consultant to be sensitive to the client's expectations and find creative ways to reframe and formulate the problems the client faces. The real art of consulting and coaching with families is helping them understand and develop a creditable rationale for learning and applying new skills.[4]

What makes developing successful therapeutic relationships more difficult in the family business environment is that the coach or consultant needs to develop a working understanding of the client's content, what they do, and also the context in which they do it. Understanding the family business context requires exploring the family business history, considering family values, looking at family norms and behaviors, and, most important, understanding family relationships and dynamics. Business families expect the coach or consultant to participate fully in addressing the issues; they want an adviser who collaborates by using their training, experience, and process skills to help the family create and apply new thinking to the family's unique context and content.

A critical issue in maintaining a strong therapeutic relationship is managing information and confidentiality. Families are private by nature and the fact that their businesses are not required to disclose financial information makes them even more private in many cases. So family advisers and coaches must be highly sensitive to maintaining confidentiality about shared information, using what they can to help the family grow without embarrassing or injuring any family members, in an appropriate manner.

ASSESSING AND UNDERSTANDING FAMILY BUSINESS SYSTEMS

Coaches and consultants who are interested in developing a family business client base should have a working knowledge of family systems and at least some basic concepts to help them look at families and understand what is happening.

An important concept in regard to structure and relationships is family boundaries. Family structures and relationships create boundaries and define dyads, triangles, and coalitions. Dyads refer to two-person relationships, often the mother and father in a family. How do the family members interact? What is the interaction between parents and children? In some families these boundaries are very blurred and children may be directly involved in making decisions or influencing the family at a young age. In dysfunctional families, triangulation and other toxic family dynamics may come to the fore, negatively affecting the company's performance. In more traditional families, the boundaries between the children and the parental dyad are very strong and clear. In general, the distribution of power and decision making says a great deal about who has the ability to make decisions and how the family manages change.

Birth order and understanding individual family member's roles are further frameworks in the coach's toolkit. Families are the first structure that we experience, so how we are positioned in the family in terms of birth order, and other factors such as gender, makes a significant difference to how we experience the world. Birth order also influences our personality development. Because of birth order and changing family circumstances, each family member grows up in a slightly different family.[5] Two brothers growing up in the same family but separated by eight or nine years will have a very different family experience, based on their parents' work and career situation, the family's wealth, and even its geographical location. The older brother may grow up in a middle-class family where his father is working all the time as he builds and grows the business. If the father becomes very successful and the business takes off, the younger son may grow up in a family of wealth where the father is widely recognized as a business leader. These two sons, even though they grow up in the same family, will have very different family experiences. As a coach or consultant, it is important to appreciate these differences because understanding how birth order affects individuals helps us understand the roles that family members take.

Gender is a major issue. In a family with several children of the same gender, a child with a different gender will be treated as a very special individual and this will shape their experience. In family businesses in more traditional societies, when there are several daughters followed by a son, he will be the anointed successor for the family business, even though he is youngest in terms of birth order. Unique living arrangements, such as blended families or living with grandparents or other relatives, can also have an impact on children's development. The quirks of the person who acts as the child's principal caregiver, the loss of a grandparent or parent, or an extended period of illness will also influence someone's growing up experience.

All families have rules and understanding these rules is an important step to understanding how the family functions. A coach or other kind of adviser to a family needs to understand the family's rules both from the standpoint of the individuals they are supporting and also for their own interaction with the family. Family rules serve several purposes and ensure the survival of the family. Rules support effective family functioning: even if it is somewhat flawed, the family's rules still provide a pattern of consistent behavior or expectations that the family understands. Family rules are deeply rooted in a family's culture and social values and they are transmitted across generations by the senior generation. They can be conscious or unconscious. In some cases the family may not even recognize that certain rules govern behavior, and an important intervention for an adviser or coach should be to help the family understand clearly the implications of the rules by which the family lives. Most importantly, they also provide a sense of control in helping the family sustain its long-term relationships.

Typically, family rules focus on helping the family organize itself. They include the definition of roles around age and gender, the structure of the family and relationships, power and decision making, cohesion and intimacy, communication and conflict, and connection and autonomy. These family rules are tacitly understood by the family rather than clearly articulated or written. Table 4.2 identifies the five major areas of family rules and some of the typical topics that are addressed.

TABLE 4.2 **Family rules govern how a family organizes and functions**

Roles and Family Membership	Structures and Relationships	Power and Decision making	Conflict	Communication
Grandfather	Boundaries	Hierarchy	Denial	Listening
Grandmother	Alliances	Status	Avoidance	Speaking
Mother	Coalitions	Power	Capitulation	Self-disclosure
Father	Gender	Change	Blame	Feelings
Siblings	Generations	Gender	Confrontation	Cooperation
Nuclear family	Dyads		Compromise	Negotiation
Extended family	Subsystems		Collaboration	Respect & regard
In-laws	Triangles			
Community				

For example, roles and family membership is an area for family advisers and coaches. Membership in families is clearly spelled out. Some families are very open and allow participation from anyone with family membership. Some families limit their definition to the nuclear family, the marriage family, or the extended family, which may or may not include in-laws or partners. It is important as a coach or consultant to understand these requirements. In Asian families, there are clear rules of hierarchy based on the Confucian culture. So a grandfather in a family business will have a very significant role as the head of the family even if he no longer has any operating or ownership responsibility in the business.

Communication and conflict are two areas that are clearly influenced by family rules. Communication is a mediating activity that helps families explore new ideas and options. Each family and family business has a clear understanding of how they listen, speak, disclose information, express feelings, cooperate, and negotiate. These and the level of respect and regard given to family members in communication may be strongly influenced by social and cultural values. One critical dilemma here is that family communication is governed by the family's rules and yet it is communication that helps a family develop new agreements about their rules. Rigid families, in which some people are unwilling or unable to try new behaviors, often lack the communication required even to *consider* new ways of operating.

The coach or consultant in a rigid family needs to act as a source of new information that can be brought into the system. Simply asking questions about how the family does things and what is working well is a significant intervention for an inflexible family, because it opens the door to new topics for the future agenda.

Families can use many different approaches to dealing with conflict, and each family will develop patterns that represent their family's coping mechanisms. All families will experience conflict created by change as individuals and the family mature and develop. Business families have further opportunities for conflicts because of the interrelationships between the family and business systems. Families develop tactics for addressing conflict that become a pattern of behavior. Businesses have mediating processes such as the board of directors and outside advisers.

HELPING FAMILIES EXPLORE THEIR FAMILY SYSTEM

While it is useful to talk about different frameworks or perspectives for exploring the family business, how is this applied in an advising or coaching situation? Family members may be intuitively aware of some of their issues, but developing a shared understanding of their family system with their coach or adviser is a different matter.

In our work at INSEAD's Wendel International Centre for Family Entreprise, we use learning exercises designed to help individuals and families explore their own family's organization and relationships. These exercises are designed to help families develop a working knowledge of the different psychological factors that influence family functioning.

Family business genogram exercises

We often begin by asking a family to complete a unique kind of family tree known as a genogram. The genogram is a map or organization chart of the family showing how it is organized and each individual's position in terms of their family of origin

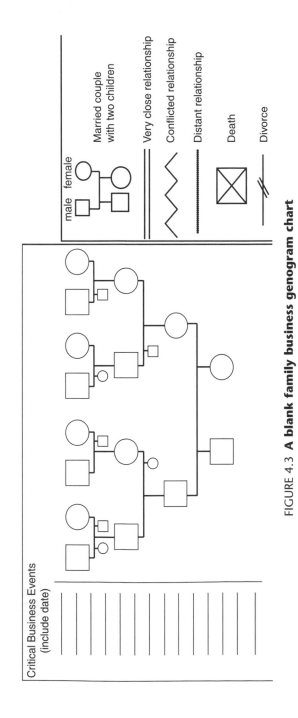

FIGURE 4.3 **A blank family business genogram chart**

and generation. It is also a history of family experiences, as the family business genogram can be used to give dates of birth, death, and marriage, as well as details about education and other significant information, which makes it a good schematic to help coaches and advisers understand how the family is organized (Figure 4.3). Using the family business genogram as a tool for family assessment and interpretation requires training beyond the scope of this chapter, but I want to emphasize here that important information about relationships can easily be identified from discussion with the clients. Family members can identify who has particularly close relationships with whom and any conflicted or severed relationships. It also prompts the family to share stories that explain the distribution of decision making and power, and the alliances within the company.

CREATING THE FAMILY BUSINESS GENOGRAM

Using Figure 4.3 as a model, the family is asked to draw a three-generation schematic of their family adding names, dates of marriage, birth and death, and describe relationships using the symbols suggested in the box on the right. They add critical business events on the left side of the genogram to display events that shaped different generations of the family.

Once a family business genogram has been completed, the family can start to consider the implications of both the generational and family patterns, and also how the family business has influenced the development of the family itself. To help the family accomplish this, we guide them through other exercises, all based on family systemic thinking.[6]

Questions for interpreting the family business genogram. Using the completed genogram, the family is asked to write answers to questions like, "Who has particularly strong or conflicted relationships?" and "What significant family events have affected relationships?" These questions help them think about where they come from, the nature of their relationships, and other significant family events or information that influence how the family functions.

Family and business timelines. By noting important events in chronological order, the family discovers how these events are interconnected and create impact across generations. Most family businesses do not keep a careful family business history, and coaching becomes a critical issue during transitions between generations because coaches are hired to help facilitate the development of the next generation of family business owners and leaders. The family business timeline can help the coach explore with his or her clients the family and business events that have influenced the family. Analyzing these life events and transitions can help prepare for future events, and can also show patterns of behavior that may recur in the future and need to be addressed as part of the coaching process. To help families see patterns in family events, we ask questions like: "Are there life events or life transitions that are still unresolved and challenging your family?" "Describe two life-cycle transitions that your family may face within the next five years."

Exploring the impact of birth order and family roles. The next phase of the workbook looks at family roles and birth order. In simple terms, it is demographic information, but structured in such a way that families and family members can start to understand how birth order may influence the different roles family members play. We all talk about our little sister or someone who plays "mom," or the brother who is a rebel or the "good" daughter. All these are roles in the family influenced by birth order and the personality of individual family members, as well as the family's experiences. Thinking about these roles and how different family members interact with one another is another important tool in the coaching process.

Understanding family rules. Families are often not fully aware of their own family rules and values. In this exercise, families identify and discuss the rules of origin, extended family system, and society and culture in their family. As discussed earlier, family rules are the guidelines that shape individual and family behavior. This exercise looks at some of the critical issues within the family related to respect for seniors, individual needs, gender roles, marriage, and addressing conflict, and helps the family think about what rules are important in shaping family behavior.

Assessing family expectations about communication. Here, the family completes a questionnaire about their communication styles. They are asked to rate their family on statements like: "Family members are good listeners"; and "Family members calmly discuss problems with one another." We then look at the scores with the family, and discuss areas where communication could be improved. Communication is an important tool in families because communication helps families renegotiate their relationships, develop new shared narratives to explain problems or difficulties, and understand one another's perspectives. Families with weak communication skills have a difficult time developing viable plans for their family in business. It is the issue of communication in the family system that often explains why the family has an inherent weakness in its planning and development when compared to the business. Businesses demand communication because of market forces and the participation of multiple stakeholders. It is very difficult for an entrepreneur not to communicate with his or her suppliers, key employees, and large customers on all aspects of the business, but that same entrepreneur can easily avoid communicating with his own children, siblings, parents, or even spouse about personal issues. There are limited external forces or influences in the family system, and, particularly in the entrepreneurial stage, if the entrepreneur or founder or owner chooses to neglect communicating with their family, there is very little the family can do about it. Often these patterns develop over years and are first confronted when the children enter the family business. We might see a situation where the father desperately wants his son or daughter or even a group of siblings to be part of the family business, but does not know how to discuss involvement in the company with his own children.

Dealing with family conflict. Business families have multiple reasons for conflict because of the interrelationships between the family and business systems. This exercise presents typical conflict tactics (denial, avoidance, capitulation, blame, and so on) and asks family members to list the five tactics their family uses most frequently, and the behavior associated with these tactics. This helps families think of action they can take to prevent or address future conflicts in their family system.

These exercises help coaches and consultants working with family businesses to understand better their family client's unique situation. The family business genogram reveals family structure, how the family is organized by hierarchies, and how alliances influence decision making, family dynamics, and relationships. By looking at family roles in terms of birth order, factors that influence individual family members' personality and behavior within the family system become visible. A discussion of family rules helps people to see the way in which the family's unique identity shapes and affects individual behavior regarding decisions, gender, boundaries, emotions, conflict, and communication. Through discussing their family's ability to communicate, the group hones a fundamental skill for bringing new information into the family system that will support new behavior, such as renegotiating relationships that must adjust to reflect individual and family development. Closely related to communication, modes of family conflict reflect differences in the individual and the family system perspective. Conflict is inevitable in families because transitions create loss and families experience loss with significant emotional responses, but communicating well about how to deal with conflict can be very helpful.

The exercises are intended to be a learning experience for individuals and their families. Each individual or family completing the exercises needs to be responsible for how he or she chooses to use the information. It is important to remember:

1. if an individual family member or the family as a group experiences high levels of conflict or discomfort while doing these exercises, then it may be helpful to seek outside professional support;
2. the exercises focus on the *family system* and problems in that system, so it would not be appropriate to attribute problems to an individual or subsystem of the family.

Fair process

Fair process is critical in family businesses because fairness itself is an ambiguous concept based on the perspective we apply. If we define fairness in terms of family needs, then fair means

71

meeting the needs of all family members, e.g. everyone gets a job regardless of qualifications. If we define fairness in terms of ownership, then fairness means allocating rewards pro rata, based on ownership position; and if we define fairness in a business context it means equity, and the individual who contributes the most should be rewarded the most. It is clear that this can create serious conflicts if one family member applies family thinking (needs) and another applies business logic to their contribution.

Fair process is a philosophy of interaction that helps families create more justice in the family system and in their dealings with one another, reducing conflict.[7] Families are inherently unfair because of individual differences, traditions, decision making, and hierarchies. Fair process addresses these issues by suggesting an improved approach to planning and decision making within the family by using the following behaviors:

- *communication*, allowing a voice to all family members;
- *clarity*, sharing accurate and timely information with the family;
- *consistency*, uniformly applying agreements to all members;
- *changeability*, the willingness to change rules as the situations change; and
- *culture* of fairness, a commitment by the family to use fair process because it benefits the family through better decisions and stronger family commitment.

Fair process stipulates a set of behaviors to create transparency around decision making and planning so that all family members recognize why and how decisions are made. It does not create fairness in the outcome.

Consider the case of a coach hired by the owning family to work with two next-generation family members. Both siblings have expressed interest in working for the family business. The family wants to provide both siblings, but especially the older one, with every advantage to help them develop their skills and talents. The younger sibling has developed strong business skills after completing an MBA degree and five years' successful executive experience outside the family business. The older sibling did not complete a college degree and has migrated through a series of jobs without much success. He has now decided that he wants to work in the family business as an executive.

If merit is used as the measure, the sibling with the stronger business skills and training should be placed in a position of greater responsibility and authority than the other. This can create significant issues of fairness, particularly if the less-prepared sibling is the older one. In many families, the older sibling should have a position of more responsibility to be "fair," but if business decisions are made according to family fairness rather than merit, the talented family and non-family executives may leave, putting the business at a competitive disadvantage.

Using fair process, the family needs to agree what policy they will use for hiring family members after discussion and sharing relevant information, and that this policy should then be applied consistently to all family members. Fair process does not ensure that the outcomes are always fair, as in the case of the two siblings, because the older sibling will be hurt if he is not given the job he wants. What it does ensure is that the decision will be made in a fair manner based on transparency. Applying fair process helps a family prevent conflict in a situation like that described above because the family uses fair process to create family justice in how the siblings' careers are handled.

ASSESSING YOUR PERFORMANCE AS A FAMILY BUSINESS COACH

Coaching or consulting in a family setting is very different from other organizational settings because of the emotional impact and the personal involvement of the coach or consultant, not only in business activities but also in the family's relationships and dynamics. For this reason, it is critical that a coach or consultant understands how his or her actions influence the family and how the family assesses the coach's performance and overall contribution. This can be done informally on an individual basis with a coaching assignment, or as a questionnaire on a large-scale family assignment or intervention. Generally, coaches need to be aware of two overall measures of their effectiveness. Are the coach or consultant's actions contributing to the family achieving its goals? And does the coach or consultant's behavior and personal style support a constructive, therapeutic relationship with the family?

One tool to help coaches and advisers in the family setting is to develop a simple questionnaire that can be used to guide an ongoing discussion during the project and as a formal written evaluation at its completion. Effective coaches and consultants need to have a clear understanding of how their actions influence the family. Critical issues include:

1. Did our work help create better options for individuals or the larger family system?
2. Did the coach or consultant understand and appreciate individual family and business goals?
3. Did the coach or consultant help the family learn new processes (how we do things) rather than specific content or recommendations?
4. Did the coach or consultant address sensitive and difficult issues or problems in a respectful and helpful manner to help the family resolve them constructively?
5. Did the coach or consultant demonstrate objectivity in dealing with individuals and the family?
6. Was the coach or consultant a good listener, demonstrating an understanding of family issues or emotions?
7. Did the coach or consultant maintain a supportive relationship with the individual or family?
8. Last, and probably most important, did the coach or consultant treat the individuals and family with respect, earning their trust and confidence?

The use of some type of formal evaluation or assessment of the coaching or consulting relationship closes the circle of many of the ideas and issues that we have discussed in this chapter. It is an important learning step for the coach or consultant's personal development, because they then have the family's perspective on how the family was influenced by the coach or consultant's work and how they perceived the coach or consultant. It also gives the coach or consultant a chance to understand better their skills set in terms of working with family systems and appreciating the impact of a family system on a business organization.

The overriding theme of this chapter is the uniqueness of each family business due to family experiences, history, relationships, culture, and values. This is very different from most business organizations where, while they may have different cultures, the actual business processes and practices become rationalized as the organization professionalizes its management structure and processes. In family businesses, this rationalization often does not occur because of informal reporting relationships, and the direct involvement of family members at all levels of the organization. There may be co-CEOs, rotating CEOs, or even no CEO but a group of family partners with one family member taking the leadership role. There can be many, many different structures, so an important aspect of assessing our work with families is to ensure that we are sensitive to the needs of the family that we are coaching or consulting. There are no prescriptions for helping family businesses.

NOTES

1. Anderson, R.C. and Reeb, D. (2003). "Founding Family Ownership and Firm Performance: Evidence from the S & P 500," *Journal of Finance*, 58 (3), 1301–1328.
2. Kets de Vries, M.F.R., Carlock, R.S., and Florent-Treacy, E. (2007). "Family Business," entry in Clegg, S. and Bailey, J. (eds), *International Encyclopaedia of Organization Studies*, Thousand Oaks, CA: Sage.
3. The Family Firm Institute (FFI) is an international professional membership organization dedicated to providing interdisciplinary education and networking opportunities for family business and family wealth advisers, consultants, educators, and researchers, and to increasing published awareness about trends and developments in the family business and family wealth fields.
4. Sprenkle, D.H. and Blow, A.J. (2004). "Common Factors and Our Sacred Models," *Journal of Marriage & Family Therapy*, 30, 113–129.
5. Toman, W. (1993). *Family Constellation: Its effects on personality and social behavior*, New York: Springer Publishing Company.
6. For more information on obtaining and using the WICFE Business Family Systems Workbook contact Prof. Randel S. Carlock, family-firms.fb@insead.edu.
7. Van der Heyden, L., Blondel, C. and Carlock, R.S. (2005). "Fair Process: Striving for justice in family business," *Family Business Review*, 8 (1), March, 1–21.

5

GOODBYE, SWEET NARCISSUS: USING 360° FEEDBACK FOR SELF-REFLECTION

MANFRED F. R. KETS DE VRIES, ELIZABETH FLORENT-TREACY, PIERRE VRIGNAUD, AND KONSTANTIN KOROTOV

Although few would readily admit it, many business leaders are a bit like the mythical Narcissus: standing in front of a mirror in the morning, they see the person they love most in the world. At the office, many top executives are surrounded by people who tell them what they want to hear. In most instances, their subordinates do not have the courage to speak critically. Colleagues are happy to work with them as long as they are effective, but if they start to slip, the colleagues are likely to focus on protecting themselves. Other members of the executive team may wait until the board is forced to take action, rather than confronting anyone with their concerns.

The best leaders avoid this trap by creating well-balanced top executive teams, each with skills and strengths in specific areas. They create an organizational culture where executives have a healthy disrespect for their boss. They *want* to have a culture where people speak their mind. Unfortunately, however, few leaders–too few, in our experience–seek honest feedback from their colleagues. In many cases, even the best of them are reluctant to give direct feedback about a CEO or chairman's seemingly irrational behavior. Although they may not go to the extreme of being pure yea-sayers, it is very difficult for anyone, including members of the top team, to take the distance necessary to reflect on the person's leadership style and personality characteristics, and even more difficult for a colleague to help a leader change his or her behavior.

Given this reluctance to seek and receive honest feedback, it is not surprising that roughly 70% of executives believe they are in the top 25% of their profession in terms of performance.

Many of them are truly unaware of the way in which their behavior impedes functioning–their own, and others'–in their organization. The result is a serious gap between what many leaders *say* they do, and what they *really* do; that is, between their self-perception and the perception others have of them. Although many of them say that they want feedback to enable them to learn and develop, it is human nature to accept feedback that is consistent with the way we see ourselves, and reject feedback that is inconsistent with our self-perceptions. Introspection can be, after all, a journey into a dark and frightening place.

Some executives, perhaps more courageous and curious than most, decide to work with a leadership coach, or participate in an executive seminar, in order to receive unbiased advice on their own blind spots. The person may know where they want to go–what their personal goals are–but most likely, they will have little idea of just how to proceed. Like any journey, the process of executive development and change is facilitated by the use of robust instruments that can guide them on the journey from where they are to where they want to be.

We have found that properly designed 360° feedback questionnaires and assessment tools can be very useful. They can be the beginning of an introspective journey, and set into motion changes in behavior. How do 360° instruments help us arrive at an understanding of individual character and leadership strengths and weaknesses? They are not diagnostic or navigational tools in an empirical sense, but they provide a useful way for leaders to compare their self-perceptions with the observations of colleagues or others who know them well. The results of a 360° survey exercise give ample insights for a constructive dialogue about the way the leader functions, and insights into those aspects of his or her implicit and explicit behavior that need further development. They can help redefine superior-subordinate relationships, setting the stage for a more open, network-oriented organizational culture. They can be used to create more effective executive teams. And last, but certainly not least, they can contribute to establishing a better work-life balance, for example, by helping the person deepen their relationship with their significant other, or accept the need to take time to care for an aging parent.

WHY USE FEEDBACK INSTRUMENTS IN A MORE CLINICAL WAY?

There are a number of so-called diagnostic tests around of debatable value. It is not enough to label someone as, for example, "timid," "controlling," or "honest." Simply declaring, "The results of the survey show that she is not the best candidate for CFO," for example, is not enough. The unanswered question is: "What exactly are her strengths and weaknesses?" To complicate matters even more, until we understand a person's inner theatre—the dramas and major scripts that play within all of us from birth—we will not have a holistic understanding of her behavior and character attributes, let alone be able to establish how those attributes affect her leadership style, and how to change it where necessary.

How deep can we go? Outside a psychotherapeutic context, not very far. One of the first rules of executive coaching is to do no harm, to avoid going deeper than the coaching relationship, and the leadership coach's training, allows. But, using leadership diagnostic tools as a starting point for observation and reflection, we *can* identify behavior and action patterns, and compare these with individual self-perceptions. Most of us want feedback about our effectiveness. We want to know how we can change, if change is needed, either for the better or simply to adapt to changing circumstances. However, since most academic studies on leadership pay attention only to surface manifestations, most leadership feedback instruments, in turn, are not concerned about the psychodynamic processes that underlie leadership rationale.

To address this gap, at INSEAD Global Leadership Centre (IGLC) we develop and use 360° feedback instruments based on the clinical orientation to the study of leadership. This approach provides not only insight into leaders' manifest behavior but also a more complete analysis of their driving forces. The clinically oriented feedback process that includes specially designed 360° survey instruments, face-to-face presentation and discussion of results (often in a group setting), and resolution through the development and followup of action plans, can have a significant behavioral impact and will have action implications. The process, similar to what is described in the chapter on the systems approach to developmental coaching, is rather like peeling an onion: as the outer, superficial layers come away, our core life experiences are steadily revealed. With this new insight, we can design action plans for development, and ask our family, friends, and colleagues for support as we implement these changes.

WHY USE 360° FEEDBACK?

In designing our IGLC instruments, we have emphasized the importance of including observers in the process, which is why this type of instrument is called *360 degree* or *multiple source feedback*. The multiple feedback approach minimizes the phenomenon known as the *social desirability factor*, which reflects the conscious or unconscious tendency among many people to present themselves in a more positive light by scoring themselves favorably on many of the questions they reply to.

Research clearly indicates that 360° feedback systems give a much more accurate picture than self-assessment of what executives really do and how they actually behave,[1] and so for us, 360° feedback became the operational method of choice for the instruments we design and develop. Some of the most interesting and useful information is gathered not from the individual scores, but from a gap analysis, or close study of the *differences* between self and observer scores. When interpreting the results of the questionnaires, however, we also remind participants that people are too complex to be summarized in a simple 360° questionnaire. We also emphasize that no single person is excellent in all dimensions measured. It is perfectly normal to be stronger in some areas than in others. Furthermore, we also point out that many developmental areas are really strengths overdone. Our goal is to help participants identify personal strengths and weaknesses, and then consider action plans to "fill in the gaps" through personal development, or in other cases, by creating well-balanced executive teams whose members complement one another's strengths and weaknesses in specific areas.

In sum, our survey instruments are designed to help people:

- Deal with the "shadow side" of their personality
- Gain insight into their strengths and weaknesses
- Expand their behavioral repertoire and discover more creative ways of solving difficult interpersonal problems

- Become more effective at career management and professional advancement
- Become more effective at operating in teams and organizations
- Acquire a greater capacity to cope with stress
- Better manage the tensions between their professional and private lives
- Draft a developmental agenda and a program for change.

A WORD ABOUT THE PSYCHOMETRIC DESIGN OF OUR INSTRUMENTS

Given a target audience of executives from around the world, our objective is always to construct simple, conceptually sound diagnostic instruments with a psychodynamic focus. The questionnaires are aimed at a "normal" population (that is, our norms and standard deviations are constructed using our database of high-achieving business leaders from many national cultures), and are to be used as the basis for a discussion about individual behavior. We strive to develop tests that are easy to complete, easy to understand and interpret, and easy to translate into action aimed at improvement. *We strongly discourage people from using them as a basis for performance review.* Using this type of 360° instrument can be a delicate proposition, as many people fear that the information gathered will be used as fodder for demotion, unwanted lateral moves, or other unpleasant consequences. Therefore, we only give the feedback report to the individual concerned, and let him or her decide with whom they wish to share the information.

We are also extremely rigorous when it comes to the psychometric properties of our instruments. In fact, we began designing our own instruments because we were unable to find instruments that were robust enough, or comprehensive enough, to meet the needs we perceived among the executives we work with. Our development team consists of Professor Manfred Kets de Vries, Professor Pierre Vrignaud, and several other colleagues with academic backgrounds and psychological training. We use specific psychometric analysis and methods that respect the data structure (dependency between observers who are observing the same individual) of the 360° process.

80

In designing a new survey instrument, we begin by studying top executives from all over the world who have participated in leadership programs at INSEAD. Leaders who participate in these seminars are typically at a very senior level of their career ladder. They come to the program with the intention of taking some time to reflect on their life goals, both professional and personal. Therefore, this group of leaders is the ideal place to begin testing our theories on leadership behavior, and to distil the theories into measurable dimensions for 360° instruments.

Identifying the dimensions. To identify the dimensions we wish to measure in a specific questionnaire (for example, dimensions of global leadership, personality traits, or leadership styles), we have interviewed hundreds of senior executives to uncover what issues are most important to them in their day-to-day work, and what kind of behavior contributes to their effectiveness. In some cases, they are also asked to discuss concerns about life balance and stress.

These exploratory interviews are conducted in a semi-structured fashion over a period of many years. Each respondent is approached with a list of open-ended questions pertaining to major concerns. Depending on the responses of the group as a whole, themes are dropped, revised, or retained. Supplemental observational data are collected in the form of notes taken while studying the various executives in meetings and while participating in a large number of action research projects and strategic interventions. In the course of this fieldwork, we arrive at a set of hypotheses about various preoccupations of the participating executives; in other words, while engaged in the process of hypothesis-formulation, the researchers delineate connections, patterns, and themes, continuously modifying their hypotheses as dictated by emerging material.[2] The observed patterns of behavior are then integrated with knowledge about the growth and psychological development of people and the findings of developmental and clinical psychologists on the functioning of human personalities. The constructs that emerge from the in-depth interviews with top executives are content-analyzed by our research team, and then grouped in terms of themes relevant to leadership.

Writing the questions. We then proceed to design the survey instrument itself. We devise a series of statements that reflect the constituent constructs in each dimension. These statements are triangulated during group discussions.

Developing a pilot questionnaire. In order to turn the statements about leadership into a questionnaire with a minimal amount of ambiguity about each of the items, the questionnaire is pretested. The initial pilot questionnaires are distributed to a large group of CEOs who comment on the clarity and the face validity of the questions. After two or more subsequent pre-tests with other top executives and MBA students (for a total of at least 200 respondents) the number of questionnaire items is narrowed down.

Validating a new questionnaire. The psychometric reliability and validity of each new questionnaire is studied in three stages: (1) by checking the internal consistency within each dimension using a classic psychometric approach; (2) by evaluating the structure of the questionnaire through confirmatory factor analysis at both the item level and the dimension level; and (3) by conducting a study of the effects of the characteristics of subject groups (gender, nationality, age and experience, among others).[3]

Translating a questionnaire. Creating new language versions of a questionnaire requires another lengthy process. First, the items are translated into the target language, then back translated. The back-translated version is compared with the original language version, to control for errors of meaning. Then, the new language version is beta-tested with a large group of native speakers. If psychometric analysis shows that the new version is equally robust, it is released for use.

Once the questionnaire has passed these stringent tests, norms and standard deviations are calculated. Feedback pages are designed, using graphs that show percentile rankings, allowing the test-taker to compare his or her scores with those of the large group of high achievers from all over the world in our databases. Finally, the questionnaire is approved for use in executive seminars and courses, and by leadership coaches and consultants in companies. The questionnaires are also adapted for web-based, online use.

THE IGLC 360° SURVEY INSTRUMENTS

Global Executive Leadership Inventory (GELI)[4]

The purpose of the GELI is to investigate what it means to be a world-class leader. What kinds of behavior and actions make for leadership effectiveness? Although many 360° leadership survey instruments exist, there are no others, to our knowledge, that have a global and clinical orientation. Also, based on our exploratory interviews, we have discovered that emotional intelligence, resilience to stress, and life balance are little-explored, yet critical themes in discussions with executives about their concerns. An important objective of the GELI, therefore, is to combine an exploration of these essential dimensions in one 360° questionnaire.

The GELI allows the test-taker to rate his or her own performance, and compare their personal rating with that of a group of observers. Observers–who typically are *superiors*, *direct reports*, *coworkers*, or *others*–respond to the questionnaire anonymously, excepting the test-taker's superior(s). The GELI includes the following twelve dimensions:

Visioning: articulating a compelling vision, mission, and strategy with a multi-country, multi-environment, multi-function, and gender-equality perspective that connects employees, shareholders, suppliers, and customers on a global scale.

Empowering: giving workers at all levels a voice by empowering them through the sharing of information and the delegation of decisions to the people most competent to execute them.

Energizing: motivating employees to actualize the organization's specific vision of the future.

Designing and aligning: creating the proper organizational design and control systems to make the guiding vision a reality, and using those systems to align the behavior of the employees with the organization's values and goals.

Rewarding and giving feedback: setting up the appropriate reward structures and giving constructive feedback to encourage the kind of behavior that is expected from employees.

Team-building: creating team players and focusing on team effectiveness by instilling a cooperative atmosphere, building collaborative interaction, and encouraging constructive conflict.

Outside stakeholder orientation: making employees aware of their outside constituencies, emphasizing particularly the need to respond to the requirements of customers, suppliers, shareholders, and other interest groups, such as local communities affected by the organization.

Global mindset: inculcating a global mentality in the ranks; that is, instilling values that act as a sort of glue between the regional and/or national cultures represented in the organization.

Tenacity: encouraging tenacity and courage in employees by setting a personal example in following through on reasonable risks.

Emotional intelligence: fostering trust in the organization by creating, primarily through example, an emotionally intelligent workforce whose members know themselves and know how to deal respectfully and understandingly with others.

Life balance: articulating and modeling the importance of the need for life balance for the long-term welfare of employees.

Resilience to stress: paying attention to work, career, life, and health stress issues, and balancing appropriately the various kinds of pressures that life brings.

Sample questions
The GELI includes a total of 100 questions in 12 dimensions. Below are sample questions similar to those in the GELI. The test-taker

(and observers) are asked to respond using a scale from 1 (does not describe me at all) to 7 (describes me very well).

Envisioning *sample question*:
I establish a sense of direction for the organization.

Life balance *sample question*:
I maintain a diversity of interests in my private life.

The GELI feedback report
The objective of the GELI is to deepen awareness of the importance of the various dimensions and to encourage test-takers to undertake a close examination of their own capabilities in each of these critical areas. The report also allows executives to compare their own ratings with the average ratings of their group. In the sample feedback graph (Figure 5.1), "Franco" should ask himself why his "Self" scores are higher in all dimensions than those of his observers. It is also interesting to note that his self-perceptions compared with the perceptions of others differ considerably on factors such as Energizing, Rewarding, Designing and Aligning, Team-building, Outside Orientation, Emotional Intelligence and Life Balance. It would be a good idea to discuss the reasons for these variances. What can be done to narrow the gaps? The written comments by the observers that are part of the questionnaire and the various questionnaire items where Franco scores low can give a modicum of insight. The discussion of the variances will be of help in establishing an action plan.

The Personality Audit (PA)[5]

To be effective leaders, executives must begin with an understanding of the reasons for doing what they do. They need to study their motivation from the inside to truly understand what is happening on the outside. This requires taking into consideration their relational world, paying attention to the forces of human development and considering their emotional management. This approach creates a more three-dimensional appreciation of human behavior and helps executives obtain greater access to,

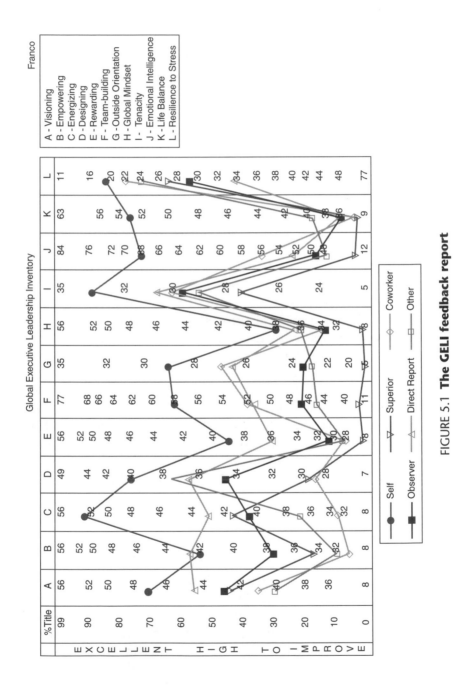

FIGURE 5.1 **The GELI feedback report**

and understanding of, their emotional lives. By providing insight into the ways in which conscious/observable and unconscious/ invisible processes influence behavior, the PA supports a better understanding of interpersonal relationships, recurring conflict patterns, and the meaning of one's actions and experiences.

The PA is a relatively simple tool with 42 questions designed to provide an assessment of seven of the major personality dimensions important in human functioning, and clarify the various motivational needs of executives. There are other assessment tools that try to accomplish this task but they are relatively difficult to use. Moreover, the administration and interpretation of most of such tests require considerable training.

The various theoretical underpinnings of today's understanding of human development form the conceptual basis for the constructs of the PA. The seven dimensions of the instrument–derived from basic aspects of personality–can help people understand the complexities of personality functioning. These dimensions, when assessed by the test-taker and others, provide a glimpse of the executive's inner world.

The PA is designed to record information given by the executive as well as to reflect the perceptions of at least three observers who represent the executive's private and public spheres. Typically, observers in the private sphere (in order of preference) include the spouse or significant other, close family members, and friends. Observers from the public sphere are from the work environment–people who know the executive well in a professional context. Unlike many assessment instruments, the observers are not anonymous. Keeping names attached to scores helps the executive recognize and understand differences in perceptions. In order for test results to reflect potential differences in upward and downward styles of leadership, it is best if at least one superior and one subordinate are included among those asked to give feedback. Of particular interest is the potential divergence in the perception of behavior in the private and public sphere.

Each of the seven dimensions of personality assessed in the PA has two anchor points, for example, high self-esteem and low self-esteem. The dimensions are listed below, followed by descriptions that characterize people who favor each anchor point.

High–Low self-esteem

High self-esteem: Feels attractive, liked, respected, valued in one's activities, confident, self-assured; is self-reliant and interested in presenting a positive image.

Low self-esteem: Feels unattractive, disliked, disrespected; belittles oneself; feels criticized in one's activities; doubts oneself, is self-deprecating, self-abasing and not interested in presenting a positive image.

Trustful–Vigilant

Trustful: Warm, empathetic, caring, affectionate, kind, friendly, open, considerate, agreeable, naïve.

Vigilant: Wary, watchful, bothered by feelings of misgiving and disbelief, skeptical, contrary, prudent, guarded, dissonant, argumentative.

Conscientious–Laissez-faire

Conscientious: Scrupulous, principled, earnest, exact, hardworking, detail-oriented, dedicated, reliable, dependable, thorough, orderly, meticulous, perfectionist.

Laissez-faire: Laid-back, happy-go-lucky, casual, carefree, undirected, untroubled, unrestricted, free and easy, unworried, easy going.

Assertive–Self-effacing

Assertive: Controlling, competitive, ambitious, dominating, mastering the situation, overshadowing, commanding, overpowering, ruling, overseeing, dictating, supervising.

Self-effacing: Submissive, accommodating, yielding, agreeable, assenting, unassertive, compliant, deferential, unpretentious.

Extroverted–Introverted

Extroverted: Outgoing, outwardly directed, sociable, congenial, amicable, people-oriented, approachable, gregarious, unreserved, easygoing.

Introverted: Self-observing, self-scrutinizing, reserved, a loner, a brooder, shy, timid, quiet, unapproachable, remote, aloof, distant, unreachable, standoffish, self-contained, self-reliant, private, withdrawn.

High-spirited–Low-spirited

High-spirited: Optimistic, ebullient, exhilarated, vivacious, sparkling, excited, enthusiastic, lively, cheerful, bubbly, buoyant, lighthearted, animated; has élan, gaiety and passion.
Low-spirited: Pessimistic, somber, unhappy, sad, melancholic, blue, heavy, disheartened, glum, cheerless, solemn, dejected, disconsolate, discouraged, depressed.

Adventurous–Prudent

Adventurous: Inquisitive, searching, venturesome, curious, eager for knowledge, original, nonconformist, creative, exploratory, daring, incautious.
Prudent: Conventional, conformist, conservative, rigid, prosaic, methodical, habitual, careful, orthodox, pedestrian, cautious.

Conscientious–Laissez-faire *sample question*:

I prefer to take care of problems …		
BY MYSELF	1 2 3 4 5 6 7	WITH THE HELP OF OTHERS

The scale goes from left to right, with 4 being the neutral point. For example, for this statement, if the person rarely feels autonomous, he should mark number **1**. If the person feels he is somewhere in the middle of the two contrasting statements, he should mark **4**. If he always asks for help, he would mark **7**.

The PA report

The PA report consists of several graphs that summarize the self and observer responses for the seven personality dimensions. It also includes bar charts that show the raw self and observer scores for each question as well as the variance. The report also allows executives to compare their own ratings with the average ratings of their group. The PA results graphs show scores and percentiles on a bi-polar scale, with results on either end of the scale (extreme right or left side) being less frequent and less desirable. In the sample Personal Graph (Figure 5.2), we see that there are some inconsistencies in the scores. Various people perceive the test-taker quite differently. For example, the scores

89

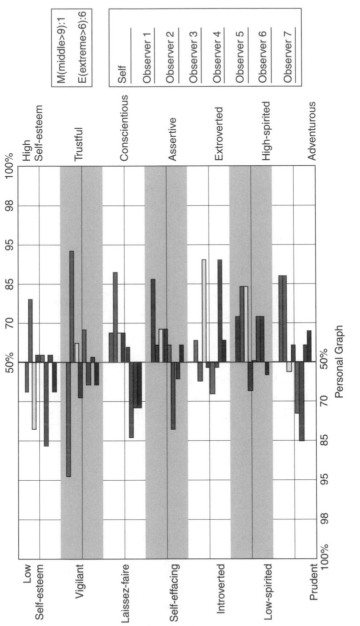

FIGURE 5.2 **The PA feedback report**

from Observer 1 (the test-taker's wife) are quite different from scores from other observers, and the executive himself. The lines in a real PA graph are color coded. In this figure, the Self results are shown in the top line, Observer 1 results are in the second line, and so on. Consider the range of scores on the Vigilant–Trustful dimension. What could the executive learn from the fact that although he considers himself to be quite vigilant, his wife feels that he is very, perhaps overly, trustful? The advantage of identifying observers in this instrument is that the executive will be able to ask his wife that very question. In the Prudent–Adventurous dimension, he might want to think about why two of his observers consider him to be a rather cautious person. Perhaps he should examine his relationship with those two people. Is he hiding a part of himself from them that others are able to see?

As with the GELI, the PA includes a number of personal questions, allowing the observers to make additional comments about the test-taker that will be helpful for the feedback process.

The Leadership Archetypes Questionnaire (LAQ)[6]

Personality theorists recognize that certain constellations of character traits–archetypes–recur on a regular basis. A leadership archetype characterizes the way in which leaders deal with people and situations in an organizational context. These archetypes represent prototypes for ideas, a template for interpreting observed phenomena and understanding behavior.

Effective leaders have two roles–a charismatic one and an architectural one. In the charismatic role, leaders envision a better future and empower and energize their subordinates. In the architectural role, leaders address issues related to organizational design and control and reward systems.

Both roles are necessary for effective leadership, but it is a rare leader who can fulfill both roles seamlessly. Usually, alignment is only achieved within a leadership role constellation when it is constructed of team members with complementary archetypical leadership styles. A group of carefully selected individuals can become a highly effective team that delivers much more than the sum of its parts.

The eight leadership archetypes included in the LAQ are *strategist*, *change-catalyst*, *transactor*, *builder*, *innovator*, *processor*, *coach*, and *communicator*.

Strategists are good at dealing with developments in the organization's environment. They provide vision, strategic direction and outside-the-box thinking to create new organizational forms and generate future growth.

Change-catalysts love messy situations. They are masters at re-engineering and creating new organizational "blueprints."

Transactors are great deal-makers. Skilled at identifying and tackling new opportunities, they thrive on negotiations.

Builders dream of creating a new organization and have the talent and determination to make their dream come true.

Innovators are focused on the new. They possess a great capacity to solve extremely difficult problems. They like to innovate.

Processors like an organization to be a smoothly running, well-oiled machine. They are very effective at setting up the structures and systems needed to support an organization's objectives.

Coaches are very good at developing people, to get the best out of them. They create high-performance teams and high-performance cultures.

Communicators are great influencers, and have a considerable impact on their surroundings.

The LAQ helps leaders understand the way they deal with people and situations in an organizational context, identify situations in which a particular leadership style could be most effective, and think about what it is like to work with people who demonstrate certain dominant behaviors. It also helps them determine the best roles for each team member, the best way to manage and work for people with certain dominant characteristics, and which combination of styles works well and which to avoid. Finally, it can help leaders create teams of executives best suited to particular challenges, for example, merger integration, new product development, or transition periods. The test-taker responds to each statement using a 1–7 scale, with the anchor points "does not describe me at all" (1) to "describes me very well" (7).

Communicator *sample question*:
An important part of my role is representing our organization to outside stakeholders.

Builder *sample question*:
I am most happy when I am creating something new in the organization.

The LAQ report
Ideally, the LAQ 360° process is undertaken by a group of executives working together in core teams. The questionnaire should be completed by the individual and also by members of one or two of the core team(s) to which the person belongs (for example, colleagues from the same department, and fellow members of an executive team). A third category includes all interested others inside or outside the organization (for example, clients or people from other departments or subsidiaries). Each individual will receive a graph showing his or her score on each archetype and a graph of the scores of the others (a graph for all others and a graph for each team). This circumplex model is interesting in that it also shows the relationships between dimensions; proximity conveys similarity (for example, Builder and Processor) (Figure 5.3).

For example, in the graph (Figure 5.3), we see that the test-taker scores high on many of the leadership archetypes, indicating a great flexibility in dealing with different situations. His lowest score is in the coaching area, suggesting a need to work on that dimension of his style or make an effort to have someone in his team take on a complementary role. In addition to the personal report, the self-score, core team score(s), and others' scores of all the members of the organization participating in the test are then averaged and mapped on another spider-web grid (Figure 5.4), where congruencies and discrepancies for a team as a whole become immediately visible. The example (the scores of the other

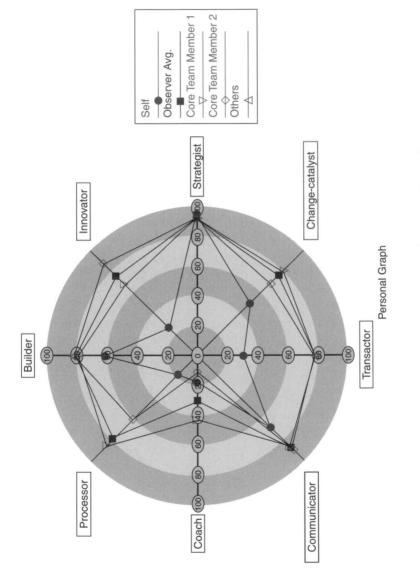

FIGURE 5.3 **The LAQ feedback personal graph**

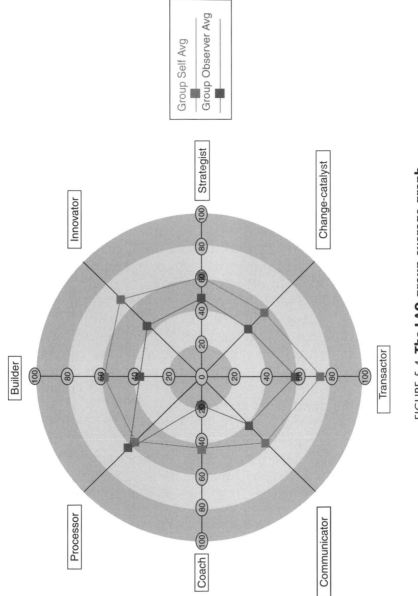

FIGURE 5.4 **The LAQ group average graph**

members of the team of the previous test-taker) shows the self and team average lines. At a glance, we see that this team lacks individuals with coaching skills. In particular, their observers suggest that coaching is something that barely exists. This could signal future problems for this fast-growing organization. There doesn't appear to be enough leadership development taking place; has thought been given to succession issues?

As with the GELI and the PA, the LAQ also includes a number of questions attached to the questionnaire where the observers can make additional comments.

INTERPRETING 360° FEEDBACK SURVEYS

Just as leaders come in many different forms and shapes, many different combinations of scores on the various dimensions can make for leadership effectiveness. Because the dimensions on the various instruments described above are highly independent, an "excellent" or "to improve" score in one dimension does not imply a similar score in other dimensions. Similarly, it is common for an individual to have a more pronounced tendency toward one pole in some dimensions of a personality test, and be rather nearer the centre of other scales. And, of course, a well-balanced team by definition requires people who have clear abilities in some areas, but not all. By comparing scores and dimensions, in fact, we can differentiate leadership styles and encourage a person's natural tendencies and inclinations.

Furthermore, depending on the position of the individual in the organization and the type of organization, certain dimensions will be more relevant than others. For example, dimensions such as Global Mindset or Outside Orientation may be of less importance to some people. It should be remembered, too, that leadership must always be considered in the context of a specific situation. The socioeconomic and political environment in which a leader operates helps determine which leadership style is more appropriate in a given situation, as do the nature of the industry and the life stage of the company. In addition, one should keep in mind that the data on which the normalization process for these feedback instruments are based are *not* from a random sample of the working population, but rather a large number of top executives. In the case of the GELI, it is important to keep in mind when using this comparison base that an *average* score is already quite high.

The objective of the 360° feedback process is to deepen the individual's understanding of the importance of the various dimensions and to encourage test-takers to examine their own capabilities in each of these critical areas. Although there is no such thing as a perfect score on all dimensions, a high score on certain dimensions can indicate greater leadership effectiveness (again, depending on the context). As we mentioned in our discussions of the different IGLC instruments, above, insight into one's position relative to the norm comes through such questions as these: Which scores are high, which are average? What leadership style do these results describe? Is this style congruent with the environment in which the person works? Once again, what is important is not only the test-taker's relative position compared with the norm but, in particular, the comparison between the self and observer scores. Are the differences higher or lower? Are there similar or different amplitudes across the dimensions or scales?

OBSTACLES TO IMPLEMENTATION

The introduction of a 360° feedback process frequently triggers resistance. One perceptive cartoon has two executives talking in a hallway. One says to the other, "It's not the 360° appraisal that worries me; it's the 360° reprisals that follow." This highlights a very real problem: human nature being what it is, negative feedback can lead to defensive reactions on the part of the person being assessed, dooming the development process in that organization.

Some executives–those for whom position and authority are important–view this type of exercise as the overstepping of boundaries by subordinates. Others fear that the process will jeopardize working relationships by delving into problem areas; they would rather let sleeping dogs lie. Finally, some people worry that there might be negative political implications, scores might be manipulated, or misused as a part of a performance review.

If the feedback process is launched without acknowledging these issues, people may resort to a multitude of defense mechanisms to deflect attention from their feedback results. Among the most common defenses we see are as follows:

- *The mathematics defense*: calculating and recalculating the numbers in an attempt to make them add up differently; questioning the validity of the norms and standard deviations
- *The bad-timing defense*: blaming poor results on upheaval in the organization
- *The negligence defense*: not following up with observers to be sure they fill out their questionnaires
- *The scapegoat defense*: attempting to guess which observer was responsible for a low score, and arguing that this individual's score skews the graph unfairly
- *The IT defense*: "I couldn't make the web platform work, so I gave up."

Even though most people agree that 360° feedback is valuable to both individuals and organizations, for most people, it requires a great leap of faith to really listen to feedback and use it as a part of their personal development journey. To start a constructive dialogue even before the process begins, we ask executives: How often do you elicit feedback? How do you feel when you receive feedback? We feel it is essential to take the time to build an environment of trust before asking people to embark on this type of journey. Constructive dialogue *before* and *during* the process helps to build a foundation of commitment and accountability to the action plan and change process.

THE IMPORTANCE OF FOLLOWING UP

The real challenge of 360° feedback is to do something with the information received. The value of the questionnaire is that it offers a jumping-off point for reflection and discussion leading to a development plan for improvement. For example, a discussion about the dimensions with fellow respondents helps clarify the different sides of an executive's personality: the one she shows, the one she has, and the one she thinks she has.

For the process to be successful, executives need to do the following:

- Pay attention to the feedback, keeping an open mind and striving to minimize defensive reactions. Executives should ask themselves such questions as, "Does the feedback make sense? Is the information to the point? Does it reveal a new perspective? Does it provide useful data about my possible blind spots?"
- Thank the respondents for their efforts, to validate the candor and courage that are required of observers (particularly when the feedback is given by subordinates).
- Share the feedback with others–their spouse or significant other, their manager or their coach. This process of exchange serves as a reality check and helps the executive identify possible routes to improvement.
- Return to the people who gave their feedback, sharing with them ideas for improvement, asking for their reactions, and enlisting their help to work toward change.
- Develop and implement a plan for change.
- Review progress every three to four months; consider taking the same 360° survey again, with the same observers if possible.

LEADERSHIP COACHING GUIDELINES

A critical part of the leadership development feedback process is ensuring that it is constructive. We use these instruments as a part of a group intervention process: leaders discuss their feedback results with their peers (from the same or different organizations) in a group, guided by an executive coach who facilitates constructive discussion, praise and criticism, and the identification of concrete action steps. By creating a safe, transitional space for the members of the group, the executive coach taps into the powerful group effect on supporting change through engaging the collective mind, heart, and experience of the group. Here are some suggestions for making the most of the 360° feedback process:

TAKE THE EXECUTIVE'S PERSPECTIVE

Look at some weaknesses as exaggerated strengths. For example, *conscientiousness*, one of the character traits measured on the PA, is important for a finance executive. The numbers must add up. However, when it is overdone, conscientiousness can lead to micro-management and a lack of delegation, both of which can have a stifling effect on subordinates.

Remember that persistent behavior patterns must have had benefits at one time. But behavior that was effective for someone at one point in his or her career might not be effective at another point. As the person moves forward, other qualities increase in importance.

Keep in mind that assuming that others think and act like we do can lead to unrealistic expectations. People do not usually think and act the same way, and that is especially true when we deal with people from different cultures.

Be aware of outdated, distorted perceptions that an executive might have of herself. For example, parents or teachers may have stated that a person is not very good at certain things. Such statements often become self-fulfilling prophecies, with the result that the person stays in her comfort zone and avoids experimentation. Your task as a coach is to challenge such assumptions.

FACILITATE REFLECTION

Ask lots of open-ended questions. Closed questions – those that can be answered "yes" or "no" – provide little useful information. Open-ended questions encourage people to decide what issues are important.

Ask executives to evaluate their own performance. Evaluating themselves offers people an opportunity to assess their ability to be discriminatory and permits insight into their capacity for reality testing.

Encourage people to develop their own solutions. Only in rare circumstances, such as critical situations, should executive coaches prescribe what their clients should do. The task, instead, is to encourage clients to find the solutions by themselves, making for greater commitment and a greater likelihood that things will change.

Establish a relationship of trust. The relationship of trust and mutual respect within a group helps individuals move beyond their comfort zones and take the risk of exploring new behaviors. A positive working alliance is essential for the 360° process.

Address defensive reactions immediately. An executive coach needs to acknowledge and address negative feelings, in whatever form these appear, immediately. In dealing with defensive reaction, the coach should not address these head on, but play "resistance judo" by doing it in a subtle way. To put a new twist on an old saying, "strike when the iron is cold." When the iron is too hot–when people get too emotionally wound up–they stop listening. The coach should not be sidetracked by requests to recalculate the scores, or identify the one observer who brought the executive's average down.

Encourage leaders to experiment with new approaches and strategies. In the group discussion of feedback results, people can help one another explore different options for new ways of thinking and acting. The group can provide a safe environment for individuals to test some of these new approaches.

Reinforce learning from other's experience in a group coaching session. Group members serve not only as powerful supporters in the process of a group coaching session, but also provide great material for vicarious learning based on other's varied experiences.

Allow executives time to change. The "working through" process takes time because people need to take small steps to build up their self-confidence in finding new directions. We strongly recommend follow-up sessions, and regular communication among members of the group.

101

Strive to create greater self-awareness. The goal is for the executive to become a reflective practitioner, a person who doesn't merely act, but also reflects on the implications of his actions.

CONCLUSION

In a global environment characterized by continuous and discontinuous change, successful organizations are characterized by a distributive, collective, and complementary form of leadership. To create and maintain these forms of leadership within an organization, we must identify leadership role configurations that contribute to greater performance and adaptability within a specific context. 360° feedback instruments are among the tools that help us engage in this type of leadership design, by informing us about the qualities, skills, and competencies leaders must have to be effective, the roles they must play, and the way these various roles complement one another. In addition, because a clinically oriented 360° feedback process provides feedback from both the private and the public spheres, it can help executives make connections between patterns of conflict at work and interpersonal and emotional problems within the family.

Although individuals on their own can use 360° instruments, these tools are used most effectively when working with an executive coach, a counselor, a consultant, a psychotherapist, or in group settings such as workshops and retreats where a facilitator can help the executive understand and apply the results. In general, discoveries about oneself are difficult to process unless they are shared with other people, whose observations help to clarify personal reflections and encourage new ways of thinking, feeling, and behaving, enabling a coming to terms with the difficult task of identifying previously unacknowledged parts of the self.

In the case of senior executives, self-reflection facilitated by a clinically oriented feedback process may well have a beneficial effect on overall organizational functioning, not the least on the multitudes of stakeholders–employees, customers, suppliers and shareholders, and even family members–who are affected by the leader's decisions.

NOTES

1. London, M., A.G. Wohlers, and P. Gallagher (1990). "360-Degree Feedback Surveys: A Source of Feedback to Guide Management Development," *Journal of Management Development* 9: 17–31; Hazucha, J.F., S.A. Hezlett, and R.J. Schneider (1993). "The Impact of 360-Degree Feedback on Management Skills Development," *Human Resource Management* 32: 325–351; Kluger, A.N. and A. DeNisi (1996). "The Effects of Feedback Interventions on Performance: A Historical View, a Meta-Analysis, and a Preliminary Feedback Intervention Theory," *Psychological Bulletin* 119: 254–284; Walker, A.G. and J.W. Smither (1999). "A Five-Year Study of Upward Feedback: What Managers Do With Their Results Matters," *Personnel Psychology* 52: 393–423.
2. Glaser, B.G. and A.L. Strauss (1967). *The Discovery of Grounded Theory: Strategies for Qualitative Research.* Hawthorne, NY: de Gruyter; Argyris, C. and D. Schön (1978). *Organizational Learning: A Theory of Action Perspective.* Reading, MA: Addison-Wesley.
3. For greater detail on the psychometric design and testing of IGLC 360° survey instruments, see Kets de Vries, M.F.R., P. Vrignaud, K. Korotov, and E. Florent-Treacy (2006). "The Development of the Personality Audit: A Psychodynamic Multiple Feedback Assessment Instrument," *International Journal of Human Resource Management* 17 (5): 898–917; Kets de Vries, M.F.R., P. Vrignaud, and E. Florent-Treacy (2004). "The Global Leadership Life Inventory: Development and Psychometric Properties of a 360-Degree Feedback Instrument," *The International Journal of Human Resource Management* 15 (3): 475–492; Kets de Vries, M.F.R. (2005). "Leadership Archetypes: An exposition," INSEAD Working Paper 2005/75/ENT.
4. For a complete discussion of this test see Kets de Vries, M.F.R. (2005). *Global Executive Leadership Inventory: Participant Workbook*, San Francisco, CA: Pfeiffer and Kets de Vries, M.F.R. (2005). *Global Executive Leadership Inventory: Facilitator Guide*, San Francisco, CA: Pfeiffer.
5. For a complete discussion of the PA see Kets de Vries, M.F.R. (2005). *Personality Audit: Participant Guide*, Fontainebleau, INSEAD Global Leadership Centre and Kets de Vries, M.F.R. (2005). *Personality Audit: Facilitator Guide*, Fontainebleau, INSEAD Global Leadership Centre; Kets de Vries, M.F.R., P. Vrignaud, K. Korotov, and E. Florent-Treacy (2006). "The Development of The Personality Audit: A Psychodynamic Multiple Feedback Assessment Instrument," *International Journal of Human Resource Management* 17 (5): 898–917.
6. For a complete discussion of the Leadership Archetype Questionnaire see Kets de Vries, M.F.R. (2006). *Leadership Archetype Questionnaire: Participant Guide*, Fontainebleau, INSEAD Global Leadership Centre and Kets de Vries, M.F.R. (2006). *Leadership Archetype Questionnaire: Facilitator Guide*, Fontainebleau, INSEAD Global Leadership Centre.

PART TWO: COACHING PROGRAM DESIGN

6

EXECUTIVE DEVELOPMENT AND LEADERSHIP COACHING

MARTINE VAN DEN POEL

During the last 25 years, executive education has taken its place next to graduate education in the world's business schools. In the 1980s, most business schools witnessed substantial growth in their open enrolment programs. At the same time, many of them started to engage in an emerging market for customized programs.

The 1990s were marked by two phenomena: a confirmed growth and increasing demand for customized programs on the one hand, and on the other, a new, fast-growing need for leadership training, fueled by the shift in requirements from traditional management development to leadership development. The purpose of this chapter is threefold. Here I will:

- outline reasons why leadership development coaching has become an essential part of executive development;
- look into the context and conditions under which leadership coaching can be developed for optimal results within the executive development context and
- assess (to the extent possible) the impact the leadership coaching processes can have on behavioral change.

THE NATURAL LINK BETWEEN EXECUTIVE DEVELOPMENT AND LEADERSHIP COACHING

As director of INSEAD's customized programs (1992–1995) and subsequently of all its Executive Education Programs (1995–2000), I witnessed a number of early signals and changes in perspectives:

The limits of traditional executive education teaching

INSEAD, not unlike other leading business schools, had three important General Management Programs as the mainstay of its executive education portfolio, for senior managers, middle managers and young managers. Their main mission was to deliver continuing education at a high level in a number of functional areas, including operations, marketing, finance, strategy and organizational behavior, adapted to the particular level of the manager.

Analyzing a large number of program evaluations, I was struck by the difference between overall scores that were generally excellent, and comments in the fine print. Answers to the question about "issues that need to be addressed more" almost invariably included comments like, "I wish to understand myself better both as a person and as a manager," "I want to improve my impact as a manager," "What leadership style do I have or should I have?" "How am I perceived as a manager?" "How can I better manage my work-life balance?"

The prevailing sense was that the participants were satisfied with the up-to-date practical knowledge, theories and concepts of better management they had been exposed to. Given the INSEAD environment and perspective, they had also learned a considerable amount about working with different cultures in their group case discussions and simulations. But it appeared that issues of personal concern, and questions about their identity as leaders, had not been touched at all, except in some rare cases where a faculty member dared to mix a few self-assessment exercises and emotional elements into his or her teaching.

The growing importance of 360° feedback and the response processes on the job

By the mid- to late 1990s, most Anglo-Saxon and Nordic multinationals had systematically introduced some form of 360° evaluations for executives into their organizations. The degree to which this was accepted by the executives and facilitated into workable action plans for dealing with some of the gaps in their leadership profiles varied widely from company to company.

Some companies diligently provided feedback support and professional debriefs to their executives afterwards, while others just dumped the 360° feedback results on individual managers with little after-care. The results of 360° feedback were also sometimes linked to bonus compensation schemes, thereby eclipsing the opportunity for non-threatening developmental benefits. Most critically, however, a large number of the 360° reports were totally unlinked to the larger leadership and broader executive development needs of the executive, and his or her potential future leadership transitions.

At that time, the Centre for Creative Leadership (CCL) was the only professional organization that linked in-depth 360° feedback (*Benchmarks* was their key 360° instrument) to leadership and personal development. Beginning in the 1970s, in their one-week Leadership for Development Program and customized programs, CCL also used small group work and one-to-one feedback processes, by and large made possible by an economic model that allowed much lower margins than traditional business schools. A number of companies, mostly American, and subsidiaries of those companies, regularly sent their managers to the CCL program. The field of self-assessment and leadership development was expanded further by offshoots from CCL, such as Personnel Decisions Inc, who also developed their own instruments, such as *Profilor.*

Yet, for many executives and many HR executives, leadership development was still largely developed on the job or through an in-house 360°, or through a special leadership program in a stand-alone organization. Classic business schools, and particularly their organizational behavior departments, were very wary of bringing the self-assessment process within their main teaching portfolio. An exception was Ashridge Business School, who introduced these processes through a joint venture with CCL in the 1980s, and in 1995 created Ashridge Consulting, which offers leadership consulting and coaching.

In 1991, INSEAD started the three-week *Challenge of Leadership Program*, created and directed by Professor Manfred Kets de Vries, and based on the clinical approach to leadership development, with a number of 360° instruments and a very innovative pedagogical process, which constituted a real "identity laboratory" enabling executive change and transformation. (The identity laboratory concept is discussed in Chapter Seven.) Though the program was, and still is, very successful, it was an outlier in the overall executive education offering of the early 1990s, and best practice was not transferred to our other programs until later that decade.

The growing need to make executive development stick: linking personal and professional development

The 1990s saw an increased demand for measuring the return on investment from executive education. In addition, more and more companies and HR managers were looking for ways to make those investments, particularly in open enrolment programs, stick. They expected some lasting personal change as a result of the process. Demands for specific "take-aways," "tools for Monday morning back on the job," re-entry strategies, personal action plans and so on were voiced everywhere.

In addition, just as in the medical world, where there was a growing acceptance that physical wellness and emotional wellness are interlinked, in the business world more and more executives and HR managers realized that personal development and professional and managerial development in the leadership area were interdependent. Questions such as "What holds a manager back in his or her leadership development?" opened up the way for deeper questions: "What are the major themes in this person's personal setup or profile that explains these blockages?" "Which processes can help this person first increase his or her self-awareness, second, analyze the perception gap and third, act upon this gap through behavioral change?"

Similarly, it became accepted that change begins to happen when there is an emotional experience, when one has an opportunity to share and delve into one's own story, when one moves from being a passive recipient to an active, involved person.[1]

Eventually, a number of business schools started to act on this realization, integrating some form of 360° feedback and leadership coaching, usually beginning with general management programs. Once the high impact of such activities was recognized, there was no stopping them.

Currently, leadership coaching at INSEAD is not only a core part of all general management programs, it is also part of many customized programs and has led to a boom in specific leadership development courses. This development has been enabled by the creation of the INSEAD Global Leadership Centre (IGLC) in 2003, instigated by a report from the Boston Consulting Group to the INSEAD faculty that suggested that the school had a lack of focus on leadership. Manfred Kets de Vries was invited by the Deans to become the product champion to enable such a focus and be the Director of IGLC. Over time, IGLC has developed a series of innovative leadership programs (including the in-house diploma program, Consulting and Coaching for Change, which promotes the development of a pool of highly qualified international coaches) and has introduced the series of 360° feedback instruments (described in Chapter Five).

OPTIMAL INTEGRATION OF LEADERSHIP COACHING AND EXECUTIVE DEVELOPMENT: KEY INGREDIENTS AND A VARIETY OF PROCESSES

As our experience with the integration of leadership coaching in executive education grew, the ideal conditions under which leadership development activities and coaching processes could be successfully integrated into our executive programs became clear.
We have identified seven key ingredients for successfully integrating leadership development coaching into an executive development program.

A natural time for reflection

The very first condition for any leadership development process is reflection, in other words, creating a state of mind where the executive can think freely, without specific time boundaries and with a true notion of slack time. Any executive development program, be it a four-week advanced management program, a three-week program for young managers, a ten-day company-specific customized program on our campus or in any other neutral place, sets the stage for this "away from everyday business" feeling. Within this favorable context, the leadership coaching leverages the slack time. We commit a minimum of one or one- and-one-half days to our leadership coaching process, giving the executive time to reflect deeply on his or her leadership challenges with a small group of colleagues.

The importance of high quality, thoughtful and broad feedback

Understanding your own blind spots and the various different perceptions that others may have of you as a leader is a key ingredient to starting the process. INSEAD's Global Leadership Centre 360° instruments (The Global Leadership Inventory, The Personality Audit, The Leadership Archetype Questionnaire, the Personal Feedback Page) give a very rich, complete and in-depth leadership profile and assessment. We usually also combine the feedback from the work environment (the full 360°) with feedback from the personal environment (family, partner, friends, children) that assures a more holistic perspective. This feedback is gathered electronically via a web platform, four to six weeks before the executive attends the program.

Critical influence of the small group coaching process

The small group coaching process is a unique pedagogical process for leadership development that we developed over the years at INSEAD.[2] It combines a number of critical success factors, such as the cultural and functional diversity in each group, the (contained) self-disclosure process that gives a feeling of catharsis and letting go of emotions, the process of understanding oneself through hearing the stories of others, the power of group pressure for dealing with important issues combined with the power of group support for change and finally, the atmosphere of confidence and security created by the coach. A group coaching session is a process whereby participants take turns to present their stories, supported by a self-portrait, a debrief of the result of the 360°-leadership feedback package, a review of personal feedback from work and non-work environments, and observations and reflections of other participants.

The profile and competence of the leadership coach

Generally, we work with coaches who combine a degree of clinical training with some managerial experience. The coaches need management experience and maturity to accelerate the understanding of the issues discussed, and to build empathy with each member of the group. The coach must also have sufficient international sophistication to gauge the cultural subtleties of each individual and the multinational (or family firm) the individual works for. The clinical training of the coach will allow him or her to understand and manage the underlying psychological issues, potential pathologies and the group dynamics in the team. Finally, a good leadership coach will have a strong notion of common sense to allow for practical discussions and action plans. The majority of our coaches are graduates of our Consulting and Coaching for Change Program, an Executive Diploma Program in Clinical Organizational Psychology.[3] This assures a consistency in outlook, familiarity with instruments and allows for seamless coordination between the coaches, added to the rich background and experience that each one of them brings.

A variety of processes for follow up

While the initial coaching process for all programs leads to an Individual Action Plan (also called a Personal Action Commitment or Setting Your Leadership Agenda, SYLA), each program has its own dedicated follow up process. For a number of programs, such as Leadership Transition and Coaching and Consulting for Change, we follow up on Leadership Action Plans through group conference calls to discuss progress between on-campus modules. For the year-long Executive MBA Program, there are two full-day, small group leadership development coaching sessions at the beginning and the end of the program, and specific action plans are followed up with one-to-one phone calls from the coach between these sessions.

For other programs (for example, the Advanced Management Program) we have introduced an additional half-day coaching session on how the *leadership* action plan interlinks with the executive's *business* action plan after the initial coaching process and one-day action plan session. The same small group works together on the potential pitfalls and positive re-enforcements between the two action plans. An example of a positive re-enforcement is a situation where one's leadership action plan calls for increased delegation and where one's business plan calls for increased investment in new business development, in other words, the success of the second action plan is highly dependent on the success of the first action plan.

For other programs, for example the three-week Management Acceleration Program (MAP), we combine two-thirds of a day of small group coaching with one-third of a day of individual one-to-one coaching on campus, followed up 100 days later with a group conference call facilitated by the coach. (See Appendix One for a detailed description of the full leadership development process in the MAP. See Appendix Two for a case study of the conference calls with a group of MAP participants.)

In other customized programs, we developed a "six-months after," a second 360° degree Global Executive Leadership Inventory (GELI) survey to allow the executives to measure their progress also in a more quantitative way.

In most leadership coaching processes, participants are asked to choose a learning partner (also called *peer coach*) within their small group with whom they commit to follow up on each other's progress via e-mail or telephone on mutually agreed up dates over a three-month period following the program.

A relevant question is, of course, to what extent do these follow-up processes work and do they even happen? As a general rule, follow-up group conference coaching calls and one-to-one phone coaching sessions in between modules of programs have a high success rate because there is a higher commitment by the members of the group and from the participant himself or herself because progress will be discussed when they come back to campus for the next module. For follow-up telephone

114

coaching with the small group or one-to-one after the end of a program, the success rate is less clear and seems to average about 50%. (Later in this chapter, we will address the deeper question of "Did the leadership coaching session really lead to any behavioral change?")

Linking moments and integrating the coaching within the overall program

It seems critical to us that the leadership coaching process is closely integrated with any other experiential learning process within the overall program, such as outdoor group experiences and simulation exercises, and with the basic organizational behavior and strategy concepts. This allows the coach to integrate the various feedbacks into the group session and it allows the participant gradually to bring leadership concepts and practice together. Within the general management programs, coordination among the coaches is assured by an IGLC program director who coordinates with both the overall program director and other faculty members involved.

As a result, leadership is a theme that runs like a thread through the overall program, as illustrated by the case of our MAP.[4] On our highly successful three-week general management program for young managers, participants may attend either the continuous program on the Fontainebleau campus twice a year, or the modular program offered during two weeks at our Singapore campus and one week in Fontainebleau.

While the leadership development coaching process has been successfully integrated into the Advanced Management Program and the International Executive Program since 2000, the process was first introduced in the MAP in 2003, following the growing realization that leadership can be coached at a relatively young age, when managers are facing their first managerial positions and either managing their first teams or having a staff function where influencing without authority becomes a leadership challenge.

Within the customized programs, the IGLC program director ensures that the coaches are knowledgeable about the company's strategy, the corporate culture, the leadership competency grid and the possible link or overlap between the company's 360° and IGLC 360° instruments. In addition, key senior executives are interviewed beforehand by the IGLC program director regarding major leadership challenges before the coaching process starts. Regular feedback loops are put in place between the company HR professionals and the IGLC program director to adapt the process in between the modules or between different cohorts.

As an example, we developed a leadership coaching process together with SAP in their Global Leadership Development Program (GLDP) started in 2004 (see Appendix Three for a detailed description of the SAP GLDP). This program was developed for SAP's global executives worldwide, with the objective of giving them the tools and develop new skills to execute SAP's global strategy. As Peter Boback, SAP senior consultant for Executive and Management Development, explains: "Leadership team coaching is a situation of Leadership Culture in Action. While receiving feedback and valuable support from the professional coach and the peers in their team, the executives actually build and improve their capabilities to act as coaches themselves. The team leadership coaching also constitutes a microcosm of the current leadership culture at SAP."

Different leadership coaching themes in different leadership transitions

We have identified several key leadership challenges for executives over the years.[5] While many leadership challenges are general and relate to core themes, such as relationship with conflict and its origins, relationship with authority, a need for control, a desire to receive protection or give protection, an inability to say no, a lack of self-esteem, the "imposter syndrome,"[6] an undigested experience with loss and separation, a strong need for emotional attachment, or a need for exploration and assertion,[7] we do see specific leadership challenges crystallizing around specific job stages and specific life cycle stages.

For participants in the MAP, for example, the ability to empower, inspire and motivate one's first team constitutes a major challenge, just as the ability to manage one's boss is rarely a natural task for these young executives. For the middle managers that we encounter, the tension between the emotional attachment to a specific company (and company culture) and the need for exploration and moving on is a difficult challenge. For senior managers in our Advanced Management Program, issues of working identity,[8] the transition to pre-retirement, the management of a major disappointment in missing a promotion, boredom, the desire to pass one's knowledge on to the next generation, the skewed work-life balance and a different notion of time, for example, constitute a new set of issues that may not have been faced before.

In addition, a number of special programs have been developed entirely devoted to leadership. One such program is Leadership Transition directed by Professor Herminia Ibarra, who defines transitions as "key junctures or the inflection points in a person's career at which they either learn how to lead or become derailed."[9] When an executive is given a stretch assignment, this calls for a fundamental role change, which in turn calls for new skills, relationships and styles of interacting with others. The program, spread over two modules, looks at what leaders do, who leaders are, and how leaders evolve.

THE ETERNAL QUESTION: IS THERE ANY IMPACT AND HOW DO WE MEASURE IT?

All executive development experts are familiar with the "happy sheets" at the end of a program, the evaluation sheets filled out by the participants. It certainly gives a great sense of value-added when the evaluations of the leadership coaching process are systematically highly marked and include very positive comments.

However, the questions remain: What happens to the diligently filled out action plan, with the success measures and obstacles the participants spent hours talking about and creating? After they return to their companies, do they respect the timeframes they committed to? Do they enlist the help of enablers and support persons as part of the action process that the coaches recommended?

We know that the business world changes so fast that often during the follow-up phone calls, barely 6 to 12 weeks later, the context may already be different: promotion, a company merger, a private equity firm having bought up the company, a major restructuring where participants might be fired and so on.

Nevertheless, we hear remarkable stories of real change and of life-changing insights: from the senior manager who realized that his obesity was a way of coping with unbearable stress and who lost 15 kilos over the following three months and asked for a job change, to the young manager who wrote a letter to his coach thanking him for his suggestion that he needed to work with a therapist after the program to go deeper into his suicidal and self-destructive behavior.

Appendix Two gives an example of enacted change, in a "100-days after" group conference call with the participants and coach of a MAP. These are simple tales of four young managers acting on their action plans in ways that they are comfortable with and with goals that they find attainable. They are also the output of a mere 1.5 day investment on leadership coaching in a three-week program, and have no comparison with the deeper change and renewal processes that happen as a result of much longer leadership programs over multiple weeks in multiple modules and with recurrent coaching sessions in between, and even follow-up modules years later. One group of participants of the four-week Challenge of Leadership Program, for example, still meet in their original groups and have met regularly with the program director-coach for the last 10 years. Of course there are also other stories of participants from the MAP who went back to the job, filed their leadership action plan neatly in their drawer and never looked at it again.

LEADERSHIP COACHING IS HERE TO STAY

In conclusion, we think that leadership coaching in executive education can only continue to grow in importance. Innovative ways of integrating the process into a large number of executive development initiatives will be developed, particularly in the follow-up phase. Business schools might also develop parallel processes with leadership coaches worldwide working with executives who are following a functional, general management or even company-specific program in several modules on campus. Flexibility and customization is the name of the game for business schools; for leadership teachers and coaches, solid training, high ethical standards and real value-added contributions are essential.

APPENDIX ONE

A CASE IN POINT: MAP AND SYLA

During the three-week MAP (Management Acceleration Program), the integrated leadership development process is referred to as SYLA (Setting Your Leadership Agenda). An integrated collection of events and processes focusing on leadership and personal development and culminating in an action agenda, SYLA was developed by the MAP Program Director, Charles Galunic, together with IGLC.
SYLA's objectives are:

- To pro vide instruments for self-assessment (personal and 360° feedback) designed to support the participant's leadership and personal development
- To provide team-based outdoor challenges (IMPACT training) to facilitate learning about teams (team dynamics)
- To provide facilitated group coaching sessions focusing on leadership development
- To help the participant prepare an action agenda for re-entry into business life after the program
- To follow up with the participant and his or her group 100 days after the program to review progress and insights on change.

The five main parts to SYLA are briefly summarized below.

Week One

- GELI Self-Assessment Instrument: A focus on leadership characteristics. The 360° GELI evaluates the participant through

119

100 questions on 12 key leadership dimensions and is filled out on line by the participant and the observers before the start of the program. The GELI has two components. First, there is the Self questionnaire, a series of questions which, once completed and processed, gives the participant a picture of his or her leadership behaviors as seen by the individual himself or herself. Second, there is the Observer question-naire, a series of similar questions and additional qualitative responses that gives the participant a picture of his or her leadership behaviors as seen by others (superiors, coworkers, direct reports, others, for a total of about ten observers).

Outputs: Results of the Self survey are used in the first Organizational Behavior Session in Week One, which focuses on leadership, and the Group Coaching Session in Week Two.

- IMPACT Training, Half-Day: A focus on how teams work … and how the participant tends to work in teams: Time is spent on leading teams in the second Organizational Behavior Session. Closely following this, a half-day of outdoor activities is organized by IMPACT Training, an organization dedicated to helping individuals develop themselves and their teamwork skills through the use of outdoor events and challenges.

Outputs: This half-day session helps the participant to develop further insights into teamwork and dynamics and offers another opportunity to learn about him or herself ("How do I work in teams?"). This serves as additional input for the Group Coaching Session in Week Two.

Week Two

- Group Coaching Session: A focus on leadership and personal development: In the second week of the program, a day is devoted to group coaching sessions facilitated by a professional coach and run in conjunction with the IGLC. Each coach provides their own structure to the group session (group size is approximately five people), but the common purpose is to help participants think through their leadership challenges for the future. Inputs for the day include: (A) the Self and Observer responses to the GELI survey, (B) IMPACT Training experience debrief page and (C) biographical information.

Output: Initial discussion and work in preparation of an action agenda for re-entry.

Week Three

- Drafting the Action Agenda: A step toward commitment: The coaching sessions have prompted the participant to develop an action plan. Before departure, the participant will hand in a memo (or letter of intent) outlining his or her plans for development, along with targeted actions.

Outputs: The letter of intent with the participant's action plan is written and sealed in a self-addressed envelope. A copy of the action plan is given to the coach and the participant's learning partner in his or her group.

100 days after the program

- Small group conference call to gauge progress of change: A small group conference call of two hours, facilitated by the coach, reviews progress and insights on the action plan; a review of contacts with the learning partner during the 100 days is also evaluated.

APPENDIX TWO

A CASE IN POINT: THE GROUP CONFERENCE CALL WITH A GROUP OF FOUR PARTICIPANTS 100 DAYS AFTER THE MAP

For confidentiality, all names of participants and the countries they live in have been changed.

121

The conference call was on and all four participants of the MAP Group were present: Patrick, the German Banker; Samir, the Kuwaiti engineer; Boris, the Hungarian real estate professional and Francine, the French data manager.
We all heard in the background the calls to prayer in Kuwait and thus the coach suggested that we start with Samir so he could step out to pray and then call in again, which he did.

Samir had lost his mother when he was very young and was raised, together with his older brother, by his father. The feedback showed that he suffered from extreme moodiness, had very low resilience to stress, was good on global mindset, low on tenacity, high on emotional intelligence and teambuilding but low on empowerment. In the discussions with the group during the program, he had realized that he had very low self-esteem, linked to fierce rivalry with his older brother, who systematically got higher grades in school. He shared with the group that he hadn't talked with his brother for three years. At work, he never managed to say no and was very attached to and protective of his team, in many ways caught between a very demanding boss and a team he didn't delegate to. His action plan was to be stronger in boundary setting with his direct superior, delegate more to the team and express his frustrations earlier. Samir told us that upon his return after the program he had decided to re-initiate a dialogue with his brother and that they had talked for many hours, beginning the process of clearing up major misunderstandings. On the work front, he had debriefed his 360° feedback with his boss, re-adjusted the expectations of his workload and asked for more resources, which he got. He had also started to delegate half of his engineering projects to the team.

Boris was a different story altogether. Boris was a real go-getter in the real estate business, working 80 hours a week and having every breakfast, lunch and dinner booked with clients seven days a week. Boris's 360° feedback showed a strong overestimation vis-à-vis his observers, a significant "low" in designing and aligning capability (setting objectives, performance standards and deadlines for his team), a high score on vision, low on emotional intelligence and very low on stress resilience. During the discussions in the program, he had acknowledged his conflict avoidance, his disproportionate need for recognition, his total lack of time management and priority setting, and the fact that he was in a permanent seduction mode with everyone. He also shared with the group a deeper fear of success because he did not have a university degree and he realized that the "imposter syndrome" was part of his problem. His action plan was time management, focusing on key clients, protecting himself from complete burnout, and lowering his own expectations. Boris told us that he had started by asking his personal assistant to schedule two two-hour meetings a week with himself for reflection and planning time in his agenda. He had also, for the first time ever, started keeping two evenings a week for himself without client dinners, and he had asked his CFO to help him with a client margin analysis to allow him to set priorities in his work.

Patrick had news for the team: he had originally been in a staff function with a German Bank and, since finishing the program, he had been promoted to a function in Structured Finance and was now manager of a team for the first time. His 360° feedback showed a low on energizing, teambuilding and emotional intelligence, and a high on outside customer orientation and tenacity. He was also perceived by his observers to be stubborn, impatient and arrogant. His action plan was to develop seriously his listening skills and to choose his corporate battles. Patrick told us that he had enacted one simple behavioral change which was extremely difficult for him: to ask more questions than give answers, he had instilled with his new team a climate of trust and was trying very hard to give a voice to his new team by letting them enact certain decisions.

Lastly, **Francine** also had news of a new job: from a staff position in data management in the French division of a large American IT company, she had now been asked to be in charge of demand generation for new products, coordinating the various actions in five European countries. Her feedback had shown an overestimation of herself vis-à-vis her observers, a high score on energizing and teambuilding and a low on global mindset and emotional intelligence. She was perceived as a very quiet, very loyal but very opinionated person. During the coaching discussion, she had realized that being an only child and having two teachers as parents, she was a real perfectionist. She was also a very black and white person–grey was not a color she liked, and if things weren't going her way she would just take a flight attitude, isolating herself in her group.

Her action plan was to lower her perfectionist, idealized standards and to start giving praise and credit to others. A second point was her desire and need to be more outgoing and socialize and network more in the company. She had enacted two behavioral changes: one was to systematically give specific positive feedback to others for a job well done; another was that, after accepting that she had a certain power in the organization, she initiated a network of professional women working for the company in the five countries in Europe that she was coordinating in her new job.

At the end of the two-hour conference call, the atmosphere was very positive and the coach detected a sense of real support for one another among the team members, asking their learning partners to stay in touch and already planning to reunite in Paris later in the year.

APPENDIX THREE

SAP GLDP[10]

The purpose of the program is to develop SAP's global executives to become global leaders, and to provide new tools and develop new skills for executing SAP's strategy. Typical participants are senior vice presidents, managing directors, CEOs, general managers and high potential executives not yet in global positions.

The program content of the GLDP is organized around three pillars:

1. Leading an Organization:
   a. Building a best-run company
   b. Becoming an effective leader (including leadership coaching and development)

2. Strategic Business Issues:
   a. How to become more efficient in the new SAP organization
   b. Volume business
   c. Business model innovation
3. Execution Excellence:
   a. Cascading strategy
   b. Creating high-performance organizations

The program is organized over two modules: a 4-day module and a 3-day module. An integral part of the first module of GLDP is input on leadership styles and a leadership team coaching exercise. The GLDP participants complete a SAP proprietary 360° feedback survey (Management Excellence Evaluation) before the start of the program. They receive the feedback reports for debrief and coaching the night before the leadership team coaching day. To add to the analytical data from the feedback reports, participants are asked to complete a biographical note and create a personal portrait for the coaching exercise.

Why use leadership coaching in the context of this program?

- The leadership team coaching provides the attending global executives with a professionally supported opportunity to assess their current "role performance" (360° feedback report). They are encouraged to plan development actions based on the results of the feedback.
- The leadership team coaching is a situation of leadership culture in action; while receiving feedback and valuable support from the professional coach and the peers in the team, they build and improve their capabilities to act as a coach.
- The leadership team coaching is a microcosm of the current corporate leadership culture; it is an opportunity for staging relevant individual and cultural themes and topics.

NOTES

1. Kets de Vries, M.F.R. (2003). "Can CEOs change? Yes, but only if they want to," *INSEAD Working Paper*; Kets de Vries, M.F.R. (2006). *The Leader on the Couch*, London: Wiley.

2. Kets de Vries, M.F.R. (2005). "Leadership group coaching in action: The Zen of creating high-performance teams," *Academy of Management Executive*, 19 (1), 61–76.
3. For a description of the program see www.insead.edu.
4. This program, which has been offered since 1979, was formerly called Young Managers' Program.
5. Kets de Vries, M.F.R. (1995). *Life and Death in the Executive Fast Lane*, San Francisco, CA, Jossey-Bass Publishers.
6. Kets de Vries, M.F.R. (2005). "Feeling like a fake: How the fear of success can cripple your career and damage your company," *Harvard Business Review*, 83(8), 108–116.
7. Kets de Vries, M.F.R. (2001). *The Leadership Mystique*, Great Britain: Prentice Hall.
8. Ibarra, H. (2003). *Working Identity: Unconventional strategies for Reinventing your career*, Boston, MA: Harvard Business School Press.
9. Ibarra, H.(2004). *FT summer school: Tough lessons on the road to leadership*, FT 24/09/2004.
10. Leadership Coaching in the context of SAP's GLDP, developed by Peter Boback, senior consultant for Executive and Management Development at SAP, and Professor Roger Lehman from IGLC. INSEAD program director of SAP GLDP: Professor Morten Hansen.

7

EXECUTIVE EDUCATION FROM THE PARTICIPANT'S POINT OF VIEW

KONSTANTIN KOROTOV

Programs at business schools, particularly those aimed at experienced managers, are positioned more and more as change-making opportunities for executives. Completing such a program is portrayed as a special kind of experience that goes beyond the purely academic exercise of mastering theories or learning about management tools. Many programs aimed at executives are described as "transitional," "career and life changing," or "transformational." Ironically, however, regardless of the glossy brochures and flashy media advertisements, to date there is not much research and common understanding, even among providers of executive education, as to how such transformation is achieved and what needs to be done to increase the chances of successful change facilitated by an executive course.

Moreover, there has been little research on what brings individuals to executive courses at business schools and other educational institutions, and how they experience the learning process. Previous research in this area concentrated primarily on the organizational perspective, leaving individual agency, the personal choices of executives, untouched. Thus, researchers in the past have indicated that executive programs help companies to meet their needs by upgrading the skills of their employees and supporting the implementation of change efforts.[1] More recently, several more explanations have been added to the previously identified reasons for attending executive programs. The reasons are as follows: a recommendation from a boss or a colleague who has done a similar program and benefited from it; a desire to advance one's career outside the current employing organization; or a desire to take a break from current work responsibilities – "fundamentally, executives attend [executive education programs] mainly for personal reasons, not organizational ones."[2]

In fact, individuals coming to an executive program may be using it for finding their true selves, ridding themselves of the false layers imposed by life or work circumstances. Going back to school may be helpful in finding a new sense of professional self. Attending an executive education program, particularly a leadership development one, is often seen as an acceptable way for leaders to start a journey of personal psychological growth, a way of maintaining their mental health.[3]

To add to our understanding of how executive programs can be of help to people looking for change, transformation, or new opportunities, the work presented in this chapter takes the above ideas further and looks specifically at what happens to an executive when he or she joins a transformational business education program and how he or she deals with realizing a personal goal. It is a truism that without taking participants' experience into account, HR and learning and development practitioners and business educators cannot design a meaningful program for those who attend it. This chapter is based on research conducted in the context of multi-modular executive development programs at leading business schools,[4] and teaching and consulting experience of the author and other contributors to this book.

Before going into the specifics of participants' experience in educational programs, it makes sense to say a few words about current thinking on transformational opportunities for individuals. With changes in the world and life, people are increasingly seeking favorable conditions for self-renewal and transformation. Some thinkers even suggest that learning personal change and reinvention is a critical competence for today's professional and personal success. Recently, there has been a renewal of interest in the potential offered by the psychodynamic concept of transitional space[5] and the anthropological concept of liminality (from *threshold* in Latin)[6] in exploring ways of how people achieve personal and professional transformation.

In one model of the identity transition process associated with radical career change, for example, there is special room given to liminal experiences and transitional phenomena.

Liminal (in-between) experiences are traditionally character-ized by a feeling of being between identities, being suspended, being in no man's land, and the ugliness of being in the mid-dle.[7] Nevertheless, regardless of their possible negative sides, such experiences are also thought to give opportunities for people to imagine new alternatives to their current situation, failure to do so often being the biggest stumbling block on the road to personal and professional transformation. Transitional phenomena (i.e., phenomena similar to transitional objects in their function[8]) are conceptualized to provide resources and conditions for people to put identities into play (in other words, opening existing identities to question and change and trying out new possible selves). Recent literature on transitions draws researchers' and practitioners' attention to the concept of tran-sitional spaces, or special privileged areas that are set apart from mainstream activities and have a legitimate status as a place for experimentation and creativity.[9]

Transitional spaces create opportunities for play and experi-mentation, help the people inside them overcome change-related anxieties, offer novelty that gives an extra boost to desire for changing the self, impose certain rules and structures that are counter-normative to what exists in the world beyond the transitional space, set psychological, temporal and spatial boundaries, and offer a menu of guiding figures to people inside the space. All these elements together create the potential for identity experimentation and renewal. There have been specific indications in literature and in practitioners' work that adult education programs can create spaces conducive to identity exploration and experimentation.[10]

The novelty of the executive education program environ-ment and the difference of the setting from day-to-day work and life mean that the experience for the participants is also new. For executives coming to a business school program, par-ticularly a longer, multi-modular one, there are several stages in their experience that can be roughly categorized as pre-entry, initial surprise of getting into the executive program's space and learning to use it, engaging in identity exploration through examining past and present identities, staging identity experi-ments and, finally, stepping out of the executive program.

PRE-ENTRY EXPERIENCE

The pre-entry experience of participants contributes to the formation of expectations and fantasies about their forthcoming learning and experimentation experience. When the executive program admission procedure requires a significant contribution and commitment from the participants, the latter become engaged in the learning process even before the program begins.

Thus, in some of our leadership programs, before entry, candidates are subjected to a heavy dose of essay writing and a mandatory, in most cases face-to-face, interview with a program director. Officially designed to assess the fit between a candidate and the program offerings, these instruments in themselves trigger some of the initial learning that will later grow as the course unfolds. The essay questions often include a description of an entirely different, imagined life; fantasies about the future; stories that people tell about the person applying, assessment of one's achievements; and so on. As evidenced by participants, the questions reveal some of the future elements of the course and trigger executives' curiosity about themselves and their professional and personal future.[11]

The mandatory face-to-face interviews give a sample of the course as a novel and courage-demanding experience, and as a program rule-setting mechanism. Thus, participants get an indication of the amount of personal involvement that will be required and observe the faculty's seriousness about making participants follow through on the learning commitments made. Interviews serve as individual psychological contracts and commitments to future actions,[12] such as readiness to engage in the course at the cognitive, behavioral and emotional levels.

Pre-entry experience gives participants a preview of what lies ahead, sets expectations about the rules, and also contributes to the initial feeling of psychological safety of being on the course. The pre-learning process serves as a first exercise in dealing with the anxiety associated with the unusual experiences offered to participants during the program. In particular, it shows that the faculty, albeit challenging and demanding, is not psychologically threatening. Going through the interviews also helps participants develop a view that other participants, having gone through the same kind of selection process, are of equally high quality in terms of suitability for the program.

SURPRISE – AND LEARNING TO USE THE SPACE OF THE EXECUTIVE PROGRAM

Despite the development of initial expectations based on pre-application information gathering and pre-entry experience, the actual initial transformational program experience often turns out to be different from both the expectations and any kind of previous educational experience participants have had. The beginning of such programs often brings about surprise.[13]

In programs that claim to be unusual and different from the typical educational experience for executives, the major dimensions of surprise are usually about the experimental nature of the learning and opportunities that are perceived as opened by the course and not necessarily available in other parts of life. In other words, the surprise often comes from the contrast between the program and life beyond it. One of the types of surprise is usually associated with the need to engage oneself as an object of study, having self as a perspective through which personal and interpersonal, team, and organizational issues are to be understood, explained, and predicted.

Another type of surprise often seen in leadership programs, particularly at IGLC and at the European School of Management and Technology, is associated with bringing the clinical organizational psychology theoretical lens to bear on a plethora of organizational issues. The use of theories and approaches that are traditionally viewed as belonging to the domain of deeply personal issues and not related to work to understand business issues is surprising to those participants who have experienced traditional executive courses.

All in all, the experience, as indicated in program brochures but not necessarily totally expected by the participants, turns out to be novel and unexpected. People come to executive programs from organizations where they might, for instance, be expected to keep their thoughts, concerns and anxieties to themselves, and suppress any expressions of their feelings, despite the often very neurotic nature of their jobs and company culture. Having to look at their feelings and express and openly discuss them is not in line with the set of expectations they have developed through years of professional and life experience.

131

Similarly, it is possible to assume that participants have pre-conceived notions (or "coordinates") regarding the theories and the teaching approaches used in business schools in general and executive education programs in particular. Transformational executive program situations may represent a surprise stemming primarily from a certain loss of those coordinates. It should be noted that a loss of coordinates has been described as a feature of going through the liminal state, which, as mentioned above, opens up opportunities for personal experimentation and change.

However, the strangeness of the situation, when realized and accepted, is conducive to innovation.[14] Participants have to learn how to use this new environment. There are three types of issues that participants have to master:

- managing the boundaries of transitional space;
- identifying resources and instruments available and learning to use them; and
- figuring out the rules of behavior and the limits of those rules.

There are several types of boundaries that participants need to learn to master: temporal, spatial, and psychological. Temporal boundaries are about making sure that there are no interventions from the outside world into the time of the program. Spatial boundaries are about geographical separation of the program from the rest of the world. Psychological boundaries deal with the issue of perceived safety for experimentation and exploration.

Mastering temporal boundaries means finding the time to dedicate to one's own development and learning. That means not only clearing the time for being away from one's office for a course, but also having a sufficient amount of time for pre-course work, including contemplating, fantasizing, and analyzing one's thoughts and feelings. It also means dedicating time to reading; engaging in instrumentation, such as 360° feedback; having coaching sessions; going into conference calls with other participants and faculty; and so on. The residential nature of most executive education programs allows for extended days and deeper interaction between the participants and faculty. The time on the program is often a 16-hour day, with learning taking place as much outside the classroom (during group assignments, meals, social activities, and formal and informal meetings with faculty and fellow participants), as in the auditorium. Quite often, a time buffer, such as taking a day off before or after the program, is a helpful way of protecting one's experiential involvement in an executive program from day-to-day reality.

Spatial boundaries deal with the protection of the learning space from interventions from work and home. Strict rules on usage of mobile phones, timely arrival from breaks, and presence of dedicated working space, which becomes "participants' space" for the duration of the program, contribute to the creation of an environment that is specifically dedicated to experimentation and change. Spatial boundaries are also about what part of the program and its developments become known outside the program space. Participants have to manage what they communicate to their work colleagues, family, and friends regarding the experiments that they are staging and observing others stage in the program.

Finally, the psychological boundaries deal with the issues of what is safe to express, question, show, or demand during the program. Managing the boundaries in this case means finding little gateways to ease one's anxiety and develop trust in the people (both participants and faculty) involved in the program, working out how broadly or deeply they want to involve others in the process of the personal quest for transformation. Naturally, a short-term program is very limited in terms of providing opportunities for participants to start really trusting others.

Learning how to use the program's space includes mastering the rules of the process and the tools available to an individual executive attending a program. For example, participants need to work out how to make the most of the activities taking place in between the modules, such as reading, writing individual cases, analyzing one's organization, engaging in peer coaching, or completing an inter-modular project. Thus, in some programs (like the Consulting and Coaching for Change IGLC program) participants are asked to develop ongoing case studies about their work situations, and then discuss their case with fellow participants and a faculty member in a conference call. Obviously, a participant can gain full value from such an exercise only through their full engagement and the active participation of other executives.

The same rule about active participation from everyone involved in the course applies to other activities in transformational executive education programs. As part of mastering the rules of usage of an executive program's space, participants and the small groups they are members of have to learn how to deal with issues of incomplete participation by some of their fellow members. This is an interesting leadership exercise in itself, as some executives meet for the first time with people whom they need to influence in order to get full personal value out of the course but over whom they have no organizational authority.

Another dimension of learning how to use the space of the executive program is using the time of the faculty members who accompany the participants throughout the course. Our experience shows that there are some people who are more active than others in seeking consultations, advice, or just a critical ear from the faculty involved in their program. The same refers to other resources that often become available in an executive program run at a business school, such as use of library and information resources, getting access to participants in other courses taking place simultaneously, being introduced to other professors working in the same institution, gaining more information on coaching resources available, and so on.

Managing the boundaries, figuring out the rules of the program, and identifying resources and learning to use them may, overall, be seen as a part of the learning process on the road to personal change. They can be seen as contributing factors to the development of the competency of personal reinvention.

IDENTITY EXPLORATION: EXAMINING PAST AND CURRENT IDENTITIES

As an individual goes through a transformation process, they put where they are at a particular moment in their professional or personal development under scrutiny. An important part of the participants' experience in change-oriented leadership programs is self-exploration, which happens with the help of structured activities included in the program by design, as well as through an individual's overall experience of being in an unusual group, going through exercises, getting external and internal feedback, self-reflection, and interaction with other members of the class. The formal activities usually include gen-ograms (as presented in Chapter Four), 360° feedback on lead-ership competencies, 360° personality assessment (as described in Chapter Five), individual non-anonymous feedback reports, emotional intelligence instruments, and cross-cultural readiness questionnaires.

The results obtained through the use of the feedback instru-ments are particularly powerful when used in small group execu-tive coaching sessions,[15] and in subsequent peer-coaching work. Other elements of self-exploration may include presenting one's personal case to the class, involvement in fishbowl coaching sessions (being coached in front of the class), undergoing peer coaching, writing case studies and reflection papers and, in some programs, preparing a final thesis that reflects one's jour-ney. Personal case studies, for instance, help individuals put on paper the story of their journey – where they are or were before a certain tipping point. Further discussion of the case studies with fellow participants and faculty members allows individu-als to crystallize some of the problems or issues that they want to deal with, including some of the identities that they want to leave in the past.

The identity exploration stage helps executives find an expla-nation for their behavior patterns and allows them to launch an experiment with a different set of behaviors. As program par-ticipants sometimes say, transformation-oriented courses may resemble a therapy experience. It is more correct to describe such courses in terms of what many authors whose work is pre-sented in this volume call "not therapy, but therapeutic." Many therapeutic approaches, and, in particular, psycho-dynamically-oriented ones, as well as many schools of executive coaching, see helping the clients achieve self-understanding as one of their essential tasks. A significant portion of a transformational program's emphasis is on helping participants learn about themselves and make links between these findings and their effectiveness in organizations and other settings.

The process of exploration was part of a "multidimensional journey," said a participant in one such program. Various aspects of identities, beyond the professional ones, become salient and get intertwined in the process. Having gained new insights into themselves, participants seem to develop a new way of seeing themselves and their organizations. This new knowledge, or looking at oneself from a new angle, calls on them to make sense of their overall experience and the information obtained. For some participants, it becomes clearer how past experiences influenced their choices, relationship types, and responses to stimuli from the outside world.

It has been argued that sense making is the process of placing elements of one's history or one's environment into a framework, responding to surprising situations, gaining meanings, and developing interactions in order to come to a mutual understanding of events and the environment. Sense making is not a simple interpretation of things (i.e., not explaining one word by using others), but rather the phenomenon of simultaneous authoring and interpreting. Here is a description of the challenge of sense making:

> In the real world, problems do not present themselves to the practitioners as given. They must be constructed from the materials of problematic situations which are puzzling, troubling, and uncertain. In order to convert a problematic situation into a problem, a practitioner must do a certain kind of work. He must make sense of an uncertain situation which initially makes no sense.[16]

In a similar vein, participants in executive development programs often come to the course with a number of problematic situations either in their organizational life or personal careers. Very often, there is a perceived need for change or a transition, although what exactly needs to be changed remains vague. The problematic situations are given further shape through the self-exploration work. As an outcome, executives develop an explanation for themselves, primarily, and, in some cases, for the internal world situated within the boundaries of the course, about who they are and how they have got to where they are. The vague problematic situations (feeling challenged as a leader, dissatisfied with one's career, or unhappy about one's life) then take on the form of a specific set of issues that are easier to deal with. Crystallizing the need for change, and making some of the former, undesirable identities salient, forces participants to start experimenting with new possibilities. And when the meaning associated with one's preexisting selves changes, the probability of getting engaged in exploring new activities and new relationship networks heightens.[17]

IDENTITY EXPERIMENTATION

Participants in transformational executive programs also engage in identity experimentation. Executives stage both mental experiments, where they try to see themselves in a new role or with a new identity or identities, and in more tangible activities associated with experimenting with new possible identities. The mental experiments include contemplation, discussions or presentations of personal and organizational issues, preparing reflection papers with insights from a particular module, and elaborating on possible future steps and directions for development in a final thesis. In addition, exercises during such programs often require working out an action plan of some sort and discussing it with fellow participants and fellow coaches.

More tangible activities involve observations and then formal (in the plenary) or informal (in small groups or in individual discussions) debriefing of the activities or stories given by invited lecturers, guest speakers, and/or executive coaches working with the participants. By observing others in a role that may be potentially interesting for course participants, the latter are collecting a number of elements to be used or discarded in the future. The task is to see how others perform a part of the role, enact an element of the professional identity or leadership behavior (which is something tangible, observable in this case), and then try it on and see to what extent it fits the individual's desired image of himself or herself. Obviously, there are various individual antecedents that might influence the outcomes of the experimentation in general and of each instance in particular. Still, without negating the role of individual idiosyncrasies, it is important to underline the crucial role that creating opportunities for people to contemplate the various options available to them plays in a transformational executive program.

Last, but not least, small experiments are staged outside the space of the program, whereby individuals try to apply the principles studied in the class to their work situations or their side activities. They return to the group (in the next module or in a prescheduled or spontaneous phone conference) to obtain feedback on their independent experiments. Longer-term programs provide an environment where participants can evaluate the outcomes of their try-and-see experiments outside the boundaries of the dedicated trial environment. Having tried something new outside, executives return to the "laboratory" to analyze the experiment. The post-experiment follow-up debriefing opportunities allow the participants to evaluate internally whether the experiment can, and should, be taken to the world beyond the laboratory environment. Such an evaluation helps in making a decision about whether or not to continue pursuing a possible new self.

Experimentation in the executive programs may involve both professional and personal life. It often includes playing with options unthinkable or unimaginable before undertaking the course, or bringing to life some forgotten or repressed elements of oneself, such as past identities. From that standpoint, which is different from the viewing of liminal experience as unidirectional, forward-looking, "saying goodbye to the past," "being neither here nor there,"[18] the experience of going through executive education can be seen as more about being "both here and there,"[19] retrieving things from the past and trying out things from a possible but not yet certain future. From this standpoint, the above-mentioned reference to executive programs as a "multidimensional journey" is about having elements of multiple identities questioned, fantasized about, explored, and experimented with.

STEPPING OUT OF THE EXECUTIVE PROGRAM: CRAFTING NARRATIVES AND INTERNALIZING TRANSITIONAL SPACE

Executive programs, even long ones, inevitably end. As has often been observed, participants develop a certain degree of separation anxiety when they realize that the program is soon to finish. The ending of the program also means that those participants who have come hoping to facilitate a transition have reached a turning point.

It is often helpful to have some kind of soft landing or smooth transition once out of the program. Writing a graduation thesis may be a way of consolidating one's learning experience and launching the change process. Participants often choose to use their thesis writing for the purposes of developing a business plan, preparing a new in-company initiative, or just rewriting their personal story. Writing a thesis is a form of telling a story. These identity narratives, or stories, serve as a means of signaling to self and others about reinventing oneself, reinterpreting past identities in the light of new experiences, and putting together a coherent story about one's new identity.[20]

Post-program interviews show that transformational executive courses often terminate with the participants realizing the importance of the process that they have been through to leadership and change-management efforts in their organizations, and even in their families. Executives often leave the program desiring to implement elements of their experience in their work and personal lives. Beyond content, the process becomes an important takeaway from executive education.

Going through a transformational executive education program can be viewed as staging experiments in an identity laboratory.[21] The laboratory should be "equipped" with identity exploration and experimentation opportunities, guiding figures or facilitators, and tools, such as transitional objects that participants need to learn to use to go through the experience productively. If an educational program serves as not just a source of additional facts but also as an opportunity to experiment with one's identity and, by extension, the identity of the organization that one comes from, then it may answer the demand for business school courses that reflect the complex reality executives face and the need to deal with the often ambiguous conditions of current business practices. Executive programs with elements of identity laboratories built into them may be an answer to these types of challenges.

NOTES

1. Crotty, P., and Soule, A. (1997). "Executive Education: Yesterday and Today, with a Look at Tomorrow." *Journal of Management Development*, 16 (1): 4–22.

2. Long, S. (2004). "Really ... Why Do Executives Attend Executive Education Programs?" *Journal of Management Development*, 23 (8): 701–715.
3. Dubouloy, M. (2004). "The Transitional Space and Self-Recovery: A Psychoanalytical Approach to High-Potential Managers' Training." *Human Relations*, 57 (4): 467–496; Ibarra, H. (2003a). *Working Identity: Unconventional Strategies for Reinventing Your Career*. Boston, MA: Harvard Business School Press; Kets de Vries, M. (2006). *The Leader on the Couch: A Clinical Approach to Changing People and Organizations*. Chichester: John Wiley & Sons; Kets de Vries, M., and Korotov, K. (2006). "Creating Identity Laboratories to Enable Executive Change and Transformation." *INSEAD Working Paper 2006/36/EFE*.
4. Korotov, K. (2005). "Identity Laboratories." *INSEAD PhD Dissertation*; Kets de Vries, M., and Korotov, K. (2006).
5. Winnicott, D. (1953). "Transitional Objects and Transitional Phenomena." *International Journal of Psycho-Analysis*, 34: 89–97.
6. van Gennep, A. (1909). *The Rites of Passage*. Chicago, IL: University of Chicago Press.
7. Ibarra, H. (2005). "Identity Transitions: Possible Selves, Liminality, and the Dynamics of Career Change." *INSEAD Working Paper 2005/24/OB*; Ashforth, B.E. (2001). *Role Transitions in Organizational Life: An Identity-Based Perspective*. Mahwah, NJ and London: LEA Publishers; Ebaugh, H.R.F. (1988). *Becoming an Ex: The Process of Role Exit*. Chicago, IL: The University of Chicago Press.
8. Winnicott, D. (1953); Winnicott, D. (1965). *The Maturational Processes and the Facilitating Environment*. London: Hogarth Press; Winnicott, D. (1982). *Playing and Reality*. New York: Routledge.
9. Ibarra, H. (2005); Amado, G., and Ambrose, A. (2001). *The Transitional Approach to Change*. London: Karnac; Turner, V. (1982). *From Ritual to Theater: The Human Seriousness of Play*. Chicago, IL: Aldione; Korotov, K. (2005); Korotov, K. (2006). "Identity Laboratories: The Process of Going through an Executive Program." In: Weaver, M. (Ed.) *2006 Academy of Management Annual Meeting* Best Paper Proceedings, August 11–16, 2006, Atlanta, GA, ISSN: 1543–8643.
10. Amado, G., and Ambrose, A. (2001). *The Transitional Approach to Change*. London: Karnac; Yost, J., Strube, M., and Bailey, J. (1992). "The Construction of the Self: An Evolutionary View." *Current Psychology*, 11 (2), 110–121; Kets de Vries, M. (2006).
11. Korotov, K. (2005, 2006).
12. Argyris, C. (1960). *Understanding Organizational Behavior*. Homewood, IL: Dorsey.
13. Surprise happens when what an individual has imagined or thought of before entering a particular situation fails to materialize or is significantly different from the actual experience. See Louis, M.R. (1980). "Surprise and Sense Making: What Newcomers Experience in Entering Unfamiliar Organizational Settings." *Administrative Science Quarterly*, 25, 226–251.
14. Yost, J., Strube, M., and Bailey, J. (1992).
15. Kets de Vries, M. (2005). "Leadership Group Coaching in Action: The Zen of Creating High Performance Teams." *Academy of Management Executive*, 19 (1): 61–77.
16. Weick, K. (1995). *Sensemaking in Organizations*. Thousand Oaks, CA: Sage, p. 9.

17. Ibarra, H. (2005).
18. Ebaugh, H.R.F. (1988).
19. Korotov, K. (2005).
20. Ibarra, H. (2005); Ibarra, H., and Lineback, K. (2005). "What's Your Story?" *Harvard Business Review*, January: 65–71.
21. Korotov, K. (2005).

8

TRANSFORMATIONAL EXECUTIVE PROGRAMS: AN OWNER'S MANUAL

MANFRED F. R. KETS DE VRIES AND KONSTANTIN KOROTOV

EXECUTIVE PROGRAMS AS A TRANSFORMATION OPPORTUNITY

As already mentioned in this book, executives frequently join executive education programs or sign up for leadership coaching opportunities for reasons that go beyond the obvious ones of gaining additional knowledge and insights into the effective operation of business. Many executives enter these programs to pursue very personal agendas, including taking stock of their professional and personal achievements; dealing with hopes, frustrations and doubts; and thinking about time and opportunities ahead. The programs and coaching interventions are viewed as a chance for self-renewal and opportunities to prepare for the future.

We notice that executives often start looking for transformational programs when they become aware of certain dysfunctional behavior patterns, leading to a search for a way to deal with them. Sometimes an organization or its senior members notice possible derailment factors and make a recommendation for the manager concerned to participate in an executive program or a coaching intervention. In other situations, although an individual's dysfunctional behavior may not yet be visible, he or she feels a sense of unease, and that some form of preemptive action is needed to forestall future trouble. We also see executives who are doing quite well in their job, but feel they need something more, or different, without knowing exactly what it is that they are looking for.

Analyzing application forms, reviewing personal interviews with candidates for leadership programs, and in-program and post-program discussions with participants, we notice that there are often various crisis points that make the executive realize that some form of change is needed. Executives' desire to change themselves is frequently preceded by loss of some kind (separation, divorce, missed promotion opportunity, or job loss); developmental imbalance (with certain important life expectations remaining unfulfilled); interpersonal conflict; symptomatology reflecting inner turmoil (eating or behavioral disorders, sexual dysfunction and insomnia); perceived work-life imbalance; and quest for dealing with the fundamental questions about the meaning of existence and life.[1]

Some of the more common issues faced by executives at work include, but are not limited to, conflict-laden work relationships, the management of disappointment related to career setbacks, doubts about their managerial capabilities, feeling like a fake or failure, concerns about boredom and burnout on the job, and risky professional or personal opportunities.

In addition, there is also a frequent challenge of dealing with narcissistic problems. We know that executives subjected to narcissistic disorders have a tendency to surround themselves with yes-people. In such an environment, the executives may create their own reality disconnected with what happens in the outside environment, leading to dangerous situations for both the leaders and their organizations. Executive development or leadership coaching are often "prescribed" as a way of coping with narcissistic challenges. Furthermore, we also notice that people looking (or strongly encouraged to look) for opportunities for renewal and transformation are sometimes those who may have grown too comfortable in their current position, and lost the capacity for out-of-the-box thinking, making them incapable of dealing with discontinuous change in a creative way. Among program applicants or coaching candidates we also often recognize people who want a program or a coaching intervention to help them deal with the challenges of implementing their strategies.[2]

UNDERSTANDING EXECUTIVES' DEVELOPMENT NEEDS: THE FRAMEWORK OF THREE TRIANGLES

As this book suggests, faculty and leadership development professionals have an opportunity to help executives deal with dysfunctional behavior patterns and find ways to help these people in their journey of personal transformation. As we are talking about transformation of adults, specific developmental needs of executives have to be taken into consideration in the design of the intervention. While working on preparation of open-enrollment and customized transformational programs, we have found it helpful to use a three triangle framework to guide our course design and development efforts. The framework can be described as consisting of the mental life triangle, the conflict triangle, and the relationships triangle.

The first triangle identifies the need to take both cognitive and emotional processes into consideration if we want to create changes in behavior. The second describes how psychic conflict arises from unacceptable feelings, thoughts, or wishes that prompt anxiety and defensive reactions. The relationships triangle explains how an individual's childhood experiences can create patterns of response that are repeated throughout life.

The mental life triangle

The first element of the framework, the *mental life triangle*, links cognition, emotion, and behavior. It is this triangle that dictates the script of our inner theater, a concept we introduced in Chapter One. It serves as a distillation of people's responses to their motivational needs systems, and as the basis on which choices are made.[3] In designing transformational programs, educators have to take into account that executive change is about making new, different choices. Therefore, to have an impact, executives have to be swayed both cognitively *and* emotionally, or the change effort may not be successful. On the one hand, managers need to have a cognitive grasp of the expected advantages of the change effort. Cognition alone, however, is not enough. Therefore, on the other hand, people also need to be touched emotionally by the need for change, as specific behavior patterns are the joint product of affect and cognition.

In designing and running executive programs, faculty and consultants inevitably face the question of how best to help senior executives become even more effective, both at work and in private life. Participants gain most from such programs when they end up with a realization that they do have options, and that they can make choices. Programs need to encourage the participants' sense of efficacy.[4] Moreover, awareness needs to be created that such choices are within close reach. When seeing those options and understanding their choices, senior executives may find both a cognitive and emotional ways out of a psychic prison created by their job or personal circumstances. Well-designed programs will help them to gain emotional support for changing the life that is often devoid of learning, playfulness, creativity, and pleasure.

Psychotherapists, psychoanalysts, and psychiatrists help people to make long-lasting personal change. Senior executives, as already mentioned in this book, are unlikely, however, to search for improvement in their psychological condition via lengthy therapeutic procedures. They are looking for different, more time-efficient methods to reinvent themselves. Often, however, even getting them to this stage is not easy: executives tend to look for external help only when they are already in trouble and experiencing a considerable amount of discomfort, if not pain. Before the pain is absolutely intolerable, far too many executives avoid talking to a helping professional by keeping themselves busy with things other than taking care of their own psychological well-being and leadership dilemmas. Years of working with senior managers have made us realize, however, that signing up for a group seminar designed for senior executives is much less threatening than making an appointment with a therapist. Executive programs, therefore, may be an acceptable way of helping create healthier leaders and organizations. But such an acceptance of leadership courses does not mean that work with executives attending them is easy. It is always a challenge for faculty to create meaningful and enduring learning experiences that simultaneously deal with cognition and emotion.

In helping executives on this journey toward personal transformation and change, faculty members need to find non-traditional ways of overcoming participants' resistance. This often necessitates making people aware of problems of a preconscious or unconscious nature. Furthermore, faculty also need to ensure that changes in behavior patterns will be lasting, more than temporary "flights into health"–transient highs of the sort produced by the pulp psychology of too many self-help guides and dubious life coaches. Obviously, longer-term programs, the ones that span several modules, allow for closer observation of executives-in-change and internalization by the latter of the learning process.

The conflict triangle

An essential part of the framework that guides development of transformational programs is taking into account the *triangle of conflict*, the three sides of which are hidden feelings, defensive behaviors, and conflict.[5] This element of the framework suggests that every individual experiences conflict due to unacceptable feelings, wishes, or ideas that create anxiety and lead to defensive reactions. Ironically, defensive behavior stirs only a vague awareness of what an individual is protecting himself or herself against, because the exact nature of the unacceptable feelings rarely reaches consciousness. Defensiveness is actually about the suppression of unacceptable feelings; it acts as a painkiller allowing us to function in an otherwise difficult-to-tolerate world. Obviously, at a certain moment all of us have to stop relying on a painkiller and move to curing the cause of pain. Among various indications of defensive behavior that faculty and leadership development professionals almost inevitably meet when dealing with participants in leadership development programs include: changing the subject when certain issues are raised, denying that there is a problem or simply ignoring an admitted problem, rationalizing questionable acts, and even acting out. Taking into account the triangle of conflict and respective developmental needs of the executives, creators of transformational programs need to think how they are going to help participants learn to act as psychological detectives in order to find out what they are erecting defenses against when demonstrating such behaviors.

The challenge for executives is to learn to recognize and overcome defensive barriers and identify the central issue(s) they should deal with. In a transformational executive program they should not be alone in this particular task. When designing an intervention, educators should think how the issues faced by executives can become better defined through a process of confrontation and clarification by faculty and fellow participants.[6] For example, in many of our programs, participants work on their issues by presenting them to faculty and classmates in a plenary or small group setting in what we describe as the critical incident technique. From a process point of view, *confrontation* takes the form of questions about issues and patterns of behavior that the presenting executive appears to be avoiding or ignoring. These questions, and the kinds of responses they elicit, help make the participants' defenses more explicit, allowing a better understanding of the underlying feelings and conflicts.

The concept of an executive education program as an identity laboratory (described in the previous chapter) presupposes that many risky things can be done within the psychological safety boundaries of such transitional space. As evidenced by our participants, when they come to such workshops many of them find themselves for the first time in an environment where they can be genuinely challenged without hidden agendas and/or career or personal repercussions. What makes the process effective is that each executive not only finds himself or herself in a challenging situation, but also one where people care. The faculty and the other participants serve as guiding figures and sparring partners.

The issues that are brought to the fore through confrontation are then analyzed more closely and brought into sharper focus through *clarification*. The latter helps to sort out cause-and-effect, and systemic relationships and fosters an appreciation of the connections between past and current patterns of behavior. Clarification sets the stage for various forms of interpretation and the creation of greater insight about a specific issue faced by the executive.

The outcomes of the confrontation and clarification stages usually lead to personal insight, and lay the groundwork for a considered and detailed reappraisal of career and life goals and for readiness to experiment with new alternatives to deal with organizational and personal issues. Ideas and action plans emerge through this process. Importantly, confrontation and clarification serve to decrease ambiguity about what an individual really would like to accomplish, leading to greater peace of mind and an ability to concentrate on the issue at hand and the resources available to resolve it. The empathy expressed by the other participants leads to the appreciation that other people truly care. In turn, such developments encourage executives to take greater control of their professional and personal lives.

Designers of transformational programs have to dedicate sufficient time for confrontation and clarification to take place. They also have to take into account that while it is important that the faculty leading these seminars remain empathic, the supportive role of the group is critical. People who are engaged in self-exploration and experimentation need to feel that other group members are supporting them in dealing with change. Program designers may need to take into account the need to help the group learn to be supportive of its members in their transformational efforts.

The relationships triangle

The *relationships triangle*, another critical element of the framework that helps to understand developmental needs of executives, points out that all of us, in all situations, have to deal with two kinds of relationships.[7] First, there is the "real" relationship between the person and the "other"–a relationship between two colleagues at work, for example, or between an employer and an employee. This real relationship becomes the context for another, more elusive relationship grounded in the past–what psychologists call the "transference relationship." As described in Chapter One, the concept of transference suggests that no relationship is a new relationship, and that all relationships are colored by previous relationships. Obviously, the relationships that have the most lasting potency, coloring almost every subsequent encounter, are those that we have with our earliest caregivers. Our adult behavior has its roots in those privileged, early relationships.

As adults, we may find ourselves responding in the same way to present situations as we responded to situations in the past. In other words, without even being aware of it, we are often confused about person, time, and place. With our past relationships having solidified into organizing themes in our personality structure, in our everyday life, we experience attitudes, thoughts, and emotional responses that, although appropriate to the interpersonal processes governing our earlier years, have become maladaptive. Anyone hoping to make sense of inter-personal encounters at anything but an intuitive level needs to understand (and be alert to) these transferential processes.

Leadership programs can use the relationships triangle–with its three sides of self, present-other, and past-other–to illustrate the effects of transference. It helps participants understand that the earliest feelings they experienced toward others are repeated in relation to people in the present–including, for the duration of the program, the course itself, the other par-ticipants and the faculty. This triangle provides a conceptual structure for assessing patterns of response by pointing out the similarity of past relationships to what happens in the present. It helps explain certain interpersonal problems that the executive may be experiencing at home and at work. Trans-ferential interpretation is a crucial tool in the personal and organizational change toolbox that executives need to master to make the link between present relationships and the past meaningful. When an individual understands old patterns of interaction and then learns to recognize that such patterns are no longer functional, given the current relationships, he or she is more likely to succeed in achieving personal change and overcoming barriers to organizational transformation. Learn-ing about transference and counter-transference and being able to recognize them allows executives to change how they super-impose long-standing and maladaptive past patterns onto cur-rent relationships.

IMPORTANT QUESTIONS FOR DESIGNERS OF TRANSFORMATIONAL PROGRAMS

A leadership program within the context of a business school gives a legitimate reason for an executive to look into the patterns of his or her behavior and start the process of self-exploration. Since nobody would argue against the statement that leading others involves understanding oneself and the way we present ourselves in interactions with others, faculty in leadership programs have great opportunities to help executives to be more effective and contribute to creating better functioning organizations. To get the best out of people, designers of such programs need to address several critical questions.

Who is the program for? How will participants be selected?

The first important issue concerns the target audience and the criteria for selecting program participants prepared to engage in a change effort. In order to create a truly productive, safe environment where executives can experiment with cognitions, emotions, and behavior, participants need to be able and willing to engage in self-exploration and self-experimentation. Given the stress that such programs put on their participants, only relatively healthy people will have the psychological strength required to participate and, importantly, be of help to themselves and others. Fortunately, many successful executives possess a considerable degree of emotional stability. In spite of that, however, we need to be vigilant in assessing the executive's capacity to gain from such transformational programs.

Among the criteria for the design of the program and subsequent acceptance of participants are: work and life experience; the level of motivation to learn and change; the capacity to be open and responsive; interpersonal connectedness; emotional management skills; a degree of psychological mindedness; the capacity for introspection; responsiveness to the observations of others; the ability to tolerate depression; and flexibility. Ideally, all these criteria need to be assessed before the start of the program through a combination of personal interviews with the program faculty and assessment through application essay writing (which will reveal the level of a participant's skill at putting thoughts into words). The process of application and interviewing gives the candidate a sneak preview of the program he or she is applying for, and the opportunity to evaluate the initial fit between the course and his or her perceived developmental needs. An in-depth acceptance process also allows faculty to assess whether the candidate will be able to cope with the psychological demands of the designed program and whether he or she will fit with the expected group of participants. As shown in other chapters of this book, such pre-program work can become a powerful first step in the change process, as it brings many psychological issues to the fore and stimulates readiness for personal exploration.

How will participants look for their focal issues?

The second issue concerns the identification of the focal problem(s) that each participant needs to work on and how to fit this into the overall structure and content of the course. The program should allow executives an opportunity to become clear about what it is that they really want to change. They have to identify their central problem(s) and need to be able to formulate explicit, tractable improvement goals. When people tell their history (and listen to the stories of the other participants), they are often able to identify specific themes that began in their past and continue over time into the present. Their challenge (which is also a challenge for faculty and other participants) is to identify these themes. This means not only having a better understanding of one's own story but also making sense of other people's stories. Very often the stories told by others allow executives to gain better insights into their own seemingly insoluble dilemmas grounded in misguided perceptions of the world and the world of others.

In putting programs together, it becomes important to allow sufficient time and conditions for work with personal narratives.[8] Telling life stories is an important way of exploring the self. Executives should be given an opportunity to deal with such questions as: Who am I? Where am I going? How will I get there? Through storytelling, executives gain a way of working through internal crises and developmental challenges. Stories also help to arrive at meaningful personal life integration. Other people's stories lead to learning empathy, psychological astuteness, and further self-reflection.

Program designers should think how to maximize the benefits of storytelling by creating opportunities for people to tell their stories and for the other participants to identify the issues together and talk them through. Every story will reveal specific present-day dilemmas that have grown out of underlying problems–dilemmas that can be remedied by addressing those deeper issues. These dilemmas will be the basis for "contracts" between the presenter and the rest of the participants.

151

We believe in the need to create in executive programs opportunities for each participant to present their stories to the rest of the group. Narration of one's own history and future challenges is an important structuring experience. Storytelling can be done by giving a hot seat to each participant at a certain moment in the program, or by running parallel small group coaching sessions in which participants take turns to present their stories, supported by self-discovery tools described in this book. However, to make sure that storytelling works, faculty has to pay attention to the issue of trust within the boundaries of the course. As we stress throughout this book, the old Hippocratic dictum – "Do no harm" – should be constantly remembered by program designers and teachers.

Normally, as the program unfolds, participants develop the trust necessary to be able to open up and learn from one another. It would be unrealistic, however, to expect deep trust among participants who come for a short-term, one-off executive program. We have observed that courses consisting of several modules that give people an opportunity to interact over a longer period of time and that allow for both in-class and out-of-class activities (dinners, joint assignments, teleconference discussions of case studies, peer coaching interventions, or visits to one another's organizations) have a significantly greater chance of creating higher level of trust, allowing for deeper and more challenging discussions, and eventually making a lasting impact on executives.

How will a safe transitional space be created?

The third issue concerns the creation of a safe transitional space. An educator or a leadership development professional should never forget that exploring oneself, one's emotions and one's behavioral patterns is a stressful undertaking for anyone. Change is difficult, and changing oneself is often the most difficult task executives have to handle in their life or career. Even the best-intentioned people rarely manage it single-handedly. We have already discussed in this book that asking for help is difficult for successful executives who are closely watched by their internal and external organizational stakeholders who implicitly and explicitly expect their organizational leaders to be strong. So a major challenge to executive education providers is how to get others involved in helping the executive initiate and carry through the process of change.

There is a variety of techniques available to executive educators to encourage the sense of support that the holding environment of a truly transitional space, an identity laboratory, requires. These techniques allow the participants to acquire a sense of self-efficacy, an understanding that they can be masters of their own destiny. They also aim at helping executives learn that they can be of help to other executives in making personal and organizational change. Techniques available to leadership development professionals for teaching their participants include: positive reframing, encouragement, and the anticipation or rehearsal of difficult situations. *Reframing* is a cognitive technique used to assist people in diffusing or sidestepping a painful situation, thus enhancing self-esteem. An essential part of reframing is assessing a person's strengths–looking not only at what has gone wrong but also at what has gone right in his or her life.[9] To help deal with the conflicted areas, psychological strengths can then be drawn on. *Encouragement,* which is closely related to reframing, encompasses reassurance, praise (which, to be helpful, must affirm something that the recipient considers praiseworthy), and empathic comments. Such comments, importantly, should be coming from both faculty and fellow participants. Learning *anticipation* techniques allows a participant to move through new situations hypothetically and to weigh different ways of responding. Allowing someone to become better acquainted with a situation reduces anticipatory anxiety. *Rehearsal* allows participants to practice more appropriate ways of engaging in future events, thus expanding his or her adaptive repertoire.[10] The purpose of all these interventions is to help the person acquire a greater sense of self-efficacy, first in the context of the program, and later in day-to-day work and life. Obviously, learning the techniques mentioned here requires time and guidance from faculty and coaches involved in teaching the program.

In addition to learning the self-efficacy techniques, the program should provide space for constructive suggestions about what and how to change. Within the holding environment of the executive program, those suggestions should come from both faculty and fellow participants, who can point out better ways of doing things, building on what they have learned from listening to one another's stories and making use of the theories and models presented in the executive program. It is normal to expect participants in a high-level executive program to possess well-developed problem-solving skills. Those skills should be used productively within the context of the executive program. With the help of breakout sessions, semi-structured activities, and coaching sessions, constructive use of the collective mind, heart, and experiences of participating executives becomes possible. It requires, however, intensive interactions and ample opportunity for participants to work with one another and faculty. Often a quite large and well-coordinated team of professors, executives in residence, and trained leadership coaches is required to guide and facilitate fruitful interactions among the participants who may not necessarily be accustomed to working so intensely on their own and others' emotional issues.

Sometimes people can start the process of change by staging small experiments with their potential selves.[11] Again, a multimodular program allows participants to try new behavior patterns, experimenting outside the class, and then reporting back to the group on the results and learning points of the experiment they staged. Further clarification of goals then takes place, new alternatives are assessed and new commitments can be made.

A safe holding environment gives the individual experimenting with change a great opportunity to make a public commitment about what changes he or she would like to make. This sort of commitment accelerates the personal transformation process, because it doubles momentum: it not only influences the person making the public commitment (cementing willingness to confront a difficult situation) but also enlists the cooperation of others, a strong reinforcement for change. It creates a tipping point. By taking a public stance, the speaker issues a self-ultimatum: go through with the change, or lose face. Facetiously, we sometimes say that our major allies in the change process are the forces of shame, guilt, and hope. Hope, of course, refers to a hope for a better future. The program designers, through carefully selecting and guiding participants through the program and creating a committed learning community, can increase the chances that the commitment made by participants in front of classmates is meaningful and truly motivational for them.

How does inner transformation lead to lasting change?

The fourth issue of transformational program designers is concerned with problems of internalization and lasting change. After the focal issues are identified and alternative approaches to dealing with them practiced, the gains have to be transformed to real life, maintained, and developed further. Participants need to rely on themselves in identifying and working through future issues. In other words, they need the competencies to edit the script for their inner theater, even if they fall short of rewriting it. But this kind of inner transformation can only take place once a new way of looking at things and a new way of learning to work with one's own issues have been *internalized*.

Internalization is a gradual process by which *external* interactions between self and others are taken in and replaced by *internal* representations of these interactions. In transformational executive programs, telling (and retelling) one's own story and listening to others' stories – and recognizing similarities among them all – consolidates this process of internalization. Work between the modules, conference calls with other participants, and peer coaching sessions held as part of the learning process also contribute to internalization. Once participants leave the group, they will need to hold on to the insights they acquired through the internalization process, even though the group and the faculty are no longer there to provide external reinforcement.

Internalization may be reinforced by creating alumni groups that meet periodically after the end of the program. Participants may self-organize into mutual support or para-supervision communities. They can also get engaged in research activities with the faculty, and even become protagonists of case studies and exercises for future runs of the same program. The ways of supporting the graduates in their learning to internalize the process of change and transformation are multiple. Program designers, however, need to take into account a possible need for such support and further guidance for the alumni.

What kind of faculty and consultants can be involved in transformational programs?

The final issue concerns the faculty, facilitators, and leadership coaches who are involved in the process of creating a transformational executive education program. Designing, managing, and delivering such programs demands the competencies that are not typically found in a traditional executive education professor or consultant. One theoretical approach that offers considerable promise in accelerating the process of change has come into modern executive education from experiments in short-term dynamic psychotherapy and group psychotherapy.[12] This therapeutic approach provides a different route from long-term psychotherapy in helping people acquire insight into the way various life events and ongoing experiences contribute to their challenges. Faculty members, coaches, and facilitators trained in these techniques find that, when combined with a solid dose of empathy and psychological support, they often result in remarkable progress in program participants. Obviously, incorporating such techniques into program design is quite different from, for example, deciding on which case study to pick from the available library or how to adjust a set of off-the-shelf slides for yet another executive program.

The above discussions should make it clear that all faculty members and facilitators considered for potential involvement in transformational programs should undertake a process of their own personal self-exploration, experimentation and, possibly, change, before they try to help others. Creating a transformational program requires a deep understanding of the way the mental life, conflict, and relationship triangles function. Someone working in these kinds of programs will dispense an enormous amount of emotional energy engaging with participants, challenging them while simultaneously showing empathy and care. Program designers need to take into account the challenges associated with the required level of emotional involvement of faculty members. Not unlike the participants themselves, faculty members may need help in dealing with their own triangles of mental life, conflict, and relationships. They may also need to confront and clarify their own issues that may become salient through working with participants.

Therefore, designers of transformational programs should envisage a need for peer coaching and mutual supervision for the leadership development professionals involved in teaching and facilitating such a course. Clearly, the time commitment and the amount of resources required for preparing and delivering such programs represent a challenge in itself.

CONCLUDING REMARKS

This chapter presented a conceptual framework for understanding the developmental needs of executives coming to a transformational program. Without taking into account these needs in the design and delivery of a change-oriented program, it is impossible to create the conditions where participants would be able to explore and tackle their challenges imposed by life and work environments. Understanding the issues faced by an executive should guide program directors, teachers, facilitators, and coaches in creating courses where enough time and space will be dedicated to allow participants to work on their own, idiosyncratic issues while simultaneously helping other executives deal with their challenges and learning from their experience.

The chapter also outlines major questions that need to be addressed by the designers of transformational programs as they create workshops or other events that really help executives become more personally and professionally successful. The list probably can and should be continued. As more providers of executive education move from delivering fact-based courses to programs that enable personal and organizational change and transformation, the more we will know about challenges and opportunities faced by providers of such interventions.

From reading this chapter, it becomes clear that the costs and risks of embarking on designing and running a transformational program are high. But so are the rewards. Creating a transformational program and helping participants change is an ultimately rewarding experience. It makes both participants and faculty aware that it is the *journey* of life that counts, not the *destination*. The way we cope with the obstacles that we inevitably encounter on that journey determines the richness of our life. Participants in transformational courses learn, through their extensive self-exploration and experimentation, a lesson that can help all of us as many of our obstacles are self-made. When leadership development professionals design such programs, they get personal rewards by understanding that if they want to, they can remove or restructure the obstacles, and they can help others learn to do the same.

LEARNING TO CHANGE: A PROGRAM EXAMPLE

Every year, Professor Manfred Kets de Vries runs a program called The Challenge of Leadership: Creating Reflective Leaders at INSEAD's Fontainebleau and Singapore campuses. Twenty very senior executives are selected to participate out of a large number of applicants from all over the world. These executives, all of whom are successful in their jobs, apply to the program for a variety of reasons. The guiding theme, however, is almost always a seemingly insoluble dilemma, perhaps centred around negative feelings about the self, or on perceptions of the world and others that make fulfillment of personal dreams seem impossible. Typically, however, this central dilemma is not clearly articulated in an applicant's mind when he or she applies to the program. The workshop consists of three five-day periods with intervals of approximately seven weeks between each one, plus a final three-day module six months later. The expectation is that participants will learn more about themselves during each on-site week; then, based on that knowledge, they agree on a contract of change that delineates what they should work on at work and at home during their time away from the workshop. Because mutual peer coaching is part of the design of the program, homework assignments are monitored among the participants.

Although the basic material of the workshop is the life case study, the first week contains a number of interactive lectures on high-performance organizations, organizational culture, effective and dysfunctional leadership, best places to work, the career life cycle, cross-cultural management, organizational stress, and psychological models of the mind.

With that foundation, participants can then move on to the workshop's central model of psychological activity and organization: the personal case history. Each participant in the workshop volunteers to sit in the hot seat once during the course of the seminar, making a personal presentation. This experience is extremely important. It is a positive step toward self-discovery, in that experience and actions become sequentially organized as a person tells his or her story; but it also helps other group members who gain understanding of their own problems as they hear about the parallel problems of others.

During each case presentation, the other participants are asked to listen carefully with free-flowing attention, and not to interrupt. When a presenter has finished, questions can be asked – but purely for the purpose of understanding the narrative better. Once the narrative has been clarified, it is the turn of the presenter to be silent and listen to the associations, interpretations, and insights of the other members of the group. A considerable amount of time is devoted to the associations (fantasies, feelings, and thoughts) that the presentation arouses in its listeners. The use of counter-transference observations is essential to the understanding of the salient themes in the presenter's life. An effort is made to prevent the premature closure that results from quick recommendations. Once the feedback session is over, the presenter is given the last word, airing any additional thoughts and commenting on the various observations. The presenter concludes by presenting a proposed contract for change, outlining the things that he or she will work on in the interim period.

During the second week, some time is devoted to the processing of a number of feedback instruments. A key part of this activity is the Global Executive Leadership Inventory, a 360° feedback instrument. In addition, feedback from the Personality Audit, is conducted (both instruments are discussed in Chapter Five of this book). This includes information from each individual's private life through feedback gathered from a spouse or significant other. Additional information is collected from other family members and close friends. This broad information provides the basis for a more refined action plan in the hiatus between the second and third periods. Apart from 360° feedback about team behavior, the main focus of the third week is the consolidation of acquired insights and the internalization of change. The presentations continue, becoming increasingly multilayered and rich as the workshop progresses. The fourth workshop session furthers the internalization process.

In addition to the plenary sessions, participants spend a lot of time in small groups in and outside the class. The interactions within these groups are extremely valuable, because they consolidate newly acquired behavior patterns. Whether in subgroups or in the plenary, the 20 participants form an intense learning community—an identity laboratory. Whenever a group member backslides into a behavior pattern that he or she is trying to unlearn, the other participants offer constructive feedback. By the third week, many of the participants often know one another better than members of their own family. With that increasing intimacy, the interchange in the plenary sessions becomes extremely free flowing. The group, exhibiting considerably more emotional intelligence with each new session, turns into a self-analyzing community, so that much less intervention by faculty is needed.

A follow-up session is held after six months to see how well the action plans have been dealt with. In many instances, follow-up sessions are held year after year—thereby offering participants and faculty alike an opportunity to assess the degree to which certain new behavior patterns have become truly internalized.

NOTES

1. Frankl, V. (1962). *Man's Search for Meaning: An Introduction to Logotherapy.* Boston, MA: Beacon Press.
2. Kets de Vries, M.F.R. (1989). *Prisoners of Leadership.* New York: Wiley; Kets de Vries, M.F.R. (2001). *The Leadership Mystique.* London: Financial Times/Prentice Hall; Kets de Vries, M.F.R. (2005). "Feeling Like a Fake: How the Fear of Success can Cripple your Career and Damage your Company." *Harvard Business Review,* 83 (8), 108–116; Kets de Vries, M.F.R. (2006a). *Leaders on the Couch: A Clinical Approach to Changing People and Organizations.*

London: Wiley; Khurana, R. (2004). *Searching for a Corporate Savior: The Irrational Quest for Charismatic CEOs*. Princeton, NJ: Princeton University Press; Hamel, G. (2002). *Leading the Revolution*. Boston, MA: Harvard Business School Press.

3. Lichtenberg, J.D. and Schonbar, R.A. (1992). "Motivation in Psychology and Psychoanalysis." In Barron J.W., Eagle, M.N., and Wolitzky, D.L. (Eds), *Interface of Psychoanalysis and Psychology*: 11–36. Washington, DC: American Psychological Association.

4. Bandura, A. (1977). "Self-Efficacy: Toward a Unifying Theory of Behavioral Change." *Psychological Review*, 84, 191–215.

5. Malan, D.H. (1963). *A Study of Brief Psychotherapy*. New York: Plenum; Malan, D.H. (1976). *The Frontier of Brief Psychotherapy*. New York: Plenum; Malan, D. and Osimo, F. (1992). *Psychodynamics, Training, and Outcome in Brief Psychotherapy*. Oxford: Butterworth Heinemann.

6. Menninger, C. (1958). *Theory of Psychoanalytic Technique*. New York: Harper; Kets de Vries, M.F.R. and Miller, D. (1984). *The Neurotic Organization*. San Francisco, CA: Jossey-Bass; Etchegoyen, R.H. (1991). *The Fundamentals of Psychoanalytic Technique*. London: Karnac Books; Kets de Vries, M.F.R. (2006a). *Leaders on the Couch: A Clinical Approach to Changing People and Organizations*. London: Wiley.

7. Freud, S. (1905). "Fragment of an Analysis of a Case of Hysteria." In Strachey, J. (Ed.), *The Standard Edition of the Complete Psychological Works of Sigmund Freud*. Vol.7. London: The Hogarth Press and The Institute of Psychoanalysis; Malan, D.H. (1963). *A Study of Brief Psychotherapy*. New York: Plenum; Greenson, R.R. (1967). *The Technique and Practice of Psychoanalysis*. New York, International Universities Press; Malan, D. and Osimo, F. (1992). *Psychodynamics, Training, and Outcome in Brief Psychotherapy*. Oxford: Butterworth Heinemann; Molnos, A. (1995). *A Question of Time: Essentials of Brief Psychotherapy*. London: Karnac Books.

8. Loewenberg, P. (1982). *Decoding the Past: The Psychohistorical Approach*. New York: Alfred A. Knopf; Spence, D.P. (1982). *Narrative Truth and Historical Truth*. New York: Norton; McAdams, D.P. (1993). *Stories We Live by: Personal Myths and the Making of the Self*. New York: William Morrow and Company; Rennie, D.L. (1994). "Storytelling in Psychotherapy: The Client's Subjective Experience." *Psychotherapy*, 31: 234–243; McLeod, J. (1997). *Narrative and Psychotherapy*. London: Sage.

9. Bandura, A. (1977); Seligman, M.E.P. and Csikszentmihalyi, M. (2000). "Positive Psychology: An Introduction." *American Psychologist*, 55 (1): 5–14; Seltzery, L.F. (1986). *Paradoxical Strategies in Psychotherapy: A Comprehensive Overview and Guidebook*. New York: Wiley; Cooperrider, D.L. and Whitney, D. (2005). *Appreciative Inquiry: A Positive Revolution in Change*. San Francisco, CA: Berrett-Koehler.

10. Kilburg, R.R. (2000). *Executive Coaching*. Washington, DC: American Psychological Association.

11. Ibarra, H. (2003). *Working Identity: Unconventional Strategies for Reinventing Your Career*. Boston, MA: Harvard Business School Press.

12. Mann, J. (1973). *Time Limited Psychotherapy*. Cambridge, MA: Harvard University Press; Sifneos, P.E. (1979). *Short-Term Dynamic Psychotherapy*. Cambridge, MA: Harvard University Press; Rosenbaum, M. (1983). *Handbook of Short-Term Therapy Groups*. New York: McGraw-Hill; Strupp, H.H. and Binder, J. L. (1984). *Psychotherapy in a New Key: A Guide to Time-Limited Dynamic Psychotherapy*. New York: Basic Books; Yalom, I. D.

(1985). *The Theory and Practice of Group Psychotherapy.* New York: Basic Books; Groves, J.E., Ed. (1996). *Essential Papers on Short-Term Dynamic Therapy.* New York: New York University Press; Gustavson, J.P. (1986). *The Complex Secret of Brief Psychotherapy.* New York: Norton; Molnos, A. (1995). *A Question of Time: Essentials of Brief Psychotherapy.* London: Karnac Books; Scott Rutan, J. and Stone, W.N. (2001). *Psychodynamic Group Psychotherapy.* New York: The Guilford Press; Rawson, P. (2002). *Short-Term Psychodynamic Psychotherapy: An Analysis of the Key Principles.* London: Karnac.

PART THREE: BECOMING A COACH

9

FROM THE BOARDROOM TO THE CLASSROOM: A PERSONAL JOURNEY

JEAN-CLAUDE NOEL

"We all have a façade, a persona, a public self. What that persona does is what the world sees, but something very different may be happening deep inside, where our private self hides. The public self that we choose to share generally bears little resemblance to the private self, a self so private that even we ourselves may know it only slightly."[1]

As I was recollecting the personal journey that has taken me from many years of corporate life to a new world, this quote from Manfred Kets de Vries in *The Leadership Mystique* came to my mind. What may appear to other people to be simply an unusual career transition felt very different to me. This chapter relates my experience of self-discovery, difficult to translate into a rational process of change, and ends by offering some lessons to be shared.

My journey has taken me from the board of Christie's International PLC, where I was group chief operating officer, to life as an adjunct clinical professor at INSEAD, program director at the INSEAD Global Leadership Centre (IGLC), and private executive coach and consultant with affiliations in California and London.

My business background was primarily in hospitality, with positions on the board of Hilton International, heading Western Europe and Africa, based in Paris, and later the Americas, based in New York. Before joining Christie's, I had spent five years in a very different industry, on the management board of TNT Express Worldwide with responsibility for international business in Asia Pacific, the Middle East and Africa, and the Americas.

Christie's could have been just another career step into a new business, but it turned out to be different from the outset.

Christie's had strong brand recognition as a leader in the art world, but was smaller than the business units I had previously led and presented a very interesting challenge. As I joined, the company was going through a difficult period, leading to the internal appointment of a new CEO, and was about to face a market downturn following several years of record sales. As part of a reorganization process, my formal role was to set up a global operational structure, but I was also expected to facilitate a major restructuring and help the newly appointed CEO settle into the role. I estimated that it would take about three years to complete the assignment. This implied another career move within a relatively short time, which I ideally wanted to be outside the traditional corporate world, although I had no specific project in mind. The day I started at Christie's was in fact the beginning of another transition.

At Christie's, I had to initiate rational change by influence rather than authority in a business defined by irrationality, and deal with a wide range of stakeholders with different requirements and expectations. Soon after joining Christie's, I came across a new program, Consulting and Coaching for Change (CCC), designed by Manfred Kets de Vries, Roger Lehman, and Erik van der Loo at INSEAD. As I later discovered, this program reflected Manfred's interest in the interface between management and clinical psychology. With seven modules over the course of one year, the program intended to provide selected individuals involved in business with a clinical perspective. I thought the program could help in my role at Christie's, and this was reflected in the thesis I would later write at the end of the CCC program, "The Human Dimension of Change: Implementing Change at Christie's Fine Art Auctioneers since 1766." As I was to discover, acceptance to the CCC program would mark the point where my business life ended and my new journey began.

CREATING A TRANSITIONAL SPACE

The transition process has been described as something different from change. Transition is a necessary psychological process that allows people to come to terms internally with external change.[2] The transition process includes three phases:

- *ending*: the requirement for closure – evolution is prevented when this step is omitted;
- *the neutral zone*: an opportunity for creativity and connectivity; and
- *new beginnings*: allowing an organization or individual to move forward, provided closure has indeed taken place in the ending phase.

In the early days of the CCC program, and without being fully aware of the concept of a "transitional space," I had somehow already entered a neutral zone. I was beginning to get in touch with the idea that "reality is transitional insofar as 'now' is only a temporary resting place between the past and the future."[3]

My conscious approach to the program was focused on providing support in implementing change at Christie's, and yet an unconscious process, where *ending* and *new beginnings* would eventually find their place, was taking shape. While this transitional space was available from the beginning of the program, I only became fully aware of its existence seven or eight months later. Yet it had started on the very first day, in the first group session, through the sharing of very personal information and the immediate establishment of an environment of trust. The transitional space was a constant. Each of the seven modules of the program was a transition to the next one, and every beginning was a new beginning with an open space for reflection, association, and fantasy, right up to the last module of the program, when it became a transition back to the real world or, in my case, a move into the real world. The real opportunity given by the program was creating this awareness. Had I missed it, the journey would have been very different but I would not have known.

This experience made me aware that everyday life provides opportunities to create space in a formal or spontaneous way. It starts with a level of awareness and an ability to recognize opportunities. The more active we are, the more we need that space, but at the same time, hyperactivity can be a conscious or unconscious defense against the ambiguity prevailing in a transitional space and what acknowledging it may lead to. The change that occurred was mainly in my acceptance of this gray area. While my professional life had always been focused on finding answers, I was discovering that significant life or career changes can only happen when we address, and even find comfort in, unanswered questions, opening up perspectives that would otherwise remain invisible. Incremental change might still be achieved in the absence of a transitional space, but fundamental change would be unlikely.

I then realized that my previous career changes were in fact incremental. Changing jobs across different continents, companies, and industries may have appeared radical and adventurous, but in reality I was essentially staying in the relatively stable environment of global executive life. It became clear, however, that all these changes over time had contributed to my new awareness.

This is when coaching started to take root as a possible career path. Until then I had seen consulting as a natural evolution from corporate life, and coaching had never been a consideration. Understanding transitional space as a concept enabled me to get closer to the implications of the clinical perspective and put the coaching process in a much more meaningful context.

I also began to draw a line between reflective space and transitional space. Through the program, I had been engaged in more frequent and deeper reflection. However, reflection is inwardly directed and does not imply action, while a transitional space intertwines reflection and action, along with interaction with others at some stage of the process. From reflective space to inner transitional space, the process eventually evolves into an open transitional space without necessarily postponing action. I was exactly where I needed to be, moving away from a situation without disengaging.

DISCOVERY THROUGH SELF-REFLECTION

A book by Alain de Botton called *The Art of Travel* was given to me by a friend and colleague whom I would never have got to know, had I not gone on this journey. De Botton wrote that people often hear advice on *where* to travel, without much thought given to the *why*, or the *how* of the journey. He observed that the "art of travel" sustains a number of questions that are neither simple nor trivial, adding that the study of these questions "might in modest ways contribute to an understanding of what Greek philosophers beautifully termed 'eudaimonia' or 'human flourishing.'"[4] I was ill at the time, and reading this book provided an ideal opportunity for self-reflection, associating art and travel as two important aspects of my past and recent life, and also reminding me of the relationship between the anticipation and reality of travel. Self-reflection is, in fact, a sort of anticipation of travel, and even travel in itself.

Like most executives, I had never allowed much time for self-reflection before I joined the program. The lack of practice made my experience on the program even more intense. I had what could be considered a successful career, but work had invaded my life and created an ever-growing need for more. I started to wonder why, and found some of the answers in my early life. I grew up in a middle-class family with a very conscientious father, and inwardly rebelled against the class-driven provincial French society in which we lived. A primary school teacher may have also contributed unintentionally to a drive to prove myself that persists to this day. He could not figure out why I wanted to study Latin in secondary school while expressing interest in a career in the hotel industry. In his mind the two did not match.

My initial studies at the Paris Hotel School took me to the United States in the mid-1960s, first upstate New York for an internship and then at the newly built, 2,153-room New York Hilton at Rockefeller Centre, a few blocks away from Christie's, where I closed the loop 40 years later. It was still quite unusual for a young European to live in New York at the time. I felt I had discovered America, and with it a world of opportunity. I did not realize then that the combination of my background and this experience would shape not only my professional life, but also my personal and family life–willingly, but not necessarily reflecting everyone's preferences.

What does it have to do with the transition I was about to make? Well, quite a lot: I was living in New York, had become an American citizen, English was my working language, made my career in large global organizations, but my roots and my values were beginning to resurface. Making this connection was an essential step in defining the next part of the journey, which would involve blending the past with a very different outcome.

As part of the CCC program, several feedback instruments provided useful information on emotional intelligence (EI), through the BarOn EQ-i Resource Report, and leadership dimensions through the Global Executive Leadership Inventory (GELI). The feedback I received was very positive but several aspects caught my attention. My own assessment was generally lower than my observers', possibly indicating my never-ending desire to raise the bar. This seemed to come at a cost in terms of the level of inner stress I was experiencing, further aggravated by the energy I was spending in maintaining a perfectly calm exterior. Another aspect showed a relatively low score on empathy, a key component of EI and described by Dr. Howard Book as the capacity to think and feel deeply enough to understand the inner life of others.[5]

This last quote had such resonance that it became a beacon guiding my future choices. With it came the difficult acceptance that I may have put too much emphasis on my corporate career, rationalizing this path without giving the necessary attention to the impact it had had on others, including my family. I was clearly not alone – many executives on the program were in the same position – but while the past could not be rewritten, there was still time to write a different future.

It was becoming obvious that the ultimate point of transformation for me would be well beyond the apparent change from Christie's to a new place. I was still not exactly sure what to look for, but a search for meaning and authenticity was taking shape, setting a foundation for continued learning and diversified interests, among which executive coaching was about to take a significant place.

THE FOCAL EVENT

In *The Leadership Mystique*, Manfred Kets de Vries designates confrontation, represented by a focal event, as one of the aspects of the dynamics of individual change, along with the early manifestation of concern through negative emotions.

I was not sure I could identify a specific focal event, but looking back, it was quite clear that avoiding stagnation may have been the main expression of concern through my entire career. Claiming that my various career changes were made through careful planning, anticipation, ambition, a taste for challenge, and superior performance sounds better than honestly admitting that I was driven by fear of inertia.

Whatever drove those career changes, each change implied some level of risk taking and real challenge, and ultimately contributed to building a richer career. However, fear of the inevitable decline at some stage of any executive cycle was a key factor in each of my career decisions. Early signs of negative emotions leading to changes at the peak of each cycle turned out to be instrumental in establishing a pattern of taking ownership of my career. However, strategy was not necessarily the cause of the changes but more the end result. It also meant that I was not jumping ships like a frog jumping out of hot water. I spent many years with Hilton International, leaving and rejoining after several years, and my tenure with other companies was generally around four to five years, long enough to take responsibility and make an impact, and short enough to avoid falling into inertia. My time with Hilton International was also marked by significant position changes, from director of sales and general manager in the early part of my career to joining the board with responsibility for large operational units in my last eight years with the company.

Ironically, change had become a way to reach some form of stability. My life followed a regular rhythm of seasonal change, possibly experiencing longer springs and shorter winters, but as this latest change approached, the fear was of a different nature. I was reaching the age when the long winter of retirement was looming. This is normally the time when many executives decide by choice or by force to leave the corporate world and express extraordinary excitement about playing as much golf as they want. Thankfully, I do not play golf and I therefore had to find my next spring.

Whether or not I was entering the seventh age of the leader, to become "the Sage in his second childishness" described by Warren Bennis,[6] it was becoming clear that impending retirement was my focal event.

"POSSIBLE SELVES"

As the CCC program drew to a close, the journey I had taken had already opened a transitional space, creating an opportunity for self-discovery and along with it the awareness of the focal event that was creating the urgency.

Yet I was still unable to formulate clearly what the next step would be, or the process leading to it. In this phase of uncertainty there was a risk of consciously or unconsciously disengaging from my role at Christie's, and I knew I needed to make a commitment either to be involved for the longer term or complete the *ending* phase, which would bring closure over a period of time. I had to determine this for myself in order to embrace actively and effectively the creative *neutral zone*, exploring "possible selves" best described by Professor Herminia Ibarra in *Working Identity*.[7]

When I was going through this process, I had not yet met Ibarra and her book had not yet been published, but when I read *Working Identity* later, I could relate my own experience to her comments. Her definition of working identity asserts "that we are not one true self but many selves and that those identities exist not only in the past and the present but also, and most importantly, in the future." Referring to Hazel Markus's work,[8] she also states that "the possible-selves model reveals that we all carry around, in our hearts and minds, a whole cast of characters, the selves we hope to become, think we should become, or even fear becoming in the future."

I had learned through my own process of self-discovery that the feedback I had received was more relevant to my "possible selves" than to my current position or even to a subsequent logical transition. In fact I now use this concept in my coaching work. I understood that my transferable skills, my adaptability, and my personal values allowed me to go through several career transitions in different industries and would still take me through that next phase. Reflecting on the question "Why should anyone be led by me?" encouraged me to examine where my real interests lay, and the answer suddenly seemed quite obvious: people.

I was also aware that retaining a relative degree of independence had always been an essential consideration for me, probably also contributing to the changes I made whenever I felt that my independence might be threatened.

The revelation for me was realizing that, whatever I did next, I would need to be able to find meaning and purpose in it, to use my knowledge and experience to help others, be in control of my own destiny, and dedicate more time to my personal and family life. These criteria seemed to rule out further corporate positions as possible future selves.

This was as much as I knew at the end of the CCC program, still confused by the depth of what I had learned and what I felt I still needed to learn to transform executive coaching from a possibility to a reality. Expressing that confusion in a question to Manfred Kets de Vries on the very last day of the program, his answer was that I was ready to make it a reality if I wanted to. He did not succeed in increasing my level of confidence at the time, but he planted a seed.

FLYING SOLO

What applies to organizations also applies to individuals, as I experienced back in 1984 when I was training for my private pilot's license. At some point in the process, my instructor got out of the plane after a routine exercise and let me make my first solo flight. Had I been asked, I would not have felt ready, but I took off and landed safely. A few months later, I obtained my license and have since landed a plane over a thousand times. Being a pilot was a possible self that was realized when my competence was assessed by someone willing to take responsibility for that judgment.

In my initial days as a "shadow coach" in the Advanced Management Program (AMP) at INSEAD, a debate took place on the wisdom of involving graduates of the CCC program in clinically oriented coaching, work which had so far been conducted exclusively by psychoanalysts, psychiatrists, and psychologists. At the time, I made an association between my flying experience and being entrusted to coach "solo." I have since successfully worked with several hundred participants at INSEAD and in my private practice, and other graduates of the program have joined the team.

In both flying and coaching, trust was more important than competence, willingness, or motivation. As a result, the seed planted by Manfred Kets de Vries began to bear fruit. A later invitation to join the IGLC as executive-in-residence while still with Christie's, and my eventual appointment as adjunct clinical professor at INSEAD and program director at the IGLC, brought further evidence of that trust and contributed to making my possible self a reality.

The importance of people willing to extend their trust, support, and confidence is significant. We are easily led to believe that we succeed because of our extraordinary skills, competencies, and unique personalities. Many executives are convinced this is the case and as a result display signs of arrogance and narcissism. Leading an organization or flying a plane should be a humbling experience, with the realization that each "flight" tests your ability irrespective of how good you may have been previously.

Extraordinary people are those who believe in others and enable them to go where they would not otherwise have gone. I was fortunate to have found such people along the way and even though my interaction with some of them occurred many years ago, they all contributed to shape my life in many different ways.

The CEO of Christie's trusted me to develop an informal coaching role and facilitated my transition by allowing me to pursue my executive coaching interest while still at the company. This turned out to be a positive advantage for both the organization and myself, but such forward thinking is unfortunately not common in most organizations.

In my early career, I came across a man who was about to become my boss and unconscious mentor for many years. From the time I walked into his office in Paris, just off the plane from my first adventure in New York, he demonstrated that he believed in me. He was a renowned hotelier but also a man of few words. We did not have what could be described as a close relationship but his trust spoke louder than words. I spent the first few years working while pursuing my studies in law and economics and he appointed me as director of sales of the Hilton in Rabat, Morocco, when I was only 23 years old and just married. We came back from Rabat with a son and an amazing cultural experience that is still reflected in our lives today. This man offered me my first general manager's position at the Hilton at Orly Airport at the age of 28, and then at the Paris Hilton, considered to be one of the chain's leading hotels at the time, before I was 30. I left Hilton International to pursue other opportunities, and a few years later he hired me back as part of a long-term succession plan, and I eventually joined the board as he retired. He was taking risks while I was just taking opportunities.

We tend to see the corporate world through the visible side of public companies and too often neglect the more discreet aspects of private companies and family businesses. Several experiences allowed me to penetrate that environment. When managing director for Casino Restauration, the restaurant division of the Casino group and the largest public restaurant company in France at that time, I discovered the strong sense of values embedded in this large family-controlled business, and along with it a real passion for quality and customers, coupled with respect for their employees.

In my Christie's days, I also had the privilege to meet François Pinault, another man of few words, difficult to get close to, but who projects extraordinary power and vision. François Pinault embodies a perfect expression of possible selves. He started out with a small family lumber business and ended with a business empire that includes such names as Gucci, Chateau Latour, and Christie's–along the way becoming a leading collector of contemporary art. He would not have been aware of it, but my opportunity to observe him in various situations, including the unusual decision to transfer leadership of the business to his son at a relatively early stage, was a source of learning and inspiration, perhaps more rarely seen in CEOs of publicly traded companies. True entrepreneurs tend to be authentic, either because they do not have a choice, or simply because they are carried by their personality and can only be "themselves." They see things others do not see. Making the impossible possible is probably what drives them more than power and money, but they can also be ruthless.

In various ways, these men, and unwittingly many others, have shaped my life by playing the role of "flying instructors" and enabling me to line up for another takeoff in my personal and professional life, demonstrating that trust matters.

While professional trust is essential, the one aspect that we tend to forget or take for granted is that trust really matters personally between family and friends. Love and friendship do not start or end with a job: they are part of life. I would not have achieved what I have done without my family and I can only hope that I have contributed in some way to their own and our common achievements.

NEW BEGINNINGS

"It is not the truth that is holy but the search for one's own truth! Can there be a more sacred act than self inquiry? My philosophical work, some say, is built on sand: my views shift continually. But one of my granite sentences is: 'Become who you are'."

Irvin D. Yalom—*When Nietzsche wept*[9]

One of my "flying instructors" became a colleague and a close friend. He recently recommended Yalom's novel on the extraordinary interaction between Josef Breuer, one of the founding fathers of psychoanalysis, and Friedrich Nietzsche, the philosopher. These words by Nietzsche perfectly expressed the final destination for my journey: "Become who you are."

I may have pursued that goal for many years but, in trying to adapt to the scripted context of corporate life, it is also possible that I tried to become someone else. Either way would have been mostly unconscious. Two years after deciding to join Christie's, and having completed the CCC program, I was finding awareness of a purpose and meaning I would never reach but to which I could at least get closer. I was starting to move away from the gray area of the *neutral zone* and into *new beginnings*.

The transition was still far from over. I first had to put my learning into practice, in my work environment, and I also had to test my ability and interest in a coaching environment. I was quickly given this opportunity at INSEAD in the form of shadow-coaching, working with a number of very experienced professionals. This amazing trust and support allowed me to gain experience and eventually start to work on my own in various programs. At the same time, I was introduced to the founder of Executive Coaching Network Inc (EXCN), who immediately took me on board–another example of personal trust. Within a year, I had gained experience and confidence and could start defining my own approach to coaching.

I had to put my learning into practice to convince myself, and others, that I could do this work effectively. I was finding it difficult to assess objectively what I knew and what I still had to learn, but as I started to practice, the learning came together. To my surprise, the pieces of the puzzle fell into place quite naturally, but I was still dealing with "identities in transition," as described by Ibarra, who argues that we do not give up a career path in which we have a great deal invested until we have identified alternatives to the status quo.[10]

This is precisely what was happening; having had the opportunity to experiment, I was able to transform the alternatives into a project for the future. At that moment, I was ready to leave my job and start a new career in executive coaching. A conversation with Christie's CEO led to a different solution, not in outcome but in timing. I would stay in my COO role for another couple of years, with a focus on organizational and leadership development as well as succession planning and reorganization at board level. During that period, my working time would be reduced to allow me to develop my own activities. When I eventually left, the task was completed and my new activities were already established. Had I left sooner, the transition might not have been as smooth for either the company or myself.

The early days of my new professional life felt strange, but I could not quite understand why. I had given a lot of thought to the change and I had gone through a process, which had taken place exactly as planned. There were no surprises and I was where I wanted to be. But I had missed an important aspect: over almost four decades of working life, I had formed unconscious habits. In fulltime positions, the days are filled with activities ranging from the essential to the unnecessary, even useless at times. Becoming independent was giving me choices I never had before, nor ever expected to have. I had the scary thought that for all those years, I had probably spent a lot of energy on things that were not very useful. With this thought came the realization that long hours in a corporate role are mostly self-inflicted, for various reasons, including an unconscious sense of preservation and the related fear of "empty" space. Executives would not think of saying anything other than that they are "very busy," even though they really fulfill their role when they are available to others and make time to reflect. Experiencing this vacuum was the last step I needed to take to move away from the boardroom.

As this chapter shows, my move from the boardroom to the classroom was not the result of careful planning. It emerged at the end of an unstructured, possibly confusing, and at times chaotic process. Its foundations lie in my personal and professional life. It brings together my values, my cross-cultural background, my business experience, my deep interest in people, and the "glue" of my recent exposure to the clinical perspective. It works for me because it is as close as I can get to being me, with the whole taking over from each of the pieces. All along, my focus was on my journey, not on my destination.

The "classroom" I refer to is neither the destination nor the journey. It stands for the multiple journeys I am now experiencing as one of the "portfolio workers" described by Charles Handy, in his book *Myself and Other More Important Matters*,[11] as "people who have a number of jobs, clients and types of work." The classroom is filled with coaching, teaching, and business activities through various affiliations, all quite different but building on one another other under the umbrella of the company I created in 2002, in the early part of this process. In such a context, establishing a company was both a symbolic and practical step, manifesting the transformation in progress.

LESSONS LEARNED

I did not really make any of this happen. Others did it for me. All I did was to make transformation possible by creating the space and opening my mind to read the small signals of life. This was the main lesson, for me.

The other important lesson is that transformation takes time. From my first awareness of the need to change to the effective moment of change, almost five years elapsed, and it probably took another year to achieve full integration. Different processes take place simultaneously and, like good wine, need the time to mature. One could question whether there is truly transformation or simply a liberation of potential that was always there.

As we tend to live longer, the concept of retirement may become obsolete in favor of new forms of activity adapted to the cycle of life. Being potentially active beyond what is considered to be retirement age follows previous trends related to fundamental changes in the contractual nature of employment and the impossibility of satisfying personal needs and corporate needs "for life." A wider range of options such as self-employment, small business, consulting, not-for-profit, teaching, or volunteering have appeared in response to the relative uncertainty of large corporations. Mid-life has become a sliding scale and the line separating professional life and retirement will become more and more blurred. Reinvention or recycling now happens more frequently and earlier in life, in forms that are not limited to job and geographical mobility.

Interestingly, the clinical paradigm described in Chapter One finds its application in my specific experience:

- *Perception is not reality*: What you see is not necessarily what you get. The world around us is much more complex than it seems on the surface. Much of what happens is beyond our conscious awareness.
- *Irrationality is grounded in rationality*: All human behavior—including our uniquely individual cognitive and emotional perceptual distortions—has a rationale.
- *People are product of their past*: We cannot live in the present without paying attention to the past.

These premises were at the basis of my learning and also formed the foundation of my own experience in making this journey. Practicing these principles somehow took root in my own thinking.

I have reached a point in my journey where I feel content living the present, and with enough dreams to have no fear of the future. Is this reality or an illusion? I may never have the answer to that question but do not really need it. I like my new classroom and do not miss the boardroom that led me here.

NOTES

1. Kets de Vries, M.F.R. (2001) *The Leadership Mystique*, London: Financial Times Prentice Hall.
2. Bridges, W. (1980) *Transitions*, Cambridge: Perseus.

3. Amado, G. and Amato, R. (2001) *The Transitional Approach to Change*, Chapter Three, Some distinctive Characteristics of Transitional Change, London: H Karnac (Books) Ltd.
4. De Botton, A. (2004) *The Art of Travel*, New York: Vintage Books, p. 9.
5. Stein, S.J. and Book, H.E. (2000) *The EQ Edge*, Toronto: Stoddart.
6. Bennis, W.G. (2004) *The Seven Ages of the Leader*, Boston: Harvard Business Review on the Mind of the Leader.
7. Ibarra, H. (2003) *Working Identity*, Boston: Harvard Business Review Press, p. 23.
8. Markus, H. and Nurius, P. (1986) Possible Selves, *American Psychologist* 41, no 9: 954–969.
9. Yalom, I. (1992) *When Nietzsche wept*, New York: Harper Collins Publishers, p. 68.
10. Ibarra, H. (2003), p. 12.
11. Handy, C. (2006) *Myself and Other More Important Matters*, Oxford: William Heinemann.

10

COACHING WITHIN AND WITHOUT

GRAHAM WARD

It is the human condition to be bored periodically, but after 19 years in banking I was virtually comatose. Everything should have been peachy. I worked for Goldman Sachs, the world's premier investment bank. I co-led an incredible team of dedicated, high-performing professionals. My team had recently executed the biggest block trade in stock market history (a high risk, high capital deal: the implications of failure would have meant a significant dent in the overall earnings of the bank). For the team it was a massive adrenaline shot. We had, in the course of five years, turned around an ailing business that had been practically on its last legs. It had become a prestigious, highly profitable venture with high morale and a growing pedigree. I regularly commuted to and from the world's financial capitals first class, had sipped champagne next to Henry Kissinger on Concorde, and had even been caught up first hand in the Robert Maxwell scandal. It had been a lucrative and exciting career. Yet in my heart, something was missing.

As often happens around age 40, some major life questions began to appear. My lackluster academic record, the 70-hour week and its consequent strain on family life, my growing guilt at failing to contribute to broader society, and the accumulation of wealth with no logical rationale began to nag at me. I was not living life, it was living me. I could have easily gone to the grave with a Reuters terminal by my deathbed pumping out stock prices. My life would have been unmemorable and insignificant.

I had harbored a private interest in psychology for some time. Suffice to say this was fuelled by a rather dysfunctional upbringing, not outstandingly different from one that many children today experience. Coupled with a growing realization that, more recently, I had enjoyed the people management side of my work more than the cut and thrust of everyday deal-making, the impetus for change began to grow. I had become a notional mentor to many people at the bank, both within and beyond my purview, so looking for a people-related academic pursuit that would lead ultimately to a different career was logical. I reflected on how I had contrived to arrive at this point.

Serendipity intervened to allay my growing confusion. I was sent to a leadership offsite, a congregation of Goldman business leaders from across the globe, to focus on personal and professional development, in the dreamily bucolic setting of Connecticut. It was there, among my peers, that I dropped my bombshell: I would shortly leave the bank to pursue a career in psychology. I would leave immediately and set up shop downtown with a couch, etc. (As Richard Pascale notes, "Adults are much more likely to act their way into a new way of thinking than think their way into a new way of acting.")[1] Luckily, the skillful intervention of the facilitators steered me toward calmer seas. With a modicum of sense, they convinced me I would be better served by leveraging my considerable business experience and people skills as a coach. To that end, they persuaded me to make a leap of faith and tell the CEO of my intentions.

As a consummate risk-taker, this should have been straightforward, but this was a personal, not a capital risk. It was not an easy prospect. But the lesson for all coaches here is: take some risk, in all aspects of your life. The experiences you rack up by challenging yourself ultimately become a resource for your clients.

So it was that one dark December morning, I risked the 15 years of capital I had built at the bank and, heart in mouth, told the CEO of my intentions. The outcome was astonishing. He not only persuaded me to stay with the bank, but also offered to sponsor me through a degree in coaching. Moreover, he gave me a green-field site in the form of career development for a division with close to five thousand employees. The risk paid off handsomely.

At the outset I had misgivings about my lack of training; coaching, like other arts, is learned through experience.[2] I opened up shop at the bank in January 2000 not knowing what the future would hold. Luckily, the combination of a captive clientele and formal training was a powerful introduction to the business.

Some readers may not be lucky enough to have such a visionary as a boss. Nevertheless, consider to what extent it is within your power to take charge of and manage your own life. For three years I worked as an internal coach at Goldman Sachs. Such a position had never existed at the bank before, and regrettably it no longer does. For three years, an exclusively internal clientele had access to a senior business leader dedicated to performance enhancement, career progression, and conflict resolution. This is solely attributable to a visionary divisional CEO with enormous emotional intelligence and integrity.

As is often the case, such a leader will be instrumental in allowing prototype positions to develop. But this leadership development office was a skunk works. He deliberately positioned it to operate outside the fiefdoms and systems within the bank. And as he intended, it created a stink within the company. As it turned out this was no bad thing. As the role developed, more and more business leaders became interested and galvanized by the outputs. After all, their people were coming through my office door. In my case, the CEO played a dual role of which all internal consultants should take note. He became not only a visible and audible high-level sponsor of the position, but was also a defender and buffer for the incumbent. It was no coincidence that, later on, when the CEO himself left the bank, the position was instantly cannibalized. It was suggested that I move to Human Resources. I knew that to do so would render me toothless, and embroil me in bureaucracy. As an internal consultant you need constant, high-level sponsorship and protection. The work that you do creates not ripples but waves. If and when support recedes, head for the hills.

At first, the mandate was complex: The remit was to coach the staff (especially the high performers), set up a mentor program (for the rest), actively consider and improve diversity, and make succession planning systematic and meritocratic.

The question that naturally arose was: Why do we need such a role when HR can intermediate effectively? It is easy to imagine from which quarters that question came. There is no easy answer to this, and internal consultants face being caught between a potentially hostile HR department, who imply you are treading on their turf, and a professional base that sees you as an extra cost. One is quickly put in a position of self-justification.

In reality, my business credibility held me in good stead. My suggestion for internal consultants is to leverage that hard. When we opened shop in 2000, the CEO told me plainly he felt it would be 18 months before we would know if the experiment was successful. I was careful to pin down what the measures of success would be as far as he was concerned. Prospective internal consultants should be encouraged to do precisely that and, if possible, to get something in writing. In such an abstract field, the goalposts move often and even with a benign sponsor, performance is hard to measure.

As an ex-trader, used to quick results and instant gratification, I was not sure I had the stomach for such a marathon. As it turned out, within two months I was fully booked. I cannot attribute this to my skills, as they were at that point largely untested. In fact, it revealed the pent up anxiety that probably lurks in many organizations. For me, an early lesson was to get help ... fast.

SUPERVISION

My erstwhile facilitator from Connecticut (who by then had become a mentor) was sympathetic. I told him I had never been so exhausted. I spent eight hours a day listening to the problems, gripes, anxieties, and miseries of a group of high-functioning banking employees. "Ah," he said, "you have become what I would describe as a psychological toilet into which they flush all their ..." "Yes, well, that's all very well," I replied, "but what can I do?" My erudite friend went on to tell me that even practicing psychoanalysts take supervision, reporting the cases they are working on, in strict confidence, to their supervisor. Why should it be any different as a coach? I took little convincing and immediately sought help via the Tavistock Centre for Group Relations in London, where the CEO agreed to supervise my work. I consider this to have been a vitally important step for me. All would-be coaches, whether coaching internally or externally, should do the same.

As a coach in training, I learned more from my supervisor than any study program or book could ever have taught me. He had over 40 years in the business as coach, psychoanalyst, and consultant. At times he offered stunning psychological insights, which I believe accelerated my abilities. At other times he simply let me unload. I have come to believe that any coach who does not take supervision is bordering on irresponsible. No coach has the monopoly of wisdom and an experienced supervisor is a *sine qua non*, an extra mirror to the work. All potential coaching clients should check if their coaches take supervision. If they do not, they should consider seriously whether the coach should be hired.

BUILDING TRUST

I cleared the rather large hurdle of trust easily as I had been at Goldman Sachs for over 12 years. If you do not have that luxury, then a systematic process to garner that trust must be put in place. My suggestion is to work from the bottom up, meeting key stakeholders one-to-one, and making internal presentations to important constituencies. And from the top down, a powerful sponsorship communication from on high will generate credibility quickly.

In order to be effective as an internal coach, one very narrow waterway has to be navigated. The question that arises time and again is: Are you loyal to your client or to the firm? As an employee of the firm, how do you manage this conflict?

Imagine the scenario: a young woman comes into your office and tells you her career has not been going well lately, she has been overlooked for promotion by her "tyrannical boss," she performs better than some male colleagues yet earns less than most, she feels her team is a boys' club and she is now having difficulty sleeping, and sometimes returns home in tears in the evening.

A professional *external* coach would, in the first place, probably recommend that she visit a doctor/psychotherapist to check for clinical depression. Only when that had been assessed, might she proceed to work on her professional competencies and relationship with authority figures and male colleagues. As an *internal* consultant you have far less room for maneuver.

In the first place, you will probably know the tyrannical boss personally. This lends itself to creating predispositions. Maybe you quite like him and do not view him that way, or you already disliked him before the woman came and told you her sorry tale. Obviously, in order to be truly helpful you need to be highly objective. Casting aside one's initial prejudices is not easy. Moreover, you need to understand the alternative view. There always is one and it rarely correlates with what you have been told. How can one do this without opening the can of worms that every complaint represents, and which, if not handled properly, can lead to the client being penalized?

Second, if one suspects that an employee is depressed, does one have a moral or fiduciary responsibility to address that and tell someone? After all, your company could be on the receiving end of litigation if the situation ended in a constructive dismissal allegation or, worse still, a suicide attempt. So to whom does one owe loyalty, the company or the employee? And if after investigation, it turns out that an unfair compensation policy is being used, how can one address that without (to adopt another image) stirring up a hornets' nest?

These are not easy questions, and external coaches will seldom face them. However, I was faced with this type of situation on more than one occasion, and my response was clear cut.

In the first place, it was essential to clarify with my sponsor that, in every case, my responsibility, loyalty, and prerogative were to the employee not the company. I said as much to each client before I began the work. I suggest internal coaches do just that. I also told the CEO that I would not be sharing any information with him about my clients, but that from time to time, if themes developed where he as CEO could implement strategic change for the benefit of his workforce, I would inform him. He always respected that. Had he not, the position would have been untenable. Other business leaders did not, however, and there was sometimes pressure for me to reveal what their people had been telling me. I never did. Moreover, I think the Hippocratic maxim of "Do no harm" applies to coaches as much as any other professional helper.

To coach someone is to share his or her inner world, hopes, fears, fantasies, and aspirations for a period of time. Coaches assume a fairly powerful position that must never be abused. *Whenever a coach suspects that the territory has shifted into areas beyond his or her competence, i.e., mental health, a referral or other outside help must be immediately sought, irrespective of whether it compromises the company or the coach himself.*

It is vitally important that, if one finds oneself in this situation, rigorous detailed notes are kept. The client should be informed that this is happening, but it is also a form of self-protection for you, the consultant. If the client claims that he or she told a coach something that was not addressed, for example, sexual harassment or bullying (and these things come up a lot in internal coaching), the company and the coach are potentially exposed. *Write up every meeting religiously.* If you do come upon a situation that is potentially litigious, it is your job to convince the client gently that they need to take it further, usually by informing HR. Otherwise, you might find yourself sitting on a time bomb.

What became clear early on is that for every protagonist there is an antagonist. And the antagonist may very well end up being the person sitting in front of you. Sure, they might complain about rough treatment at the hands of their peers or superiors, and pour scorn on the strategy of their department, but sometimes they have failed to take any responsibility for their present situation. Occasionally, that is the only material that you work on.

Naturally, an external coach has no access to the cast of actors that surrounds the client. The internal coach does, and the irresistible temptation is to test reality. *Do not do this.* If you believe the maxim that reputations are built over decades and lost in minutes, talking outside the confines of your coaching office is a surefire way to test the theory to its maximum detrimental effect. Your internal credibility will be instantly destroyed. What you can do, however, is assess the state of the department. Perform a forensic check of the performance and compensation records of the department. Read the 360-degree reviews of the client and any other members of the team, if there are any. Again, negotiate this possibility up front with your sponsor. Without it, you will not have sufficient understanding of the context to do the job. Do anything within your power to assess the situation without creating disruption. Establish clear boundaries and guidelines for your work and agree them with the key stakeholders. You could attempt to divine the mood of the business, look at recent results, and study the environment that is contributing to the situation. It could be worth walking over to the area to see where the client sits in relation to his or her peers. An internal coach sometimes needs to think like Sherlock Holmes. Sniff around picking up clues without betraying your presence. Every nuance is important and, particularly if you work as an internal coach, the more you can discern without having to talk to other parties the better.

I believe that one cannot operate optimally as a coach until one has learned and integrated some form of group dynamics training. As an internal coach, where one has vast quantities of organizational resources and knowledge at one's disposal, this type of training proves invaluable. Group interplay inevitably impacts individual performance. The unconscious impact of a person's place in a group hierarchy affects their output in ways of which they are unaware. But the various transference effects of group relations are only understood if one spends time studying the theory, which adds considerable context and contributes enormously to one's effectiveness as a coach.

One of the drawbacks of coaching internally is negative image management. This is usually not a problem for an external coach. You meet a prospective client, assess the chemistry, and agree to proceed or not. The relationship exists and is visible only to the coach and the client. There is a neutrality of context. Internally, that is not the case. Often one starts to attract a reputation as a certain type of person.

When the office was set up at Goldman Sachs, my most frequent clients were senior women who had hit the so-called glass ceiling. Further exploration of the issues faced by women within the firm led me to discover certain inequalities that needed to be addressed. I tried to do this systematically. While it was a good outcome for the firm (and the women) to have someone focused on this area, the trade-off for me was that I became the "women's champion." The more women I helped, the more came to see me, and in the end I became not only typecast but a container for women's issues within my division. I do not necessarily see this as a negative, since naturally one's impetus to coach stems from a desire to help. The problem was more one of being trapped in a certain type of work, precluding other assignments. The consequent payoff was that I was regarded as some kind of *über*-feminist, thus ostracizing other constituencies from my client base. This is something to be aware of and manage actively.

BUILDING AN EXTERNAL COACHING PRACTICE

Waking up on January 1, 2005, I felt like a puppy poking its head out of the front door and seeing snow for the first time. I had finally left corporate life. Twenty years of infrastructure support were behind me. The psychological apron strings of the organization were severed and I was on my own, with the ambition to build a consultancy from scratch. Most men approaching 40 face passages in their lives for which they are unprepared.[3] I had undergone a revolution.

Goldman Sachs had gone public in 1999. In turn, this led to the retirement of many of the talented partners who had previously so impressed me. The firm was left in the hands of a new breed of executive. Younger, hungrier, and less farsighted, the emphasis on human capital seemed to shrink and I was asked to return to the business, which I did, albeit half-heartedly. Within a year, the motivation to stay at the company that had done so much for me evaporated and by mutual agreement, I too left the firm.

Paramount in my mind during this disruptive period was the ongoing well being of my family. It was not a hard mental leap to decide to spend more time at home and develop a business that would theoretically enable me to be with them more than my 70-hour week investment banking lifestyle had allowed. But the three major negatives about home businesses weighed heavily: you are constantly job hunting, work-life balance is hard to maintain, and, statistically, your pay drops by 30 percent.[4]

I dismissed my first inclination, which was to tout myself around the financial community in Scandinavia, leveraging my experience and contacts in the business. Strangely for me, I decided that the best course of action was to do nothing. Suppressing my predisposition to hyperactivity, I started taking long walks in the woods with an ever-thinning but happier Labrador, figuring out exactly how my professional future should look and, more importantly, how and what I should make happen.

The time was well spent. I recall feeling tremendously anxious at the time, fantasizing that I was washed up and might never work again. In spite of this anxiety, I was not going to make the mistake I had made 20 years previously and reflexively execute a flashy dive off my burning platform into a sea full of great white sharks. Was this not the time to exorcise my ghosts? Those ghosts of a trading career, however, were still lurking in the shadows.

I, like many others in the same position, retreated momentarily into the past. Setting up a trading account with a London broker, I managed to blow through several family holidays of cash in a couple of months, largely out of boredom. What I quickly discovered was, the gas that fuelled the flame of excitement for trading was exhausted and I recalled the words of the market wizard Ed Seykota, who once proclaimed that "everyone gets what they want from the market." Well, I certainly did, and I squashed any further thoughts of trading for a living. If I was going to be successful, I would require focus, energy, and stamina. To dilute my efforts would mean to fail at both. It will always be tempting for people going out on their own to sabotage themselves in this way; after all, the path of least resistance is to do what we know, not what we can. In the words of Shakespeare's Lady Macbeth, "Nail your courage to the sticking place." Running your own consultancy business will be a massive challenge but the rewards, both from the freedom it affords and the satisfaction it brings, are enormous.

That said, building a career again from scratch is a tall order requiring confidence and character. The latter, I inherited from my mother. The former needed bolstering, and it was to my old mentors that I inevitably turned.

Conversations with both my professor and supervisor saw them converge in the opinion that it would be folly to dismiss the learning in human relations that I had accumulated over the last few years. Why had I embarked on such a course in the first place, if I was now to discard it all?

While plowing my furrow at Goldman Sachs, my *alma mater*, INSEAD, had set up the International Global Leadership Centre (IGLC). The centre runs a number of high-level programs for executives, and, during my time at Goldman Sachs, I had been invited to work alongside the team of coaches they had built.

It would have been a conflict of interest to do this while at Goldman Sachs, but freed from those shackles, this was one area for exploration. The scope of the job would be a greater challenge than I had so far faced. The task would be to coach groups of five to six executives intensively for nine hours. It occurred to me that this would be a good proving ground. It would not be an onerous demand on my time, since the programs usually ran over one day. It would be an acid test to see if I could coach outside a firm that I knew intimately and it would, if successful, give my confidence a kick through a couple of gears. So I resurrected the invitation. The reality was that, even at full throttle, the opportunity only amounted to 12–14 days' work a year. I needed other strings to my bow.

When setting up a consultancy it is elemental to use basic management technology. In the first place ask yourself the question: "What am I going to do and how am I going to get there?" I tried to simplify the answer. I wanted to be on *Fortune Magazine*'s list of the world's top ten coaches within ten years. I agree it is a lofty target, somewhat ambitious, and not completely at odds with the ethos of my former career. So that is what I wanted to do. The way to get there had to be broken into bite-size chunks, and the following was my template for creating the business.

GET BRANDED

I believe the first step is to create your brand. What do you want to look like in the marketplace, what does your stall look like, and which clients are you trying to attract? Had I woken up one morning and decided to be a coach? Not really. In essence it had been an evolutionary process. I was not, however, content to drift around touting for business. If I had learned nothing else from my time at Goldman Sachs it was that you had better be differentiated. When building a brand, "you shouldn't settle for saying who you are and what you do, you should state what you believe in."[5] My training in the psychodynamic perspective was a big plus and a relative rarity. Twenty years of top-drawer business experience was another. I believe all coaches can find a way to express their individuality. My surmise was that not to do so would ultimately mean failure. Figure out who your audience is, and brand yourself accordingly. Get a logo that fits your brand, just for fun. Start to feel yourself as part of that brand and make the brand a part of you. Choose a name that has meaning to you and talk about it at every opportunity.

GET PLANNING

Your company will need a legal structure. Think about where it is to be based from a tax perspective and whether that fits with the brand. I made the initial mistake of branding myself a "Nordic Consultancy." This was too limiting and luckily was easily remedied. Start as broadly as you can and then narrow your focus according to the business landscape.

It is also important to consider whether you will be employing other coaches or simply affiliating with them. I decided early on that I wanted to work alone, as a sole proprietor. What I subsequently discovered was that, as a sole proprietor, you need fairly substantial personal liability insurance.

It is vital to find a target audience for your services. This will help to define your own brand and keep you focused when marketing. For instance, you might want to work at board level, or maybe you only want to work with female executives. Are you a life coach, a career coach, or a leadership coach? By narrowing down and zeroing in on your expertise and interest you will deliver a punchier message to any potential client. Do not make your scope too narrow but find yourself a niche to exploit. Make sure that when somebody asks what you do, you can tell them in one line.

A common mistake for sole proprietors is not to make a business plan. In order to systematically plan, organize, brand, and market your consultancy to your potential customer base, a good business plan is essential. I was tempted to wing it for a while. The result? I ended up being drawn down a number of blind alleys. Although an element of experimentation is to be expected, a loose framework is the very least one should build in order to avoid unnecessary diversions.

Your fee structure is an important differentiator. In order to get this right you may need to tinker with the initial structure.

I rather liked the Marshall Goldsmith ethos that if you don't like what you get, you don't pay, so that is how I started off. If cash flow is an issue, this methodology may not be for you. However, it is bold, puts pressure on you, the coach, to perform, and potentially allows you to ultimately command a higher fee. It resonated with me because I feel it is unjust to charge a client if they receive no benefit. Moreover, if one is relying initially on word-of-mouth recommendations (and that is to be expected at first) then you can assume that those that have paid are satisfied and therefore more likely to refer you. At least those that were not satisfied are less likely to blacken your name because the experience has not cost them. Some coaches have a two-tier structure, a higher fee for corporate clients and a lower one for individuals. I personally favor this, as the average corporate fee is preclusive to individuals, other than those in banking or successful entrepreneurs. However, try to stick to your fee structure. Nothing is more infuriating to a client than to hear that they are being charged 20% more than the next person for the same service. Your reputation is at stake. Do not discount your service. Work on the premise that good coaching is worth paying for.

In order to focus on your business and your coaching, it is also important to put the entire infrastructure you need in place up front. Bank accounts, tax accountants, bookkeepers, and auditors are all paid servants of the sole proprietor. If you organize this cadre and define exactly their role in your business, you will have plenty of time to be strategic. To do this after you open your doors will waste valuable time.

GET OUT THERE

The singular most important characteristic for would-be consultants is networking ability. This was far from my strongest suit and there were tough lessons during the start-up phase, especially given my locale. My early mistake was to focus very tightly on the financial services industry in Stockholm. I wasted a lot of energy writing letters to small local boutique operations in the hope that my international banking credentials would catch me a fish. I received very few replies and garnered no business. At first, my exuberance led me to send a second wave of letters. In order to shape up, I had to get irritated. When no replies came back from the second wave I hastily (and wrongly) identified the parochial nature of the Swedish as the problem. That gave me the energy to consider playing on a bigger and broader stage. So ...

... SPEAK PUBLICLY

The first time I spoke at a coaching conference, I not only felt queasy but had stayed up all the night before reviewing most of what I was going to say. It was not necessary. Most people who go to conferences are either on an information-gathering mission or networking, and typically the whole exercise is one big marketing jamboree. This is the place to get your newly differentiated brand on display while at the same time contributing to the field. Find out where these conferences are in your area and go along. Meet the organizers and offer your services if you see gaps in the market. Do not expect to be paid. The organizers will know why you want to speak. It is a fantastic way of reaching a broad audience of potential purchasers swiftly. Many heads of HR spend their lives at these gatherings (say no more). As a Goldman Sachs mentor told me, if you want to make an impact, "be large and in charge." If you are going to be a coach then you cannot hide your light under a bushel.

BUILD A WEB PAGE

There are many coaches out there. The chances you will be hired at the first meeting with a client are small. They will (and should) want to check your background, client references, career history, and most of all your accreditations. Pointing a potential client to a web site covers all those bases in a click and you will stand a better chance of converting client potential into hard currency. If the customer has to telephone people for references, or has to undertake other laborious processes to research you, they will probably take the path of least resistance and go with someone who is easier to check. If you feel really energetic, write a web log and attach it to the site. This not only serves as a diary to your practice, but also works as a marketing tool: millions of business people read these blogs every day. If it is interesting enough, business may follow. The worst thing that can happen is that you spend five minutes a day keeping an electronic record. To add to this, any form of publication will aid your professional cachet. If there are relevant publications to which you can contribute, then it could be a good idea to submit articles or even ask for a regular spot. Write to the local paper. In time you might even write a book!

GET ACCREDITATION

I believe our fragmented industry will consolidate. Hordes of coaches have hung up their brass plate and opened for business in the last few years. Coaching can be well paid and liberating. There are also many charlatans who have no business in the field. The problem for clients is to find a quality assured service: there are just too many to choose from. A few umbrella organizations have started to set some fairly rigorous standards for the profession. Those coaches who are prepared to raise their game and meet the standards will in my opinion be the winners in the long run. The International Coaching Federation has the highest profile among these organizations. Even if you do not start your coaching life with a formal accreditation, it seems expedient to work aggressively toward one.

TAKE IT FURTHER

Join the local Chamber of Commerce, which will almost certainly hold high-profile speaker events, business breakfasts, and social gatherings. Find out whether there are consultancy associations in your area, make sure you are part of any alumni network from colleges you have attended or other courses and if you have been in business, particularly a corporation, stay connected. This can be one of your biggest sources of revenue. Look for professional organizations that constitute your target clients. These are fantastic opportunities for handing out your business card. Remember you are a walking business. Carry the tools of your trade with you everywhere. Make sure you have an answer for any potential client who asks you what you do. "I coach and develop business leaders at the senior management level," (or whatever your target segment is) is better than "I am a coach"–define and refine!

Pro bono work is another way to get your name out there. Offer friends or former colleagues within your target segment the opportunity to be coached by you for free for a month. Practice your new skills and work with people on the tacit understanding that they will tell others about you. But set your boundaries early on and limit the time you are prepared to spend in this way. Affiliate with larger consultancy organizations that need coaches for their bigger assignments. There are plenty of medium-sized firms who call for air cover when they win a big contract. Put yourself on their radar screen.

Finally, the Ice Queen of marketing, cold calling. Not many coaches, myself included, are happy to ply their trade by dial and trial. If you can stomach this, remember that you will probably not get two bites at the same cherry. Heads of HR are the gatekeepers to coaching services, but they do not ultimately pay for such services as they themselves are a cost centre. If you can make a connection with a head of division or even a board member (who might then refer you to HR but at the very least give you high-level sponsorship of sorts), you will probably be better off.

Your coaching training and the opening of your business are just the beginning of a long journey. Ongoing education is essential to foster a thriving business. The field is evolving constantly and clients will want to know that your work is current. Think about your areas of interest and make a prioritized list of the courses that would help your practice.

THE EVALUATION MATRIX

Finally, the best piece of advice I can give to anybody setting up a coaching practice is this: every single time you pitch to a client, think about what the return on *their* investment is going to be. Touting your wares, telling people you are a better coach than the competition, being super qualified, etc., are no bad things. But for a moment put yourself in your client's shoes. They are going to pay you either from their own or their company's taxed money. You need to assess quickly not just how you are going to help them improve in whatever area they need, but how that improvement is going to pay a material dividend either to themselves or to their company. The intended result of coaching is that they are going to get better. But when the manuals tell you to make the goal measurable, you need to take that to an extreme. Moreover, you need to help with the evaluation procedure.

Let's take an example. You are coaching Vincent, the manager of an advertising division at Latitude, a multinational media company. Vincent does not delegate well, and stays in the office until midnight working on high-profile client projects and layouts that should be turned over to his designers. He attends two divisional strategy meetings a week, yet his client focus is only average. He is seen as too internally focused and not a team player.

Now, any coach worth his or her salt is going to be able to deliver a pretty cogent strategy for helping Vincent improve. Let's assume that, using all the usual tools and checking in just after halfway through your coaching series, Vincent and his colleagues all recognize an improvement in his delegation skills and the team is functioning better as a result. Vincent himself feels you have added value. Do you then cruise through the final three or four sessions, giving yourself a resounding slap on the back and collect your fee? Resoundingly, *no*.

SOME CRUDE MATH

Take a look at Vincent's situation. He makes $160k. Do some 360-degree feedback from the outset. Pose the question, "How much of Vincent's time is spent doing work that he should delegate?" Let's say the answer is 20 percent. In that case, $32k is spent on wasted time. Find out where that time would be better allocated from the employer's perspective. Ask what the expected benefits will be from a number of different business perspectives, i.e. improved productivity of the department, improved personal productivity, time spent developing strategy, increasing sales, etc. You decide what the criteria are with your client. But then translate them into a hard figure.

After coaching, Vincent's personal productivity was unchanged. He spent the same amount of time in the office. But his time was spent more strategically. He visited more clients and won two major contracts. His department productivity went up by 15% (annual sales $1.2 million increased to $1.38 million).

Other benefits might be intangibles, such as improved internal and client satisfaction, better teamwork, better morale, and better leadership skills for Vincent. But in hard dollar terms it looks like this:

Cost of coaching (including materials, transport, local taxes, etc) billed to the client:

*(10 × 1 hour sessions = $6000 plus expenses, etc., **Gross billable = $7500**)*

Benefit to Latitude Inc.:
***$180k gross sales increase** per annum*

Thus return on investment is 240% in year one. Put in those terms, most companies will retain you. While the above example is a little rough, I hope you see the point. Your coaching is a business proposition, not executive therapy. While you may spend a proportion of your sessions helping the coaching client through bottlenecks by talking, the real output should be a gross financial benefit to the client. If you keep this in mind, you will build a worthy business. The intangibles are the icing on the cake. Excusing this rather crude example, those who wish to look at a more crafted and systematic template could do worse than refer to Anderson and Anderson.[6]

CONCLUSION

The question I am most regularly asked by my clients is, "Why did you make the transition from investment banker to coach?" Many of them find it remarkable that one would trade a prestigious job at the cutting edge of commerce for one that is viewed by many as "soft." I am not a subscriber to the notion that coaches are overwhelmingly in the business to help others, although most profess that to be their rationale. Most people are in business to be successful. To be a successful coach you manage transition and change effectively. To be a successful coach you solve puzzles by skillful questioning. Most parents rightfully feel a swell of pride when they successfully teach their children to ride a bike or acquire some new skill. Coaches get that same wave of satisfaction when their clients break through and extend their boundaries. In short, coaches, like any other business people, are in it for themselves: they just get their rewards vicariously. And that is OK. Acknowledgment of that allows the coach to rise above himself or herself and truly help.[7] At their most effective, coaches can be the butterflies whose wings stir ripples that can, over time, create hurricanes of change.

NOTES

1. Pascale, R.T., Milleman, M., and Goija, L. (2001). *Surfing the Edge of Chaos*. New York: Three Rivers Press.
2. Gallwey, W.T. (2002). *The Inner Game of Work*. Mason, OH: Thomson Texere.
3. Sheehy, G. (1998). *Understanding Men's Passages*. New York: Ballantine Books.
4. Bolles, R.N. (2004). *What Colour is Your Parachute?* (revised edition) Berkeley, CA: Ten Speed Press.
5. Drucker, P. (1996). *The Concept of the Corporation*. Somerset, NJ: Transaction Publishers.
6. Anderson, D. and Anderson, M. (2005). *Coaching That Counts*. New York: Elsevier.
7. Downey, M. (2003). *Effective Coaching*. Mason, OH: Thomson Texere.

11

COACHING EXECUTIVES ACROSS CULTURES

ANN HOUSTON KELLEY

The ability to lead across cultures is a key competency for today's international executives, and coaching skills are even more essential in this context. Global executives must recognize and adapt to cultural complexities on many levels, and steer their organizations in a rapidly changing world. Doing this well can mean the difference between economic success and failure. Consider the impact of cultural misunderstandings just in the world of mergers and acquisitions at the time this book was written, for example:

- Mittal's acquisition of Arcelor;
- UniCredit's acquisition of HypoVereinsbank;
- the rumor of an attempt by PepsiCo to acquire Danone;
- the merger of Daimler-Benz and Chrysler (followed by plunging stock prices);
- the failed merger of KLM and Alitalia;
- Viacom's failed merger with CBS; and
- the merger of GE and Honeywell blocked by the EU Commission.

Although it is important not to oversimplify the reasons behind the drama in each of the examples above, it is possible to argue that miscommunication and misunderstanding, coming from subtle differences in culturally influenced viewpoints, added to the confusion. In some of these cases, we see a culture clash on a macro level–such as the prevailing anti-American sentiment in the minds of some Europeans, which may have fuelled the debate over a possible acquisition of Danone by PepsiCo, and in others on a micro level–with stockholders reacting badly to the authoritarian statement from Daimler-Benz CEO Jurgen

Schrempp that the deal was never really intended to be a merger of equals.

These examples add to the evidence that there is a growing need for executive coaches who are skilled at working across cultures *between* organizations and *within* organizations, as well as with individuals. Developing leadership competencies in today's executives is impossible to imagine without helping them master the challenges of real diversity (going beyond traditional, textbook-type differences) that are increasingly present in today's organizations.[1] This chapter is intended for international executives who want to interact more effectively in cross-cultural situations, and who need to develop their own coaching skills, and the executive coaches (both internal and external) who support them in this task.

LAYERS OF CULTURE

A typical cross-cultural coaching assignment involves working with executives from one nationality who need to work with colleagues from another culture or nationality. Differences in language or ethnic group present a fairly common challenge. Consider the case of a French Belgian manager working for a Flemish Belgian company which is taken over by a Canadian firm. He first had to learn Flemish and now must master English in order to be heard in the new company. There may be differences between head office versus regional office culture. Many regional corporate executives struggle to maintain an appropriate balance between head office requirements for standardization and the specific needs of particular regions/locations for flexible solutions. Corporate divisions may have very different worldviews, but their top executives must know how to harness the best of each division in making the company more profitable. Professional identity (for example, finance, engineering, or legal) is another issue. Social class and educational background can affect a leader's status in some cultures. In more traditional companies in some countries, executives with less tenure may have difficulty making themselves heard, especially when they are trying to bring in new ideas.

Although these situations are not easy to resolve, many experienced global executives are already aware that these types of issues may cause misunderstandings or miscommunication, and are willing to address them. However, in some cases, the task at hand may be complicated even further for an executive coach by *unrecognized* cultural differences, leading to misunderstanding between a coach of one nationality and a client of another nationality, or between clients who refuse to acknowledge cultural differences. Here the executive coach must realize that the problem at hand cannot be resolved simply by giving advice on cross-cultural business practices. This added complexity illustrates that, while it is extremely important to consider obvious national cultural differences when coaching across cultures, there are deeper layers of culture that may also have significant influence.

Although a detailed discussion of culture is outside the scope of this chapter, I recommend that any coach who is contemplating work in a cross-cultural context should read the seminal academic work in this field. André Laurent identified differences in perceptions of business practices early on, when there were far fewer multinational or global corporations.[2] Ed Schein created a framework that integrates different perceptions and definitions of culture, and tools for deciphering cultural values and meaning. Schein proposed that culture reflects a deeper level of shared, basic assumptions and beliefs that are often taken for granted, or even unacknowledged in an organization.[3] Susan Schneider and Jean-Louis Barsoux outline the ways these cultural assumptions can create threats and opportunities in global organizations.[4] Nancy Adler, who writes about cultural influence on organizational behavior, advises, "In approaching cross-cultural situations, one should assume differences until similarities are proven" and gives practical advice on managing the careers of global executives.[5] Geert Hofstede,[6] and later Charles Hampden-Turner, and Fons Trompenaars[7] conducted studies that give great insight into the way different cultures value such concepts as time, authority, status, and consensus. Robert House, leader of the Globe Study, has identified cultural variations in leadership dimensions and characteristics, among them charismatic/values-based and team-oriented leadership, humane-oriented and participative leadership, and self-protective and autonomous leadership.[8] Familiarity with basic concepts of cultural assumptions and values–going deeper than a surface knowledge of "the way they do things there"–is essential for an executive coach working with global clients.

DEALING WITH COMPLEXITIES

When coaching across cultures, one should look for *more* rather than less complexity and be prepared to address the appropriate layers of cultural difference for the client. The coach has the obligation at least to "know that he knows not" and to move toward "knowing what he (and others) know" and then to accompany coaching clients as they travel along the same route. The best coaches know their own cultural biases, and are aware of how their personal preferences may influence their coaching.

For example, a coach from an egalitarian culture may need to adjust his or her own perspective when working with a client who is operating in a more hierarchical, status-oriented setting. Coaching the client to confront a boss or others in a position of authority might be the wrong approach. Such a client may also want the coach to be the "expert" or "teacher" rather than a partner in the coaching relationship. This is an issue that may need to be discussed with the client.

Some clients will want to get directly to the business content of the coaching. Starting by telephone or videoconference may be fine with them. For others, a first, face-to-face meeting is essential with time to get to know each other as people. In some cultures, non-verbal communication and the context play an important role. In others, an executive coach who is not direct may be considered untrustworthy. This preference for relationship first and content second, or vice versa, may continue throughout the coaching process.

Regardless of whether the client comes from a task- or relationship-oriented culture, the coach will probably need to inquire about some basic preferences when beginning the relationship. For example, what language will be the most comfortable for both the coach and the client? Does the client prefer formal or informal ways of speaking? How does the client view time, punctuality, and multitasking? When and where does the client want to meet (for example, only at the office during business hours or outside of the office at a restaurant with social discussion first followed by the coaching conversation)? What preferences does the client have for communicating which types of information (face-to-face, telephone, e-mail)?

And, because even the best coaches will miss cues in coaching across cultures, the coach needs to check for understanding and ask for feedback much more often. This is the best practice in any coaching situation. It becomes even more important in cross-cultural situations because of the increased possibility for misunderstanding. Checking for understanding and asking for feedback show respect to the client and will help to deepen the level of trust in the coaching relationship.

In coaching across cultures, the issues of assessment, challenge, and support take on some additional complexity.[9] Typically, in the initial assessment phase of the coaching process, the coach will ask the client to complete one or more self-assessment questionnaires and a 360-degree questionnaire. In many companies, the use of 360-degree questionnaires is familiar and regular, but in some cultures, the notion of asking one's superior, peers, or subordinates for direct feedback (even through an anonymous questionnaire) may run totally counter to current thinking and practice. For example, just after the Asian banking crisis in 1998, I was asked to coach a number of Asian Pacific banking executives (working for a European-headquartered bank) on a leadership development program in Singapore. Interestingly enough, none of the questionnaires had been completed (either by the participants or their colleagues).

In this type of situation, an experienced executive coach will begin by identifying what "he knows not" about the cultural context; for example:

- Can one ask for direct feedback from a superior, peers, or subordinates?
- If one asks, should the other person be honest with his/her response?
- Do all of the respondents to the 360-degree questionnaire have the language ability to correctly interpret the questions?
- Have the answers to the questionnaire been influenced by other factors in the environment?

In my experience of using 360-degree questionnaires in diverse, multinational organizations, the quantitative data are helpful, but it is the comments section which is even more useful because it allows the important elaboration of the basic feedback. The interview method allows the respondents to go into more depth and clarify their responses.

Coaching across cultures requires the sensitivity to determine the right balance of positive and negative feedback for your client. Who brings the message, when, and how it is delivered are also important considerations. Much of the work of the INSEAD Global Leadership Center involves group leadership coaching with very diverse groups of international participants. I often ask them about what effective feedback looks like in their organizational culture. The answers range from all positive, to a mix of positive and negative, to mostly negative.

Support is another issue in the coaching process which is very culturally dependent. Some examples of what clients expect from an executive coach in terms of support:

- Give them "the expert answer" to their dilemma
- Deliver a tough message to a problem subordinate
- Facilitate a team meeting which they should be leading
- Drive them to an important meeting
- Intervene with family members on their behalf
- Write a positive summary of the coaching process and outcomes for their boss.

The very nature of the relationship between the coach and client, and the expectations around roles and responsibilities, will be an important factor here. As mentioned above, when coaching across cultures, expectations for the coaching relationship should be carefully and clearly defined for everyone involved. These expectations may need to be revisited throughout the coaching process, and afterward when evaluating the outcomes at the end of the coaching period.

EXPERIENCE IS THE BEST TEACHER

As in any coaching context, excellence as a cross-cultural coach comes largely through experience. In this section, I'll share some of my own experience as a coach, in case studies based on real situations (changed to protect confidentiality), as illustrations of the importance of developing competency in cross-cultural coaching.

Finding cultural synergies

Hamid, who is Lebanese, is sitting in his office in Cairo on a Sunday morning feeling overwhelmed. Two months ago, he was promoted to the newly created position of Middle East and Africa (MEA) Regional Head for his company Congentus, which was spun off from Alstpro last year. Congentus' international headquarters are in Chicago. Hamid will now be reporting to the Europe, the Middle East and Africa (EMEA) Regional Head who is British and sits in Brussels. The 13-country sales office heads in the MEA have, until now, been reporting directly to the EMEA Head in Brussels. They have been used to operating fairly autonomously but not very effectively. Congentus has big expectations of Hamid and the MEA Area. In fact, they want to see a 50% growth in the EBIT for MEA in the coming year.

Hamid has just attended a three-day leadership development program sponsored by his company at INSEAD. As part of the program, Hamid is entitled to six additional telephone coaching sessions over the next 12 months with his (Dutch) executive coach, whom he met at INSEAD. His executive coach is wondering just where to start with this case.

Commentary
This is indeed a complex situation in terms of culture. If national culture alone is considered, here is a Lebanese manager reporting to a British boss sitting in Brussels, and both are working for an American-headquartered company. Hamid would do well to try and establish a strong relationship with his British boss, with clear mutual expectations around roles, responsibilities, and communication strategies. This will probably require more direct communication than either of them might naturally be comfortable with. The results from the 360-degree feedback instrument used in the leadership development program provide some clear information to Hamid about his strengths in this process, as well as where he will need to stretch and develop.

In Hamid's region, there may be country heads (e.g. in Israel, Syria, or Nigeria) with a variety of reactions to having a new, Lebanese boss. Hamid will need coaching on how to establish trusting relationships with his new team in the most efficient way possible. He should take the time to meet with them regularly face-to-face as a group and individually while he is starting up the team. His British boss in Brussels should authorize the travel budget necessary to do this. Hamid should not make assumptions about what type of leadership individual members of his new team will expect from him.

Hamid faces two major challenges with this new team. He has to earn respect and trust from his new team members, who have been used to reporting directly to the EMEA Head, and then to motivate them to generate more growth and efficiency in their local operations.

Expectations around the amount of time and resources that it will take to turn around this region may vary greatly among the various parties. The British boss in Brussels may need to advocate with the American headquarters for additional time on behalf of this Lebanese manager, who is now overseeing a region with tremendous differences in local market conditions.

Being heard

Carola (who is Polish) has just managed to arrive in time at the local crèche in Zurich to pick up her son before it closes at 17:30. Her husband, Wolfgang, is out of the country on business this week, so the crèche drop-off and pick-up is up to Carola. She and her son arrive home tired and hungry. Carola tries to have some quality time with her son before putting him to bed at 19:30. She then spends time catching up on e-mails for the next two hours. Carola, who works for a Swiss-headquartered engineering company, is in charge of communication and public affairs for joint ventures. She is scheduled to work 30 hours per week, which usually ends up being 40–42 hours and there is always more to be done. The global head of communication and public affairs is Danish and is supportive of her decision to work part-time, although he does have high expectations in terms of her output. However, when she looks above her boss in the company, she sees only Swiss males whose wives are not working outside the home. Nevertheless, Carola is intensely committed to excellence both on and off the job. Her company conducts an annual 360-degree developmental assessment for all its managers. Carola is somewhat concerned about some of her ratings, and has decided to seek external executive coaching, which her Danish boss has agreed to fund, in recognition of her high work output over the past year.

When Carola meets up with her coach, she shares more background information about both her work and her private situation. She enjoys her profession and the good working relationship she has with her boss. Because she works on communication issues for joint ventures, she also has a great deal of contact with the executive board and the CEO. The CEO of her firm is known for his demanding nature and quick temper. Carola has been the unfortunate target of his angry outbursts on more than one occasion. This is an aspect of her job that she certainly does not enjoy. In addition to her work at the Swiss engineering company, Carola is an active participant in the Zurich network for communication professionals, and she teaches a communications class once a year in the local university.

Carola confides that she had cancer eight years ago and that she and her husband are very pleased that they were able to have a child after that experience. Nobody at work knows that Carola has had cancer. Carola and her husband would like to have a second child, which will require a trip to Dubai for specialized fertility treatment.

Carola has some concerns about her level of stress and whether she is doing all that she can at work and at home. On her yearly 360-degree assessment, Carola gets high marks from all of her raters in almost all categories, with the exception of building and mending relationships, networking, and work-life balance.

Commentary

Carola clearly sets very high standards for herself. Her desire to combine a high-powered professional career with a fulfilling family situation is certainly one that executive coaches are hearing about often these days, from men as well as women. There is no magic formula for this dilemma. The job of the executive coach, as always, is to conduct a comprehensive assessment, and challenge sufficiently while providing the right types of support. The coach did initially ask Carola, "Is all of this doable?" and she replied that it was. The executive coach has to start from where the client is.

Initially, the coach worked with Carola to see how she could work more effectively in the hours that she did spend on the job. Senior professionals who work part-time—in spite of the fact that they may work exceedingly hard to fit a full load into reduced hours—often do not have the time for the relationship-building and networking activities that other managers who are working full-time, or more, can fit in more easily. The coach worked with Carola to see how some relationship investments might help her to work "smarter not harder." Carola found she was able to enlist the support of her colleagues to develop a common strategy for dealing with the temperamental outbursts of the CEO. She also found that key colleagues accepted her ideas more quickly.

The other trap for part-time professionals with significant family commitments is that their own self-care gets left out of their busy schedules. The coach helped Carola to look at her personal life, and what she might be doing differently there as well. The coach offered a gentle challenge to Carola: if she was not taking care of herself sufficiently, then she was not going to be able to be a good mother to her son or to nourish the relationship with her husband.

And yet, despite the best of intentions, sometimes the wisdom is in knowing when to say "This is too much." The coaching had been going on for six months. It was now winter and Carola had had a series of bronchial infections, which resulted in her having minor surgery to correct the problem. Carola finally decided, after discussion with her coach, to apply for a six-month leave of absence. The negotiations with her company were difficult because they were not used to this sort of request, let alone prepared to guarantee a return to the same position, but Carola was ultimately successful. She took the six months off, relished the time with her husband and son, and became pregnant with a second child soon afterwards. When she asked to extend her leave of absence to one year, her company refused. She is now taking time off from paid work to raise her young children and she is comfortable with her choice.

The balancing act

It is a late Sunday morning in Paris in September. Robert, a Canadian, is packing his bags for a transatlantic flight to Toronto, where he will be picking up a rental car and driving to the international headquarters of his company, Soglasco, in the city of Windsor, near Toronto. He is thinking about the insight session that he just had with his executive coach that week and how he is going to report the results back to his superiors.

Robert is a long-term Soglasco employee. He started with the company just after graduating from university, and has worked his way through various positions and divisions to his most recent promotion, to EMEA Head. Most of his contemporaries in the company have followed a similar path. What makes Robert different, however, is that he has worked as an expatriate manager for Soglasco for the past 12 years (first in Mexico, then in the UK, and now in Paris). Soglasco has the majority of its operations in North America. Robert is one of a very few expatriate managers in Soglasco and he is now managing their largest foreign operation, a recent joint venture (named Sometsaa) with a Finnish-based fiber optics company. The executive boards of Soglasco and the Finnish company have high revenue growth expectations of the Sometsaa joint venture.

In the meantime, the executive board of Soglasco has asked a panel of external coaches to conduct executive assessments with five senior managers in the company who are seen to have board and/or CEO potential. These executive assessments consisted of confidential 360-degree interviews, two 360-degree instruments, and a number of self-assessment work style and personality instruments. Robert has just had a half-day session with his executive coach. When he gets back to headquarters, he is to report back on his learning to his two direct bosses, the Global VP for HR and the CEO of Soglasco.

Commentary
At first glance, one might expect the focus of Robert's leadership development to be on how he is handling the cultural business challenges of the Sometsaa joint venture. Within the joint venture, Robert has had to close down five inefficient plants across Europe over the past 18 months, which has involved many

discussions with works councils and others. In addition, Robert has had to recruit and lead a very diverse team of direct reports (including a very soft-spoken Canadian CFO, an extremely gregarious Turkish Head of Sales, and a very pragmatic Belgian VP for HR among others). In managing these challenges, Robert has done exceedingly well, both in terms of strategy planning and execution as well as in winning the hearts and minds of his management team.

In practice, Robert's major cultural challenge is improving his working relationship with key stakeholders at Soglasco's headquarters. Regional Area Heads work on a very difficult boundary in global corporations. They must manage the expectations for standardization from head office together with adapting to local market conditions within their region. Robert's situation is even more extreme. He has been away from headquarters for 12 years, so he is missing the day-to-day contact with colleagues, especially staff colleagues, which is essential for success at his level and higher in the company.

So, one major focus of the coaching is to strategize and implement effective relationship-building with his colleagues at headquarters. His clear strengths in execution, efficiency, and direct communication, which are working so well for him in the joint venture, are weaknesses for him in this area. Robert struggles to change his behavior. He is far away from headquarters so, when he has a misunderstanding with the Global VP for HR, it takes time before he can see her in person to repair the damage. Robert must fix this issue in order to be considered for later promotions to the Board.

On the private side, 12 years of expatriation have affected Robert's wife as well. At this point, she wants to spend more time with Robert. She wants to return to Windsor, Canada, so their two girls can finish secondary school there, and to be closer to her aging parents.

The needs of expatriate managers and their families change over time, especially with different life stages. Companies need to be aware of this in career planning for their expatriates. Family expatriation issues have to be dealt within the coaching setting as well.

The coach helps Robert to brainstorm some ideas to improve the current situation. Robert could be clearer and more explicit with his bosses and Global HR about what he and his family need at this point from the company in order to make this expatriate assignment work. Robert could schedule a long weekend with his wife at least once every quarter. If the family were to buy a home in Windsor, they could go there for holidays, preparing the way for their eventual return to Canada. Alternatively, Robert could move his family back to Windsor and commute from there to Europe for his job.

Robert confides that the family situation is his number one priority. Many executives express this sentiment. The much harder discussion is around what are they willing to give up or change in the work environment in order to address the family situation.

After 12 months of coaching, Robert is still working from Paris, where his family will stay through the end of the school year. Robert's 360-degree interviews reveal that his relationships within headquarters have improved significantly.

A different brand of glass ceiling

Hong Meng, who is Chinese Malaysian, is at a crossroads. He has spent the past two years working for the insurance division of BPI, a Luxembourg-headquartered financial institution. He is currently attending BPI's Global Business Manager's Leadership Development Program. Hong Meng came to BPI two years ago when his previous company, Lambert First Financial (LFF), was acquired by BPI. Soon after the acquisition, Hong Meng was transferred from Kuala Lumpur to Seoul to set up the South Korean insurance business for BPI. Hong Meng has faced multiple challenges with this assignment.

The BPI insurance business culture is very different from what Hong Meng was used to with LFF. LFF, whose headquarters were also in Luxembourg, was a very flat organization that gave a great deal of autonomy to the managers in its Asian offices, recognizing the need to adjust to local markets. BPI, on the other hand, is more hierarchical and many more authorizations need to come from corporate headquarters. Hong Meng now reports to the BPI Head of Asian Insurance Business (a Belgian) who is younger than he, and relatively inexperienced in the

Asian insurance market. In addition, his boss does not appear to exert very much influence with essential staff departments at BPI headquarters.

The South Korean insurance market is fairly volatile. There is the potential for great profits but the risks are also very high. Hong Meng speaks no Korean, so all of his business dealings in Korea must be conducted through an interpreter. The competition for talent is quite keen in South Korea, particularly for English-speaking Koreans with insurance experience. When Hong Meng and his Asian colleagues look up in the organization, they see only male, European faces. Hong Meng is not sure about the possibilities for future career advancement in BPI.

This is the first expatriate assignment for Hong Meng and his family. Seoul is not an easy posting for expatriates. His children miss their family and friends back in Kuala Lumpur. His oldest child will soon be old enough to enter secondary school. He attends an international school in Seoul during the week and a Chinese Academy on Saturdays.

Despite these considerable challenges, Hong Meng has been able to build up the South Korean business over the past two years, far exceeding his boss's expectations. Nevertheless, Hong Meng thinks that his considerable background experience and accomplishments so far in the South Korean market are not being recognized by his boss and his peers. In the group coaching session at the Business Managers' Program, Hong Meng spoke about his extreme disappointment in not receiving more recognition and support from his current boss. In a subsequent individual coaching session, Hong Meng reveals that he is being seriously head-hunted by a competitor. He asks his executive coach for advice.

Commentary
This situation presents an interesting ethical question for the executive coach. The coach has two clients in this situation, BPI and the participant. Is it ethical for the coach to urge Hong Meng to leave the company that is investing in his leadership development?

Initially the coach works with Hong Meng to explore what he can do to improve his current situation, especially his remote relationship with his boss. The situation is complex and Hong Meng feels quite isolated. Group coaching can offer the possibility for a much wider and richer range of feedback and support than individual coaching, and at the Business Managers' Program, Hong Meng hears from colleagues in his coaching group about similar situations they have faced in their careers with BPI.

In subsequent individual sessions with his coach, Hong Meng works on the developmental challenges that were identified in his 360-degree feedback survey. In addition, his coach challenges him to identify several different scenarios for his next career move and especially to consider the potential impact of the various scenarios on his family. In coaching expatriates, it can be helpful to help them to identify what their important values are both on and off the job, and then to help them identify where they can try and exert more influence on the system in order to express those values.

Creating the space for dialogue

It is 08:00 on a wintry morning and midway through the second week of an executive education program at INSEAD. The executive coach (a French woman) is in the plenary session listening to the introductory remarks and wondering just how the group coaching session will go that day. At the briefing meeting the prior evening, she heard that one of her participants, an Omani, had insisted that his non-Arab colleagues remove the bottles of wine from the table when they ate together in the INSEAD cafeteria. She thinks about the mix of participants in her group: the Omani man, a Danish man working in Greece, a Belgian man working in the Ivory Coast, a Swiss man working in Japan, a British man working in the Netherlands, and a Singaporean woman working in Singapore.

The coach greets her participants as they enter the coaching room, shaking hands with most and hesitating with the Omani to see what he would do. He does not offer his hand and averts his eyes. She begins by asking the participants to share their expectations and concerns for the day and then asks them to take some minutes to draw their self-portraits. As part of the introduction to the day, she asks the participants to share the characteristics of feedback that they have found most useful.

The coach takes this opportunity to acknowledge the differences across cultures around challenge and feedback, for example:

- where it happens;
- who can give it to whom;
- how it is introduced; and
- differences in the ratio of positive to negative remarks.

Some smiles of recognition emerge as she shares some culture-specific examples. The participants are invited to try for a balance of positive and negative remarks, but even more importantly, to try and assess what the right balance will be with the particular colleague they are coaching at the time. She indicates that the schedule of the day calls for a group session in the morning followed by short individual coaching sessions in the afternoon, and urges them to fully utilize the group session to explore their issues, instead of saving everything up for the afternoon session.

As individuals in the group share their self-portraits and 360-degree results one by one, the group develops, some working norms start to emerge and the coach reminds herself, once again, to trust the process. So far, the Danish, Belgian, Swiss, and British participants have taken their turn to be coached. The clients need to be reminded to share their own strengths and positive feedback in addition to their developmental points. The peer coaches need to be reminded to balance their challenging remarks with support, and that support is more than simply "the giving of advice."

The group then breaks for lunch. Unfortunately the Omani participant does not join the others. The lunch discussion always contributes significantly to the development of trust within the group and connection with the coach. The coach assumes that the Omani was saying his prayers.

The Singaporean participant goes next. She is struggling with a female boss who is micromanaging her, an office culture in which she is being pulled to take the harmonizing role, a very high level of stress, and significant guilt over the time she spends away from her family. Fortunately, the life-work balance issue has already been raised by several other participants. Interestingly enough, the other participants (all male) want to focus first on their family/private situation, while she actually wants to focus more on the work situation.

The Omani man is the last to go. As the coaching from his colleagues moves from positive to developmental, he grows increasingly defensive. As he grows more defensive, his colleagues criticize him for not accepting negative developmental feedback, as they had done earlier. At one point, the Omani participant scolds the coach when she uses an Arabic phrase in reflecting back to him a summary of a dilemma he describes.

Commentary

A number of contextual issues influenced the dynamics in the coaching group that day. At work, the Omani manager was having difficulty communicating with his team of non-Arabs, and that dynamic was reproduced in the group coaching session. This situation brings up the larger systemic issue of what companies should be doing to bridge the cultural gap between local management and foreign workers who are bringing in different technologies or knowledge.

In the larger, executive education group, Arabs made up the largest minority at 30%. The Omani participant was the oldest of the Arab participants. He had been pulled, and also had pushed himself, to be the "keeper of the Islamic faith" in the larger course group.

This particular executive course took place in the year when dialogue between Arabs and non-Arabs in the wider world frequently broke down. A number of news events formed the background to this course: the Danish cartoons featuring the prophet Mohammed had created great controversy that year; casualties in the war in Iraq were mounting significantly; and Israeli was bombing parts of Lebanon. Reflecting on this cultural context helped the coach deal with trying to create a space for productive dialogue within the group session.

A DELICATE BALANCE OF ART AND SCIENCE

Coaching effectively across cultures is a combination of science and art. Through the five case studies above, I have illustrated a number of themes concerning the science of coaching across cultures.

- Understanding the complexities of pursuing the business imperatives across cultures.
- Working with the relevant layers of cultural differences for the client (e.g. national, regional, gender, headquarters versus regional office, religion).
- Working with a systemic approach to the issues around expatriation.
- Knowing that assessment, challenge (feedback), and support look different in different cultures.
- Considering the wider political, social, and economic climate and its impact both on the client's world and the coaching process.

The process of coaching artfully across cultures also requires some special considerations.

- Investing time and attention in building the coaching relationship.
- Starting from where the client is willing to start.
- Knowing your own cultural programming and biases.
- Listening deeply, observing closely, and not making assumptions.
- Asking for and being ready to accept feedback.

The science may be easier to master than the art. The *art* of coaching requires a curiosity and willingness to know about oneself and others, and the wisdom to adjust one's attitudes and behavior to the benefit of the client's development. Whatever you do as a coach needs to come across as sincere and authentic to the client. The delicate balance between self and others in leadership coaching was expressed beautifully by Lao Tzu:[10]

Learn from the people
Plan with the people
Begin with what they have
Build on what they know
Of the best leaders
When the task is accomplished
The people all remark
We have done it ourselves

217

NOTES

1. Kets de Vries, M. and Korotov, K. (2005). "The Future of an Illusion: In Search of the New European Business Leader." *Organizational Dynamics*, 34 (3): 218–230.
2. Laurent, A. (1983). "The Cultural Diversity of Western Conceptions of Management." *International Studies of Management and Organization*, 13 (1–2): 75–96.
3. Schein, E.H. (1990). *Organizational Culture and Leadership*. San Francisco, CA: Jossey-Bass, p. 6.
4. Schneider, S. and Barsoux, J.L. (2003). *Managing Across Cultures*, 2nd ed. London: Prentice Hall.
5. Adler, N. (1991). *International Dimensions of Organizational Behavior*, 2nd ed. Belmont, CA: Wadsworth Publishing Company, p. 67.
6. Hofstede, G. (2001). *Culture's Consequences: Comparing Values, Behaviours, Institutions and Organisations Across Nations*, 2nd ed. Thousand Oaks, CA: Sage.
7. Trompenaars, F. (1997). *Riding the Waves of Culture: Understanding Cultural Diversity in Business*, 2nd ed. London: Nicholas Brealey; Hampden-Turner, C. and Trompenaars, F. (2002). *Building Cross-Cultural Competence: How to Create Wealth from Conflicting Values*. Chichester: John Wiley & Sons.
8. House, R.J., Hanges, P.J., Javidan, M., Dorfman, P.W., and Gupta, V. (eds) (2004). *Culture, Leadership and Organisations, The GLOBE Study of 62 Societies*. Thousand Oaks, CA: Sage.
9. Ting, S. and Scisco, P. (2006). *The CCL Handbook of Coaching: A Guide for the Leader Coach*, San Francisco, CA: John Wiley & Sons.
10. Lao Tzu (600 BC), *Tao Te Ching*.

PART FOUR: THE PROCESS OF COACHING

12

THE ART OF LISTENING

ERIK VAN DE LOO

Listening is not done by the ears, but by the mind. We hear sounds, but we listen to meanings.

W. Meissner

INTRODUCTION: LISTENING AND THE CLINICAL APPROACH TO ORGANIZATIONS

Listening is a basic human activity, and one of the most important determining factors for the quality of interpersonal and professional relationships. Skill at listening enables us to better understand and respond to situations and to others. So, in order to be an effective educator, coach, consultant, manager, or leader, we must master the art of listening.

Theoretical introductions to the coaching profession pay a lot of attention to the skill of listening.[1] General introductions typically present listening as one of the communication skills, with a focus on topics such as the relevance of verbal and nonverbal aspects of listening.[2] These sources provide information about, and insight into, the basics of the listening process, highlighting, for instance, the meaning of the nonverbal elements of speech, such as timing, pitch, and loudness. Other nonverbal signals are related to hand and other bodily movements, head-nods, gaze-shifts, and facial expression. It is evident that the listener needs to be sensitive to and capable of processing all kinds of information originating from various channels, verbal as well as nonverbal. Moreover, the listener must be aware of how his own listening behavior affects the speaker. The listener's facial expressions, nonverbal responses, and gestures are conscious and unconscious responses to what is communicated and expressed by the speaker, and may act to reinforce what has been said. The speaker and listener engage in a kind of communicative dance, known as "interactive synchrony."[3] The listener follows and often imitates the bodily movements of the speaker, and this nonverbal response represents a kind of continuous commentary on what is being said.

This chapter elaborates on listening from a clinical perspective. The underpinnings of the clinical paradigm are outlined earlier in this book. The premises of the clinical approach not only help us to understand and conceptualize human behavior in organizational life and reality, they also guide us on how to access these aspects and dimensions. One of the hallmarks of the clinical approach to organizations is the use of self as a major tool in leading, coaching, and consulting, which is touched upon in the chapter on training managers as coaches in this book.

The adjective *clinical* originates from the fields of medicine and psychology. Clinical is derived from the Greek word *klinè*, meaning bed. Clinical in our context, however, refers not so much to a location (the bed, the hospital), but to a method, an approach. It is about establishing and handling a direct and personal professional relationship. In this relationship, the client is considered as unique. The focus of the clinical approach is not on classifying clients in terms of pathology, but on developing a deep understanding of the client in his or her unique context. One of the basic methodological assumptions of the clinical approach is that the key information for assessment and intervention can only be collected in direct contact with the client, hence the word "clinical" can be applied to the domain of organizational reality. The clinical approach to organizations advocates the direct and personal relationship as the royal road toward understanding and helping the client. It should be noted that the term "client" may indicate an individual, a team, or the organization at large. Reports, statistics, and knowledge available in the public domain can never substitute sufficiently for a direct engagement with the client-system, and so the primary tool is oneself and how one handles the relationship of coach, consultant, manager, or leader.

As already indicated in this book, the clinical approach draws on a wide knowledge and theory base from the human and social sciences. In this chapter, insights, techniques, and concepts from psychoanalysis, clinical psychology, and a variety of schools in psychotherapy are used. This enables us to explore some of the most fundamental dynamics involved in the listening process: how to use oneself and one's own unconscious as one of the key tools in listening, and the role of "mentalizing" empathy, intuition, free-floating attention, transference, and counter-transference. These questions are addressed in the context of coaching.

MENTALIZING

Anybody who is listening carefully to another person is not only receiving information but is also continuously trying to make sense of what is being said. This is influenced by our capacity to understand that behavior is caused by so-called unobservable states of mind: wishes, needs, desires, feelings, ideas, hopes, fears, illusions, and so on, and to acknowledge that the state of mind of another person may be different from our own. This rather recently identified cognitive skill is called *mentalizing*.[4] As mentalizing is about unobservable states of mind, both our own, and other people's, the term refers to the capacity to think and make inferences about people and their behaviors.

Let us explore this with the help of an example. I once facilitated a leadership development seminar attended by a small group of six senior executives. Shortly after the start, I invited the participants to draw a self-portrait, without words, making use of pictures and symbols. The invitation and the task were to portray themselves by addressing themes like: What is on my mind? What I am passionate about? How do I spend my leisure time? What is in my past? What lies in the future? and so on. Participants received a flip chart and colored pencils, and had about 20 minutes to complete the task. Most participants struggled a bit initially, but found themselves on track after a few minutes.

One of the six participants, George, approached the assignment very differently. He was the first to pick up paper and pencils. Without any visible hesitation he drew immediately a pair of black shoes right in the middle of the paper. He finished in less than a minute, picked up a newspaper and started to read. This behavior puzzled and, in a way, shocked me. My first take on it was that he was not really interested in creating a self-portrait and that he might be the sort of participant who strongly resisted self-reflection and exploring dimensions of himself and his leadership. I felt irritated, wondered why he had signed up for the program, and almost regretted that he was there. I contained my thoughts and feelings and proceeded as usual, inviting the participants to tell the group a story about themselves, their life, their history, and their leadership, making use of the self-portrait.

George immediately volunteered to go first. He pointed to his self-portrait. "My story is simple," he told us. "My father left our family unexpectedly when I was one year old. The only thing that was left behind was a pair of black shoes. We have never seen him again. For the rest, I have no idea. That's it."

The story resonated strongly in the group and created a kind of shock. A long and deep silence followed, intensifying what we experienced as a deep pain, probably reflecting the pain of being deserted, rejected by your father. I felt uneasy with myself, almost ashamed by my rather strong and negative response to George initially. I experienced this as a kind of professional embarrassment: I had been wrong in my mentalization about his state of mind. I had incorrectly inferred that he was not interested in doing the task and that he was behaving in a highly defensive way. In fact, George was open to the assignment. He told the group that he had no idea what would happen in this seminar, and the self-portrait task brought the pair of shoes immediately to his mind. And that was it. He told the story almost without any emotion, in a matter-of-fact way. The group seemed to experience what George was unable to feel. As he told his story, the group emotionally mirrored to him how he might have felt. He could see how our bodies had been immobilized and picked up bits and pieces of pain, shock, sadness, and compassion in our eyes. This became the start of a very significant process. With the help of the group, George felt legitimized and supported and gradually began to feel what the group was feeling about him. The group held him in its collective mind. They could feel how he might have felt, and as a consequence, he could discover himself in the way individuals in the group experienced him.

This vignette illustrates some key characteristics of mentalizing. In interactions with other people, we start making sense of the other person, his or her behavior, and the relationship on a continuous basis. We cannot do otherwise.

Mentalizing may take two distinct forms: implicit or explicit. Explicit means consciously. For example, I was consciously mentalizing when I started reasoning or hypothesizing about George reading the newspaper: "He is not interested in the assignment or even worse, in the whole program." Implicit mentalizing relates to automatic verbal and nonverbal responses, without articulated thoughts, for instance nodding sympathetically or having a concerned look on our face. The nodding and the concerned look reveal that, one way or other, we immediately make sense of what the other person is telling us.

The capacity to mentalize starts to develop very early in life. Research identifies a secure attachment relationship–a safe, close emotional bond–as the most critical success factor.[5] A secure attachment provides a safe base not only from which to start exploring the outer world, but also to discover one's inner world. An infant cared for sensitively will see how the caregiver responds to his or her distress, for example.

The infant sees his distress or frustration on his mother's face: he feels *felt*. And two things happen. First, feeling felt, he finds his mother's empathic response comforting. Second, he begins to understand his own feelings. He sees how he feels in the face of his mother. She has his mind in her mind. He discovers his mind in her mind.[6]

Our vignette reflects an analogous process: George discovered aspects of himself in the minds and faces of the very engaged people around him. This corresponds with the finding that an infant develops emotional awareness from the outside in: the individual starts with becoming aware of the minds and emotions of other persons.

Mentalizing is a cognitive skill, a thinking capacity. As such, it is a kind of psychological meta-competency. It serves as a precondition for other skills and capacities, such as empathy. Good listening requires mentalizing. Consider the example of a dialogue in couple therapy. The wife expressed openly for the first time her need for warmth and support from her husband. He responded positively to her, but she became enraged as she detected a split-second pause before he actually responded. Her interpretation of this pause was that he was hesitating and that he was rejecting her. In fact, she had ignored the content of what her husband had communicated to her and she failed to mentalize correctly. Her own state of mind (the fear of being rejected) blocked her from being open to his state of mind (the readiness to support her).[7]

In the clinical approach, mentalizing also implies the recognition that these so-called states of mind may be unconscious. Simon, the owner of a family business, asked me to help him develop more self-control. He started by telling me that overall he was doing very well, but that his ex-wife had started a court case to demand extra money. She was accusing him of conspiring with others to conceal his true financial worth at the time of their divorce. When I asked Simon how he experienced this, he answered that he did not like it but that it now felt like something that had to be done. Period. Over the last six months, he had experienced a couple of situations where he became disproportionately angry and confrontational. He had started shouting and left meetings. He did not understand why he behaved like this. I mentalized that it might have to do with anger toward his wife that he was displacing to situations in the workplace. He rejected my hypothesis, saying, "I am not that angry any more at my wife; I am beyond that." I then asked him to describe to me the last time he had been out of control. He started talking about a conflict with one of his firm's major clients, about whom he had been feeling ambivalent for a long period of time. The meeting took place shortly before lunch. "Moreover, I arrived already stressed in the meeting." When I asked why, he answered that he had had a two-hour session with his lawyers earlier that morning to prepare for the court case. I confronted him with this coincidence in timing and suggested that it was perhaps difficult for him to acknowledge how enraged he was with his ex-wife, and that he might have unconsciously displaced his anger toward her onto this client.

EMPATHY AND INTUITION

It is important to differentiate mentalizing from empathizing. Mentalizing is a cognitive skill, while empathizing refers to the capacity to appreciate and understand the feelings of others.

226

Empathy is the ability to subjectively experience the world from another person's perspective. It is not about conjecturing what it would be like for *you* to be in the other person's shoes, but the ability to experience what it is like *for the other person* to be in his or her shoes. It is possible to mentalize about the state of mind of another person without being able to empathize with that person. The case history above about George and the black shoes illustrates that I had not only mentalized his behavior incorrectly, but that I had also been unable to empathize with how he really felt while making his drawing and starting to read the newspaper.

Empathy and intuition are modes of obtaining a quick and deep understanding. Empathy is an "emotional knowing" rather than intellectual understanding.[8] The essential mechanism of empathy is a partial and temporary identification with the other person, in psychoanalytic terms called the object.[9] The capacity for such an identification probably originates from early developmental phases, when firm boundaries between self and object (or self and object representations) do not yet exist.[10] This state of primary identification implies a primary confusion between self and object. In pathology, this confusion is reflected in severe psychotic states.[11] In normality, the "fleeting confusion" between self and object constitutes the basis for empathizing.

Mature empathy implies a temporary and intentional merging with the affective broadcast of the other person. But the capacity to remain oneself in the presence of the other is preserved. The temporary affective merging is a kind of orchestrated regression that facilitates getting to know the other person at an affective level that would otherwise not be possible. This is only helpful if the listener can return to their original non-merged, differentiated position afterwards. The listener then reflects upon and makes sense of all the rich affective data collected during the empathic stage. Empathic information is elaborated by processes of thinking, organizing, and interpretation.

Equally characteristic of mature empathy is the ability to block the transmission of affects and to isolate oneself from the emotions of others. The concept of "the empathic wall" has been described as a new ego mechanism.[12] Professionals incapable of installing an empathic wall risk being insufficiently protected when exposed to the pain and suffering of others. Medical doctors, psychotherapists, coaches, volunteers working with traumatized and helpless people, and leaders involved in downsizing activities, all are examples of professionals who need to be able to operate in empathic and nonempathic modes as necessary. In addition, one can obtain a quick, beneath-the-surface understanding of another person's subjectivity through intuition. Alongside empathy, intuition plays an important role in the art of listening.

Listening does not mean just listening to words vocalized by a speaker; it also includes listening to meaning. Hearing words is a passive component of listening, while discerning meaning is an active component. The end result of this process can be interpretation of the meaning of what has been said. Interpretations are coherent suggestions, cognitive and conscious elaborations of all kinds of material. Impressions, thoughts, ideas, observations, and feelings are collected, combined, and organized with the help of conceptual frameworks and theories.

In the case of Simon, I used the concept of displacement, an example of a psychoanalytic formula stored in the warehouse of my mind. Displacement refers to the unconscious mechanism or principle of disconnecting a feeling, impulse, or thought from the person it is attached to (for example anger), and displacing it to somebody or something else. A person who has unconsciously displaced anger or fear typically does not understand why he or she is now angry or fearful. The anger and fear appear irrational, and in fact they are. I picked up fragments of information from Simon and tried to make sense of them in my mind. I asked him how he felt about his ex-wife engaging him in a court case. His answer was emotionally a bit flat, and he did not express how he felt in terms of anger. But I experienced him at that moment as tense. His body posture was not relaxed, and it looked as if my question triggered a state of high arousal in him. My immediate thought was that there was more in the experience than he could consciously process at that moment in time. My instinct steered me not to confront him with my observation immediately, because I thought it was too soon to present him with this experience. I felt that it would be better and more appropriate to explore further the issue that had brought him to me: "Why do I at times get disproportionately angry?" That exploration provided me with the material to identify a pattern. Reconstructing the initial phase of the conversation with Simon, I had a very early intuitive under-standing of what might be behind his irrational anger. Intuitive understanding is not the same as knowing or understanding. I had an idea, an insight, that was not the result of a process of articulated and conscious thinking. On the contrary, my intui-tion became the starting point for logical and rational processes of reasoning.

This illustrates how intuition potentially plays an important role in the act of listening. Intuition is applying one's profes-sional judgment to a situation.[13] It may be approached from a cognitive or information-processing paradigm. The thinking process is conceptualized as a series of consecutive mental opera-tions. Among them are intuitive operations. These might come across as irrational or even mystical, but they in fact represent highly effective and efficient cognitive strategies. Studies of the minds of chess players and medical doctors in action reveal that the basis for intuition is specific expert knowledge combined with a lot of experience.[14]

How does the chess master decide, often within a few seconds, his next move? How can a grand master reproduce a chess posi-tion of 24 pieces correctly after having seen it for only a few seconds? The basis of this intuition (knowing without formal reasoning) is experience, previous learning stored in long-term memory. The memory of the grand master contains an enormous collection of chess patterns, with associated information about the significance of the pattern. The expert has access to his memory by means of a set of personal heuristics (rules of thumb), "which are largely intuitive in nature. In these personal strategies, per-ceptual and emotional factors play a pivotal role."[15]

Intuition should not be contrasted with, but complemented by, formal and conscious thinking. If not, intuition might not only be less powerful but also may become a dangerous, very fallible compass. As an example of this, when asked which objects – scissors, hammers, toilets, playground equipment, power saws, cooking ranges and ovens, beds, mattresses and pillows – are most associated with injuries annually (measured in hospital emergency rooms), most people will not answer correctly (they are toilets, beds, mattresses, and pillows).[16] Our fact base and our assumptions, if they are wrong, affect the validity of our intuition.

There is overwhelming empirical evidence that intuition alone is far less accurate than statistical forms of assessment and of predicting behavior.[17] This is a very sobering message for those who strongly believe in phenomena like investment intuition, clinical intuition, risk intuition, gambler's intuition, and interviewer intuition. There are many interesting examples of this, among them: "You'd better learn secretarial skills or else get married" (model agency rejecting Marilyn Monroe in 1944); "You ought to go back to driving a truck" (concert manager firing Elvis Presley in 1954); "Can't act. Can't sing. Slightly bald. Can dance a little" (a film company's verdict on Fred Astaire's 1928 screen test).[18] But there is hope: it is possible to educate oneself to use intuition in a more balanced and constructive way.[19]

It is obvious that using intuition accurately requires healthy complementary doses of thinking and testing the intuitive hypotheses. But this should not obscure in any way the relevance of processes like empathy and intuition in the application of the clinical approach to listening.

LISTENING WITH THE THIRD EAR

Listening from a psychoanalytic perspective implies being sensitive to unconscious meanings.[20] The basic assumption is that clinical listening means being open to the exploration of unconscious meanings, and empathy and intuition are therefore potential modes of data collection.

Freud recommended almost a century ago that the best way to approach and listen to patients was to offer what he called free-floating attention. Freud describes the rationale of this technique as follows:

> "It consists simply in not directing one's notice to anything in particular and in maintaining the same 'evenly-suspended attention' in the face of all that one hears.

> It will be seen that the rule of giving equal notice to everything is the necessary counterpart to the demand made on the patient that he should communicate everything that occurs to him without criticism or selection.

...[S]o the doctor must put himself in a position to make use of every-thing he is told, for the purposes of interpretation and of recognizing the concealed unconscious material without substituting a censorship of his own for the selection that the patient has rejected. To put it into a for-mula: he must turn his own unconscious like a receptive organ towards the transmitting unconscious of the patient."[21]

As a logical consequence, Freud remarks that nothing should restrict the doctor in making free use of himself, because if the therapist is constrained or conflicted, this will restrict his ability genuinely to listen to the patient and to help him or her to discover unconscious meanings. Similar advice, although phrased in a different psychoanalytic framework, is given by Wilfred Bion, who advocates listening "without memory or desire": if the mind is preoccupied with elements of memory, desire, understanding, and sense, it will be much less able to perceive elements that cannot be sensed.[22]

Although one should try to be as free and open as possible while listening, listening never will and never can be completely random and open. There is always a backdrop of concepts, under-standings, and mental operations inhabiting the listening mind: "If the analyst listens without preconceptions, that does not mean that he or she listens without conceptions."[23] At the same time, the objective is to approach listening in a "self-decentered" way.[24] The analyst is primarily focused on the patient, without allowing self-generated considerations to interfere with that process.

Listening to the unconscious is listening to what, exactly? Heikki Piha defines the nature of the elements and processes one may encounter below the surface, and the ways of accessing them. Intuition is delineated as a valuable and necessary tool for bridging the gap between the subjective reality of the analyst and the analysand. Piha argues that intuition is "like a radar in the frontline of our thinking, used to probe and explore prelimi-nary connections in the inner world of the analysand with our own inner experiences."[25] Intuition provides immediate views that are not proper knowledge, but may lead to it. The radar of intuition has access to the preconscious, where one may find "many kinds of undifferentiated forms, such as rhythms, tones and melodies of spoken words reflecting psychic meanings."[26]

The listener must have the courage and the capacity to be sensitive and open to deeper, primordial levels of the mind. He or she must be able to tolerate intense, volatile, and immediate emotions and impulses.

So the challenge is to combine a tolerance for discursive modes of thinking (linked to primary process thinking) with various forms of conscious thinking (secondary process thinking). These various forms may co-exist, and are complementary and cumulative. An example is the continuum of the affect aggression, differentiated as rage, hatred, anger, and irritation.[27] The higher the level of cognitive elaboration, the milder the affect is. Irritation is one of the mildest manifestations, while anger is more intense, incorporating cognitive elaboration of the original, and even more intense, primitive states of hatred and rage. When one listens to somebody expressing anger, the question is whether it is possible to explore deeper and potentially more primitive levels. In the case of Simon, my intuitive and empathic understanding of his aggressive outbursts was that underneath his anger was a displaced enragement toward his ex-wife.

A potential pitfall is that the listener prefers to avoid being exposed to these more primitive, incomprehensible, and fragmented elements of experience. In some cases, intuition may result in "understanding" occurring too quickly; this can be related to an insufficient capacity to tolerate puzzlement and delay.[28] Another defensive use of intuition is when it masks feelings of elation and omnipotence. One may hear cases where a person claims to operate continuously in intuitive mode, but this is obviously at the expense of reality checks, conscious thinking, and the capacity to revise intuitions in dialogue with others.

TRANSFERENCE, COUNTER-TRANSFERENCE, AND ENACTMENTS

Everything that applies to the person speaking–the unconscious, archaic modes of experiencing, and so on–applies equally to the listener. Listening is a form of interaction. How might the listener be affected by what they are listening to? How might this inform the way they listen or intervene? What kind of unconscious communications and provocations might influence the listening process and capacity? A rich source of inspiration can be found in the psychoanalytical literature on transference and counter-transference, which has been mentioned earlier in this book and will be touched on again here.[29]

Transference is defined as a displacement of patterns of feelings, thoughts, and behavior, originally experienced in relation to significant figures during childhood, onto a person involved in a current interpersonal relationship.[30] Transference represents a confusion of time, person, and place. The listener (the coach, the consultant, or the business leader) becomes the recipient of all kinds of unconscious projections. As a consequence, the listener may feel "distorted" and misunderstood.

Transference and transference-like phenomena emerge in all human relationships. Psychoanalytical treatment provides a unique opportunity to observe transference in action and to use it as a major tool for intervention. These unconscious dynamics play a part in all professional relationships, but it is not possible, and it would be not appropriate, to explore such dynamics with the client in a nonclinical setting (as will be discussed in Chapter Seventeen). The clinical approach to listening in coaching interventions brings it to an advanced level, but does not lead to psychotherapy. It is important to differentiate the various levels of a therapeutic relationship (working alliance, transference and counter-transference, and real relationship) in order to understand better to what, and to whom, you are listening.

In the case of George, I was at first concerned that he was neither willing to engage himself in the task (drawing a self-portrait) nor in the seminar at large. I became sensitive to any cues about his willingness and readiness to participate. The question running through my mind was: Will it be possible to form a working alliance with George? Listening to him from a transference and counter-transference perspective, I was focused on other cues and aspects. For instance, could it be that George unconsciously re-enacted the situation of not belonging or of being left out and rejected? Was his sitting apart and reading the newspaper a way of unconsciously provoking rejection in order to recreate the original traumatic situation?

A good listener is able to switch modes and positions very quickly. Imagine somebody asks you, in their first coaching session, to watch the time because they have to leave ten minutes early. What does this mean? The meaning may vary according to the level of the relationship. On the surface it is just a straightforward question, a request relating to an external reality, asking for some flexibility. Sometimes a cigar is just a cigar. Perhaps your client "just" has to respect an important, unexpected external commitment. But at another level, you might want to explore other potential meanings related to this question, such as, what does it say about your chances of establishing a working alliance with this client? An effective and robust working alliance requires a mutual commitment to invest time and energy in agreed time slots. One-sidedly moving the time boundary in the very first session might have a message. You may also look at the question in terms of transference. Might the question of leaving earlier represent an unconscious wish to escape from the dreadfulness projected into the coaching situation? The situation is even more complex, because your response and behavior may be colored by counter-transference reactions toward your client.

Counter-transference refers to a situation in which an analyst's feelings and attitudes toward a patient are derived from earlier situations in the analyst's life that have been displaced onto the patient.[31] Two main approaches to counter-transference may be discerned. The first essentially considers counter-transference as a dangerous and inappropriate phenomenon.[32] The attitudes and feelings of the analyst toward his patient may reflect the analyst's own unconscious and unresolved conflicts. They may interfere with the therapeutic process and the analyst should recognize and overcome them in himself through self-analysis. Analysis undergone during training, and continuous supervision afterwards, aim to prevent counter-transference. A second and more positive approach emerged in the 1950s. This sees counter-transference as providing important and useful data about the patient. "The therapist should be as free as the patient to experience a full range of feelings, thoughts and fantasies about the patient. Ideally the therapist does not struggle against or suppress these inner experiences."[33]

Transference and counter-transference reactions emerge in all relationships.[34] How capable is the listener of identifying them? Longstanding empirical research demonstrates that, for most people, these patterns are very consistent over time, and

individuals can be characterized by their core conflictual relationship theme (CCRT).[35] These themes organize behavior in a
relationship: What does one expect from oneself and from others?
The CCRT not only influences one's own behavior but also the
behavior of the other. Individuals unconsciously try to cast others
in roles in line with their CCRT. One might, for example, provoke the other into the role of enemy, rival, or helper to become
dependent on. These transference and counter-transference
reactions are neither a sign of pathology nor an indication of
dysfunctional relationships. But they may become a source of
dysfunctionality when they interfere with good and productive
relationships and cooperation.

It is therefore helpful to be aware of the most frequent indicators of problematic counter-transference. An overview of counter-
transference problems includes three categories: turning away,
activated counter-transference, and unconscious enactments.[36]
Turning away manifests itself in states of boredom, indifference,
apathy, depression, sleepiness, repugnance, and forgetfulness.
Turning away may have various functions: fighting the awareness of an important insight, reacting to repressed or directly
expressed excitement, or frustrating the needs of the helping
professional, for instance, needs to be appreciated, liked, or
helpful. Turning away tendencies make it difficult, if not impossible, to feel engaged with the other and may paralyze empathy.
I remember a striking example of turning away tendencies when
I interviewed a young woman. After a few minutes, I became very
sleepy and really struggled to keep myself awake. I was looking
for escape, how to end this meeting as soon as possible? Then my
observing ego stepped in and I asked myself what was going on.
I looked at her face and saw no emotional expression at all. She
answered all my questions but in a very flat way. I felt as though
I was talking to a robot. This awareness woke me up.

Activated counter-transference is the opposite of turning away.
The helping professional feels an unusually strong emotional
bond with the patient. In the positive form, the professional may
feel on intimate terms with the client and experience sexual
desire, admiration, or rescue fantasies. Over-identification with
the client leads to a lack of distance, which hampers proper
empathy and substitutes it with sympathy. In negative activated
counter-transference, aggressive feelings toward the client are

aroused. This may manifest itself in arguments with the client, fantasies of getting rid of the client, or behaving tactlessly.

The third category of problematic counter-transference reactions refers to unconscious enactments. Instead of experiencing a significantly increased or decreased emotional response, the helping professional unconsciously acts out a counter-transference element, for example through a technical failure (such as forgetting an appointment), or by deviating from a well-established professional routine. All these are indicators that should alert the professional to the problem and find a way to overcome it.

The best correction is to re-establish a working perspective using professional routine and best practice, as in the case of the robotic woman, where self-exploration helped me to overcome my sleepiness. It helped me to control myself and not give in to a desire to end the meeting prematurely, thus preventing an unconscious enactment.

It is important to recognize the less obvious counter-transference reactions and enactments. The way in which we listen, our silences and neutrality, may all contain concealed elements of counter-transference. Clinical neutrality, for example, may be a defense against a strong counter-aggression aroused in the coach or consultant by the client. Neutrality becomes invested with a counter-transference element: the helping professional is determined to keep his stance of neutrality. He has lost his "free-floating responsiveness."[37]

CONCLUSION

We have explored the essential processes and dynamics of listening. The art of listening from a clinical perspective is to listen below the surface. It is the art of being open and sensitive to unconscious levels of meaning and to more archaic levels of experiencing. In order to be able to access these in others, one must be capable of accessing them in oneself. Mentalizing (understanding that human behavior is caused by various and varying states of mind) is a necessary but insufficient precondition for listening. Empathy and intuition are valuable ways of connecting with out-of-conscious levels of meaning and experience. As such, they are important tools for data collection. All kinds of thinking processes help to interpret the findings and test the clinical hypotheses.

Listening is an interpersonal situation that takes place in a relationship. The relationship can be described on various levels (real relationship, working alliance, and counter-transference). Each of these levels creates a different listening position and focus. We are advised to listen with a mind as open as possible and with free-floating attention. If possible, we should listen without memory or desire. But we must acknowledge that a neutral or empty mind is an illusion; our minds are full of concepts, thoughts, and frameworks. Self-decentered listening is a more realistic ambition.

Listening to others presupposes and incorporates listening to oneself. The other, and his or her narrative, resonate in oneself. At times the listener is like an emotional mirror for the other. Given the delicate and complex processes of transference and counter-transference, it is crucial that the listener is capable of differentiating and disentangling "me" from "not me." The temporary merging and identification in empathy should be followed by moments of distancing oneself and even installing an empathic wall. Feeling and thinking can be complemented, to the benefit of listening.

One of the challenges in applying clinical skills and perspectives to listening is the capacity to use them for oneself. A major use of the clinical approach is for the consultant, coach, or leader to develop a greater ability to observe and understand through seeing more, listening more deeply, and discovering potentially unconscious meanings and patterns. But the extent to which one may start talking and working on this level depends on the nature of the setting, the contract, and the skills of the coach or consultant. There is a strong case to make for not interpreting unconscious mental life in consulting to organizations, which will be further explored in Chapter Seventeen. Exceptions may be found in particular clinical coaching situations, when the objective is to explore deeper aspects of self in the context of one's professional role and activities.

The quotation at the beginning of this chapter summarizes best what this chapter is about: "Listening is not done by the ears, but by the mind. We hear sounds, but we listen to meanings." The art of listening is at the service of personal discovery, development, and change.

NOTES

1. See for example Starr, J. (2003). *The Coaching Manual*. London: Pearson Education Limited.
2. Argyle, M. (1975). *Bodily Communication*. London: Methuen & Co Ltd; Ekman, P. and W.V. Friesen (1975). *Unmasking the Face*. Englewood Cliffs, NJ: Prentice Hall.
3. Argyle, M. (1975).
4. Allen, J.G. (2003a). "Mentalizing." *Bulletin of the Menninger Clinic*, 67 (2), 91–112; Allen, J.G. (2003b). *Mentalizing as a Compass for Treatment*. The Menninger Clinic, 1–11.
5. Allen, J.G. (2003a).
6. Allen, J.G. (2003a), p. 4.
7. This case history is taken from Allen, J.G. (2003b).
8. Moore, B.E. and B.D. Fine (1990) (eds.). *A Glossary of Psychoanalytic Terms and Concepts*. New York: The American Psychoanalytic Association.
9. Greenson, R. (1967). *The Technique and Practice of Psychoanalysis*. London: The Hogarth Press.
10. Sandler, J. (1987) (ed.). *Projection, Identification, Projective Identification*. Madison, CT: International Universities Press.
11. Eigen, M. (1986). *The Psychotic Core*. Northvale, NJ: Jason Aronson Inc.
12. Nathanson, D.L. (1986). "The empathic wall and the ecology of affect." *The Psychoanalytic Study of the Child*, 41, 171–187. New Haven, CT: Yale University Press.
13. Loo, E. van de (1992). "Intuition, countertransference and wild analysis in the clinical interview." In: L. Lapierre and V. Kisfalvi (eds.). *Clinical Approaches to the Study of Managerial and Organizational Dynamics*. Montreal: Ecole des Hautes Etudes Commerciales de Montreal, 372–385.
14. Snoek, J.W. (1989). *Het denken van de neuroloog*. (Reasoning of the neurologist). Diss. Groningen University.
15. Snoek, J.W. (1989), p. 453.
16. Myers, D.G. (2002). *Intuition. Its Powers and Perils*. New Haven, CT: Yale University Press.
17. Myers, D.G. (2002).
18. Myers, D.G. (2002), p. 189.
19. Hogarth, R.M. (2001). *Educating Intuition*. Chicago, IL: The University of Chicago Press.
20. Meissner, W.W. (2000). "On analytic listening." *Psychoanalytic Quarterly*, LXIX (2), 319.
21. Freud, S. (1912). *Recommendations to Physicians Practicing Psychoanalysis*. London: Hogarth Press. Standard Edition Vol. XII, 111–120.
22. Bion, W. (1970). *Attention and Interpretation*. Northvale, NJ: Jason Aronson Inc.
23. Meissner, W.W. (2000), p. 323.
24. Faimberg, H. (1997). "Misunderstanding and psychic truths." *International Journal of Psycho-Analysis*, 78 (3), 439–451.

25. Piha, H. (2005). "Intuition: a bridge to the coenesthetic world of experience." *Journal of the American Psychoanalytical Association*, 53 (1), 23–49.
26. Piha, H. (2005), p. 45.
27. Kernberg, O.F. (1992). *Aggression in Personality Disorders*. New Haven, CT: Yale University Press.
28. Piha, H. (2005).
29. Esman, A.H. (1990). *Essential Papers on Transference*. New York: New York Universities Press; Wolstein, B. (1988) (ed.). *Essential Papers on Counter-transference*. New York: New York Universities Press; Epstein, L. and A. Feiner (1988). "Countertransference: the therapist's contribution to treatment." In: B. Wolstein (ed.). *Essential Papers on Countertransference*. New York: New York Universities Press, 282–303; Abend, S. (1989). "Countertransference and psychoanalytic technique." *Psychoanalytic Quarterly*, 58 (3), 374–395.
30. Moore, B.E. and B.D. Fine (1990).
31. Moore, B.E. and B.D. Fine (1990).
32. Freud, S. (1910). *The Future Prospects of Psychoanalytic Therapy*. London: The Hogarth Press. Standard Edition Vol. XI, 139–151.
33. Altshul, V. and W. Sledge (1989). Countertransference problems. In: A. Tasman, R. Hales and A. Frances (eds.). *Review of Psychiatry*. Vol. 8. Washington, DC: American Psychiatric Press, 518–530.
34. Brenner, Ch. (1982). *The Mind in Conflict*. Madison, CT: International Universities Press.
35. Luborsky, L. and P. Crits-Cristoph (1988). *Understanding Transference: The Core Conflictual Relationship Theme Method*. Washington: American Psychological Organization.
36. Altshul, V. and W. Sledge (1989).
37. Sandler, J. (1976). "Countertransference and role-responsiveness." *International Review of Psycho-Analysis*, 43 (3), 43–47.

13

THE DOS AND DON'TS OF COACHING: KEY LESSONS I LEARNED AS AN EXECUTIVE COACH

ELISABET ENGELLAU

It is possible to fail in many ways ... while to succeed is possible only in one way.

Aristotle

Experience is simply the name we give our mistakes.

Oscar Wilde

A life spent making mistakes is not only more honorable but more useful than a life spent in doing nothing.

George Bernard Shaw

Early on in my professional activity as an executive coach, I was contacted by the VP Human Resources of a large US retail company. This company had just acquired a family firm in the apparel business located in France and had hired a French professional manager with vast experience in the luxury goods industry to become the new CEO. Until very recently the business had been run by two brothers (the major shareholders) in a very patriarchal way. The VP HR told me that she was keen for the new CEO to help the family business make a seamless transition to professional management. She was concerned that this transition process should go well, so had suggested to the CEO (whom I will call David) that he should engage an executive coach to help him with the transition during his first six months in the job. She also felt that David needed help to adjust his leadership style to the new situation, expressing her worry about the fit of his rather "French" autocratic style with the more participative, democratic culture advocated by the new owners. She added that the head office was going through a period of turmoil as the old CEO was close to retirement and a race was taking place to select his successor. The VP explained that she had been given my name by an acquaintance in the US who felt that I would be the right person to handle the assignment. I remember how flattered I was by that: I was relatively new to coaching. This assignment would be my most important challenge.

I agreed with the VP that I would contact David by telephone. From our conversation, which took place the following day, I could tell that David did not exactly welcome the idea of coaching and seemed to have consented only half-heartedly to the VP's suggestion. Despite his skepticism, David agreed at least to meet me to discuss the coaching proposition. Our first meeting took place over lunch a week later. It was late summer and David had been in his new position for three months. From his comments, he appeared to be somewhat at a loss. Previously, he had been a senior executive in a large, well-run organization. He was now running a much smaller, family firm that was going through turbulent times as part of a large, global operation. Being in the top job was also a new experience for David.

After a general discussion about what a coaching arrangement would mean, David agreed to a six-month trial run. The agreement was that we would meet face-to-face at least once a month for a period of two to three hours. In between sessions, we would keep in contact with each other by telephone and e-mail. A fee was agreed upon and a contractual agreement was signed. My request, however, to meet with his team and with other important players in the company, was rejected. David felt that we should wait until his new team was in place, to which I agreed. I then suggested that we should go through a 360-degree feedback process – another way to obtain more information about how David was perceived in the organization – but David made it clear that he felt that it was too early for that. According to him, he was too new in the organization.

As time passed, and although it felt like pulling teeth, I gradually acquired more information about David's activities in his new organization. I began to comprehend how messy the organizational situation really was. From our discussions, I understood that one of the brother-owners and many of the employees who worked with him had resisted the sale of the company. While the company had achieved success through this brother's creative designs, it had to be sold because of liquidity problems. The other shareholders felt that they had no choice but to sell if they wanted to ensure the future viability of the company. The understanding was that the US acquiring organization had the resources to bring the company to the next level. To help to get there, the US company had hired David. They expected him to bring in new talent in management, design, and marketing.

It became clear from our discussions that David had to deal with not-so-subtle undermining from a number of senior executives who were still loyal to the brother who had been in charge of design. Some of them felt that they were more qualified than he was for the CEO position. They viewed David as an outsider, a spy acting for the new owner. They would withhold information and fail to implement, or even sabotage, certain decisions. David was reluctant to fire them as he felt he needed their knowledge of the business to move forward. In addition, the misunderstandings and mistrust between the employees, David, and the senior executives in the US were compounded by language barriers and the very different cultures, national and otherwise, in which the two companies were operating. Yet another problem was David's indecisiveness in putting a new team into place. He appeared to be suspicious, not only vis-à-vis the "old guard," but also vis-à-vis the people from head office who were suggested to him. Compounded by the language problem, it took months for David to put a new team into place.

It did not take me very long to realize that my effectiveness as a coach was extremely limited. It was very difficult to extract information from David. At times, I wondered whether he viewed *me* as a spy who was reporting everything to the VP HR. I was further handicapped by his refusal to allow me access to any people in his organization. The only information I had about his effectiveness as a CEO were his own reports and occasional e-mails from the VP HR in the United States, who was hard to get hold of. Even that communication stopped when the individual concerned took a position somewhere else.

Whenever David and I met, both of us seemed to go through the motions, knowing that we were expected to do something, but not doing much about it. Instead, we appeared to be engaged in some kind of ritualistic activity. This was not very good for my morale. The meetings made me feel increasingly useless. I felt quite alone, confused, left out, isolated, and did not know how to move the process forward. I was not getting anywhere. I had a very hard time distinguishing between fantasy and reality. Trust was never really established between us. A working alliance never got off the ground. It was clear that David's major motivation to be present at these meetings was the strong request for him to do so by HR at head office.

During one of our meetings, David talked about a new marketing manager who had just been pushed onto him by head office in the U.S. He felt that this American woman was behaving inappropriately and not paying attention to French cultural norms. He was obviously irritated by this. I suggested that it might be useful if I were to talk to her. To my great surprise, David accepted my offer and arranged an appointment.

On meeting her and discussing the situation, I learned that head office viewed David as a loner, not very communicative, and increasingly isolated. According to her, a number of senior executives at HQ felt that he was unable to handle the complex task he had been asked to do. I listened to what she had to say and left it at that. I felt that, given my difficult relationship with David, it would not be appropriate to confront him with this kind of information by telephone. I needed to find the right moment to discuss these issues. I was also concerned that if I reported my concerns, it would further jeopardize his already difficult relationship with the new marketing manager.

Two weeks later–a week before our next session–I received a telephone call from David telling me that he had been fired. Surprised by this information, I suggested that we meet as soon as possible. When I met him two days later, he seemed to be in a state of shock. He was clearly extremely upset, very angry, and deeply hurt. He told me that he did not have the slightest idea why he had been fired. He mentioned that, only a few weeks before, he had received a salary increase with a congratulatory note from the new CEO. And now, three days ago, he had received a phone call from the same individual telling him that he was fired. To soften the blow, he was told that he would receive a one-year termination package. But what irritated him immensely was that the CEO had given him no valid explanation for his termination.

When pressed, the CEO only made a number of fuzzy comments about a change in overall strategy.

After telling me his tale of woe, David asked me what I thought he should do. Should he start legal procedures? Should he sue? I did not know what to say because I was also confused. I told David what I had learned from the new marketing director. David reacted with surprise and painted a very different picture of his relationship with head office and the new CEO. I could not offer any explanations as to why he had been fired. I felt frustrated and quite guilty, as we had not accomplished what we had set out to do.

After a couple of sessions where both of us tried to understand what had happened to him without achieving any clarity, he terminated our coaching relationship. I felt that, because of my inexperience, I had not accessed enough information and had been unable to analyze the situation well enough to get a basic understanding of the company's underlying issues, and to take all the stakeholders into account. Like David, I had not seen it coming. I was not sufficiently prepared to handle such a complex situation.

Before the David assignment, I had spent most of my time in INSEAD programs coaching executives with different levels of professional experience in small groups. This sort of coaching assignment is of a very short-term duration, a day or a day and a half, and based on the results from several 360° feedback instruments. The short time available with the executives places some very different demands on the coach. One has to work both quickly and pragmatically with the specific managerial issues and interpersonal challenges the executives face. This in turn requires listening, constantly challenging one's capacity for empathic reflection and action.

These short-term interventions are quite different from the one I had with David. There, I had been asked to help a person to be more effective in his role over a long period of time. In such situations, the relationship usually deepens as time goes by, and comes to include not only a complexity of professional issues with which the client struggles, but also very personal life dilemmas. As a coach, one has to ask oneself questions concerning boundaries of roles; confidentiality; and one's own motivations, strengths, and biases. And in David's case, I had not yet been experienced enough to handle this level of complexity. What went wrong in my effort to coach this CEO?

Thinking about what had happened, I was reminded of Sigmund Freud's first major case history, Fragment of an Analysis of a Case of Hysteria,[1] which has long been recognized as one of the classic texts of psychoanalysis. The "Dora case" played an integral part in the development of psychoanalysis. Perhaps more than any other, this case helped formalize Freud's concept of transference and its essential role in effective psychoanalysis and psychotherapy.

Let me recapitulate the Dora story. In October 1900, Freud began treating an 18-year-old woman for a mysterious cough and other signs of what were described as hysterical symptoms. The woman's name was Ida Bauer, and Freud gave her the pseudonym "Dora." Dora was brought to Freud by her father to "cure" her of her obsession that her parents should break off relations with a family friend, Herr K, whom Dora claimed had made sexual advances to her. Her father mentioned to Freud that he thought this idea was teenage fantasy. As the treatment progressed, Freud discovered a family in the middle of deep entanglements, where Herr K's wife was simultaneously carrying on a love affair with Dora's father while having an intimate emotional relationship with Dora. Freud concluded, however, that Dora was a hysteric and that most of her claims were fantasies. After 11 weeks, Dora stopped treatment, leaving much of the analytic work undone.

The Dora case entered history as one of Freud's earliest and most significant failures, and it taught him and his critics many salient lessons about psychoanalysis. Reading Freud's observations carefully, it is clear that he mishandled Dora's case badly. Although he accepted her account of the events involving the Ks (and thereby enabled her to confront them with the truth later in life), he showed little empathy for the feelings of the teenage girl. She was understandably distressed by his observations and advice.

Freud's lack of experience with the bi-personal field contributed to his failure. He was in the early stages of formulating his theories and was still unfamiliar with the concepts of transference and counter-transference, which are the emotional bonds formed between the patient and therapist. He did not realize that, during treatment, Dora had come to view him as she perceived her father and Herr K. Thus he did not understand the ways in which she reacted toward him. He did not yet understand transferential processes. He did not recognize the significance of her reactions. Through the process of analysis, Dora had transferred on to Freud some very passionate feelings, ranging from love to deep anger. After Dora terminated the case, Freud concluded that he had waited too long to bring up Dora's transference reactions and that Dora terminated the therapy because she felt deceived and abandoned as a result of her transference fantasies. Although Freud was disappointed with the results of the case, he had the honesty to say so and learn from it. Over time, the handling of transference manifestations and the patient's resistance would gradually become the centre of therapeutic interventions.

I had an uncanny feeling that there were many resemblances between my work with David and Freud's work with Dora. I wondered if I had been sufficiently empathic. I asked myself whether I should have expressed my counter-transference feelings toward David. Could I have been more perceptive and assertive? What was there to be learned from this failure?

LESSON 1: BE SPECIFIC ABOUT THE TERMS OF THE COACHING CONTRACT

There were many reasons why this coaching relationship was a failure. Flattered to be offered the assignment, I did not consider the strength of the CEO's resistance and mistrust seriously enough. I took his agreement to engage in the coaching process and his willingness to work with me on leadership development and personal change more or less at face value. Clearly, our initial contract was not sufficiently clear about expectations, boundaries, and goals. The ground rules concerning our coaching agreement created defensiveness and a lack of honesty. Given the number of people involved in the assignment, I should have clarified my relationship to David and the VP HR. As it was, David never stopped seeing me as linked to head office, possibly reporting to them on his progress. I was aware of this and, as a result, it prevented me from having any contact with people at head office. With David's consent and collaboration, we could have explored the expectations of the new CEO and the board following the acquisition, and David's role could have been clarified.

Furthermore, I underestimated what it meant for David to be a CEO. At the outset, I failed to explore his feelings about his new position sufficiently, or how I could be helpful to him. What I should have done was to have had a meeting with David and the VP HR from the US to spell out our mutual expectations, and what was needed to make the coaching intervention a success. Such a meeting would have given us an opportunity to really clarify the task ahead. It would also have been an opportunity to make sure that the desired objectives would be attainable. It is important to be realistic about what we, as professionals, can actually promise and deliver. We could also have discussed the issue of confidentiality, explaining what can and cannot be guaranteed. And finally, that meeting would have been the place to state that there was no intention of becoming the executor of another stakeholder's expectations, but that it was essential to work with the expectations of the client.

LESSON 2: BE UP FRONT ABOUT WHAT IS NON-NEGOTIABLE

With hindsight, it was clear to me that I had been pussyfooting around, fearful that if I were too forceful, David would not agree to the coaching contract. I did not insist on a more systematic approach to obtaining critical information about the context of the assignment, which was essential to assess the progress of my intervention. I should have clarified up front how important it was for David to get feedback about his performance from others. Perhaps I was oversensitive to the French cultural situation, where 360-degree feedback is not self-evident. Instead, not wanting to upset David, and due to lack of professional confidence, I had tiptoed around and never received this kind of crucial information. Only at the last minute did I receive feedback from the US marketing manager on how David was perceived at head office. By accepting David's refusal not to allow me to gather information from the people he worked with, I allowed him to make my assignment extremely difficult. I was not assertive enough in making my requirements clear to him: my wish to please and be nonconfrontational won out.

LESSON 3: USE YOUR INTUITION/COUNTER-TRANSFERENCE REACTIONS

My lack of experience also undermined my willingness to express my feelings toward David. I mentioned earlier that during our discussions, I became increasingly confused about what was going on in the organization. I had no idea how David was performing. As a matter of fact, during our sessions, he made me feel incompetent. I felt something of an impostor at having been given this assignment. What I did not address was whether those feelings were only mine, or whether David was transferring his own feelings of insecurity about his new position to me. Looking back, I am quite sure that if I had expressed my feelings in an empathic manner, it may have resonated with David, helping him to open up. It may have created a basis for trust and a working alliance that never happened.

LESSON 4: DEAL WITH RESISTANCE UP FRONT

As I explained, David did not initiate the coaching process. Flattered that I had received this assignment, I never dealt with the implications of such an arrangement. Instead, I avoided exploring how David felt about it, afraid that he would discontinue the coaching process. In addition, I never tackled the fact that the coaching process was not going anywhere. I never tried to explore his resistance, the complex relationships he had to manage, and his emotional responses. By not dealing with these issues in the right way, all I obtained instead was a serious dose of intellectualizing, the negation of most of my observations, and contrary behavior. I simply stayed in the role of the very sympathetic listener. But effective as active listening may be, obviously it was not enough to turn the situation around. It would have been much better if I (perhaps together with the VP HR) had clarified that coaching had not been suggested as some sort of last chance for a person with fatal flaws. On the contrary, we should have explained that we were trying to make an excellent executive even better, that head office had a lot of confidence in David's abilities, and that they wanted to do everything to make him a success. In addition, a discussion about what the CEO position implied, what head office's expectations were, what traps lay ahead, and how head office could be helpful during the transition would have created a very different atmosphere.

LESSON 5: PLAY RESISTANCE JUDO

During my interaction with David, he bickered many times about certain issues in his organization. Again, I had to wonder if my approach had been correct. Dealing with resistance is always a delicate process. Hard experience has taught me that directly opposing another's point has the unfortunate effect of pushing the person in the other direction. It may actually be counterproductive.

Jay Haley, Watzlawyck, and other pioneers in the field of strategic family therapy have used the metaphor of psychological judo, whereby an attack is not met with direct opposition (as in boxing), but going with the flow, using the opponent's momentum to one's advantage.[2] Had I dealt with David's resistances in that way from the beginning, exploring his feelings of ambivalence about certain issues, I could have brought about a more in-depth level of insight and motivation on his part, and may have tipped things in the right direction.

LESSON 6: HAVE A SYSTEMIC POINT OF VIEW

David was dealing with an extremely complex environment, where two companies were in the middle of a transformation process. In addition, head office was in the final throes of a succession battle. To accentuate the complexity, David had to cope with two cultures, two languages, and two different corporate culture there. He was also new to the organization and knew next to nothing about the people at head office and the corporate culture there. He had never been in a CEO position, and did not know what it meant to be the final decision maker. Furthermore, he had to deal with a number of "wounded princes" in the company he was in charge of. Instead of telling them to shape up or ship out, he was afraid to fire them, given his limited knowledge about the business he had to lead. The situation was not helped when the VP HR who had suggested me as a coach left the company a month after I started. No other person from head office seemed to have the same stake in David's success. On the contrary, the new chairman and CEO had little understanding of the different national and organizational cultures in their newly acquired company, and the change processes that were needed. Instead, they put considerable pressure on David to turn the company around and deliver extremely ambitious financial results.

Given all these changes, David needed to build relationships with the people at head office. In addition, he needed to build a working alliance with the new CEO. He also had to select the people who would make up his key team, people he could trust. All these things were happening to someone who was not politically astute. And neither was I. Given the outcome of the coaching intervention, we had been like two blind mice stumbling in the dark. David did not know how to deal with the complexity that faced him, and I had not taken a systemic outlook that would permit me to point out some of the possible stumbling points. Not knowing all the players in the organization, and not having any feedback, was definitely a big drawback.

LESSON 7: ALWAYS SUPPORT SELF-EFFICACY

As a final lesson, I felt that I could have encouraged David more about his capabilities. I spent too much time discussing areas where he could do things better. Although I believe that I am a very empathic listener, I could have done more affirming, reflecting, and summarizing. I could have focused more on his achievements. I could have tried to help David overcome his sense of insecurity in the new position. I could have mitigated his feeling of being an impostor.[3] I could have encouraged David in his belief that he had it in him to cope effectively with future situations.[4] As we all know, a strong sense of efficacy enhances human accomplishment and personal well-being. People with a strong sense of self-esteem and confidence in their capabilities approach difficult tasks as a challenge to be mastered, not as a threat to be avoided.

FINAL REFLECTIONS

The role of empathic listening

Apart from these hard lessons, my experience has taught me other things about what makes coaching effective. Over the last ten years, a large number of books have been published on coaching. Their approach varies considerably both in philosophy and quality, but there is always agreement on the key ingredient for successful coaching, which is the capacity to listen. There are obviously different ways we can listen to another person's story, but to be helpful as an executive coach I make it a priority to work constantly on my capacity to listen and to develop my empathic awareness. It is by fine-tuning this tool, honed by experience, reflection, and sensibility that I learn not only to make sense of what the client is telling me, but also to discern what is not said, the emotional quality and temperature with which the story is told, and last but not least, how the narrative resonates with me.

Some people have a natural inclination for empathic listening. They allow the other person their full attention and create a constructive, positive atmosphere for further understanding by both parties. To be able to tell your story to a sympathetic ear has a therapeutic effect, and at the same time gives the person presenting the narrative the opportunity to re-create his or her own reality, reflected in the choices made in structuring the story. The empathy that forms part of this type of listening takes into account the emotional reality of the "other," which is essential for exploring possibilities for development and growth.

What separates the professional coach from a friend or just another sympathetic human being is his or her skill in listening with the third ear.[5] It is important that a coach is always aware of the complexity of the psychological processes that come to the fore – that there is more than meets the eye. To enhance this kind of sensitivity and be able to use himself or herself as an analytical tool, a coach needs to work constantly on self-awareness. Insight into oneself and one's own psychological makeup is essential to those who want to coach others. The dialog that takes place in a coaching session is always paralleled with simultaneous

251

internal dialogs within the parties involved, and with transferential figures past and present.

REFLECTIVE TIME

One of the most important benefits of coaching, whether in groups or individually, is that it allows the client time to reflect. This reflection may concern a business issue that needs a solution, or the wish to explore important themes in life, past and present. Few of the executives that I have met during my years in coaching devote regular time to important questions in their lives, and most of them are very grateful to be given such an opportunity.

The time factor in different coaching assignments plays a major role in how successful reflection will be. Life-changing experiences can happen in a single coaching session. An individual who is given the opportunity and has the courage to tell his or her story, with all its intricacies, can benefit from insights that can lead to important changes in the person's professional or personal life.

My experience is that the concept of reflective time in leadership coaching is very fluid, whether working with a team or an individual. It is very important to manage the time available, and the clients' expectations of time at their disposal. Sometimes the length of the session is determined by the urgency of the issues explored and by the coach's and client's willingness to devote time, but most often only a set amount of time is available. Reflective time allocated to each member during group coaching has to be accepted as fair by all parties involved. Sometimes more time is needed for a participant who is struggling with an especially complex professional issue or presenting a personal trauma that cannot be ignored. The decision to spend valuable extra time on that participant is taken with the consent of the whole group. A coach needs to manage this very carefully, but the benefits of vicarious learning in such sessions can make this sort of flexibility extremely worthwhile.

Change takes time. Considering the cost of professional coaching services, it is highly unfortunate that too many organizations refrain from giving adequate resources to this process, and as a result waste both money and time on what in the end turns out to be a superficial and aborted process of change.

KNOW YOURSELF

In order to be an effective leadership coach, it is extremely important to have a sense of your own strengths, biases, weaknesses, and blind spots. Having this self-knowledge enables us to understand our clients and their issues more clearly, and makes us more effective. If coaches are not aware of their underlying baggage, it may be unpacked and transferred to the client. To use ourselves as an analytical instrument, to recognize transference and counter-transference reactions, we need an in-depth understanding of our inner motivations. There are many examples where a lack of self-awareness has a negative impact on coaching outcomes. The process of developing self-awareness should be ongoing. It is very hard to create this kind of self-awareness without having gone through a personal process of psychotherapy. Being a coach is a lifetime's work of continuous self-development and learning.

GET SUPERVISION

Supervision helps coaches to develop, and should be an ongoing process. Many very seasoned and experienced coaches have a supervisor. The form and format of supervision can vary from case presentations to videotape debriefs of sessions, to live observations and feedback (for example, in a group coaching situation). Naturally, permission from the client must be obtained before their case is discussed with another person.

Both individual and peer supervision can be extremely valuable experiences. After all, if we are asking our coaching clients to be observed and to ask for feedback, we ought to be modeling this behavior ourselves. Many well-known coaching certification programs (like INSEAD's Consulting and Coaching for Change Program) and professional associations (including the International Coach Federation, European Mentoring and Coaching Council) strongly encourage supervision on an ongoing basis.

AFTERWORD

I have sometimes heard colleagues in the leadership coaching business say that failure is good; it is the "fertilizer." Everything they have learned about coaching, they have learned from mistakes. And they may be right. After all, if you are not making mistakes, you are not doing anything. I made many mistakes in the David case, but it was also a great learning experience for me. The natural follow-up to this comment is, can David say the same thing?

I had a chance encounter with David three years later. He seemed very pleased to see me. He told me that it had taken him quite some time to get over the hurt of being fired. Fortunately, his severance package had given him time for reflection. After some hesitation–and here it helped that his wife was a psychologist–he had followed up on my suggestion to see a psychotherapist to help him to get more in touch with his feelings. He said that this experience had enriched his relationship with his wife and his children. It had also helped him clarify what he saw as his new challenge. He had realized that being a CEO of a public organization was not where he should be. I was very pleased to hear that he was now running a major nonprofit organization, a job that gave him a great deal of fulfillment.

NOTES

1. Freud, S. (1905). "Fragment of an analysis of a case of hysteria." In J. Strachey (Ed.), *The Standard Edition of the Complete Works of Sigmund Freud* (vol. 7). London: The Hogart Press and the Institute of Psychoanalysis.
2. Haley, J. (1976). *Problem-Solving Therapy: New Strategies for Effective Family Therapy*. San Francisco: Jossey-Bass; Watzlawyck, P., Beavin, J.H. and Jackson, D.D. (1967). *Pragmatics of Human Communication*. New York: Norton.
3. Kets de Vries, M.F.R. (2003). *Leaders, Fools and Impostors*. New York, iUniverse, Inc.
4. Bandura, A. (1994). "Self-efficacy." In V.S. Ramachaudran (Ed.), *Encyclopedia of Human Behavior* (vol. 4, pp. 71–81). New York: Academic Press.
5. Reik, T. (1948). *Listening with the Third Ear: The Inner Experience of a Psychoanalyst*. New York: Farrar, Straus and Company.

14

REFLECTIONS ON TEACHING LEADERS TO COACH: USING THE SELF AS A TOOL IN DEVELOPING OTHERS

ROGER LEHMAN AND KONSTANTIN KOROTOV

Leaders are now expected to be able to coach others, and their companies expect leadership development programs in-house or at business schools to include coaching skills. This chapter reflects on how coaching skills have been introduced into executive curricula, and the experience of the authors and INSEAD's Global Leadership Centre in teaching leaders to coach.

When talking about coaching skills within an executive education program, we often hear that companies want their executives to learn tools and techniques that will allow them to become effective coaches capable of unleashing the human talent and creative potential of their workforce. Progressive companies turn to business schools for help in developing their managers into coaches. At first sight, that might sound surprising as there is a nearly endless number of possible models, scripts, and tools for coaching available nowadays to the individual practitioner, HR executive, or corporate university. Bookstores are full of books offering all kinds of templates and methods for structuring a coaching conversation and building coaching relationships, including ready-made, one-size-fits-all checklists, templates of psychological contracts, and questions and statements that, allegedly, one can follow to become an effective coach. There is even *Coaching and Mentoring for Dummies!*[1] Training providers help people memorize the models and sequences of questions through mnemonics, exercises, and role-plays. While some of the models, for example GROW,[2] may make intuitive sense or become widely used, others seem to be more questionable in terms of their universal applicability. Even if they may work for some coaches, coaching clients, and coaching situations, such models may not be helpful under other circumstances.

Experienced learning and development professionals often tell us that they frequently have to turn to a business school after having tried many other ways of teaching their executives how to coach. Apparently, teaching tools like those mentioned above–something that companies have done *en masse*–does not do the trick: managers are not necessarily better coaches after they have attended a training program merely on coaching instruments. Moreover, the tools do not always work in practice, although they make perfect sense in a coaching book, training proposal, or even in the training classroom. Becoming a coach, evidently, takes more than mastering the tools, so turning to a business school, a research and teaching institution, makes sense.

When we introduce the topic of coaching to executives participating in our leadership development programs, we usually have to moderate their urge to jump straight to techniques, tools, or specific scripts for coaching others. We have to be very firm in asserting that learning coaching should not start with techniques, and that we do not distribute handouts with coaching templates, at least not at the beginning of the program. In fact, we announce at the start of our courses that mastering a specific coaching tool or set of techniques is secondary to the more fundamental task of teaching a would-be coach or would-be leader to use coaching styles in his or her work. Teaching specific techniques is not the value-added activity of a business school.

Our experience in leadership development, training of coaches, and consulting to companies and individual leaders shows that developing as a coach or as a leader actively using a coaching style starts with learning to use *oneself* as an instrument, a tool for helping others to be more effective and successful in what they do in work and life. We also claim that using oneself as a tool in coaching situations is a competency that leaders should master if they are to have a constructive impact on their followers. Eventually, the process of developing oneself as a coach will pay off as one becomes more effective in almost any professional role. The benefits even go beyond the professional role, because, as we strongly believe, all managerial jobs and personal situations benefit when we use a coaching mode to interact with others.

Despite a plethora of coaching definitions[3] and growing divergence in how coaching and its role in executive development are viewed, there are some commonalities that can be found across various schools and approaches to coaching. Coaching is fundamentally a way to help people develop, become more successful, and contribute more to the success of organizations or society. It is an activity that is highly personal in the way it impacts the coaching client, and it takes into account the individual needs and idiosyncrasies of the people involved in the process. Coaching inevitably involves interaction between individuals, and this interaction implicates dynamic relationships between the parties involved, the organization concerned, and many other stakeholders: both those objectively involved in the work or life of individuals, and those who exercise an influence on people through past relationships and fantasies. The coach or leader acting as a coach inevitably becomes part of the process, with his or her own idiosyncrasies and experiences brought into the coaching situation. It is this personal impact of the coach on the coaching client and the situation that creates a need for a certain level of "chemistry" to exist between the parties involved in a coaching situation.

Given that coaching provides a way of helping people grow and be more successful, we use the clinical approach already discussed in this book to help executives develop into an effective instrument of personal and organizational change. Using the clinical orientation in our work means that we try to help executives understand how the conscious and unconscious act together to make us who we are, and how this determines the way we behave in various situations. This applies to both the client and the coach. We seek to understand and help others understand their own strengths and weaknesses, and their impact on human behavior. In applying the clinical approach, we draw on concepts from the psychodynamic tradition, systems theory, cognitive-behavioral therapy, and other disciplines that are helpful in understanding how to make an executive a well-functioning and successful individual.

The psychodynamic tradition, an important pillar of the clinical approach and one of the foundations of our way of developing coaching skills, suggests that if you want to grow personally and develop yourself, you have to be attuned to your inner theater, a concept that has also been discussed earlier in this book. Without becoming a psychodynamic theorist or practitioner, a coach (or any person working with and through other individuals for that matter) needs to be familiar both theoretically and experientially with a number of the psychodynamic concepts. These concepts are essential for understanding oneself, and critical for a coach who needs to help their client understand some of his or her feelings and behaviors, while (a dimension that is very significant) constantly keeping a close eye on their own functioning in a coaching situation.

Recent literature on coaching indicates that the psychodynamic tradition offers useful opportunities for coaching interventions aimed at developing interpersonal or political skills (for example, understanding the behavior of board members, developing effective relationships with others, and so on), fostering a deeper understanding of self and one's wishes and desires (for example, crystallizing needs for further development or reconsidering career choices), overcoming self-defeating behavioral patterns (for example, giving up controlling or passive-aggressive tendencies), and learning to deal with difficult colleagues or employees.[4]

In teaching executives to coach, we also borrow from other traditions that deal with understanding self and others better. The approaches based on systems thinking and related concepts that have grown out of the family therapy perspective enable the coach and coaching client to take a closer look at the context in which a person operates. The behavior of individuals, when observed through the lens of the systems paradigm, is understood as a function of the surrounding environment and its demands, and the interaction between the individual and the system of which he or she is a part. Coaching literature suggests that systems thinking can be particularly powerful in helping coaching clients to understand context within their environment (see also Chapter Three). This perspective can help clients modify their approach to what they encounter in their organizations, and understand and address possible sources of resistance to change. The systems approach facilitates a simultaneous impact on both the coaching client and his or her organization.[5]

The cognitive-behavioral approach, another tradition we draw from, comes in handy in coaching situations because it helps executives learn to notice their thoughts and, if necessary, change their thinking patterns. Using the cognitive-behavioral approach, coaches can help the people they work with deal with ineffective behavioral patterns through analyzing and modifying their underlying thoughts. The approach assumes that, when a person using the help of a coach changes their thinking, they will also begin to change both their behavior and feelings related to these thoughts.[6]

Working with others through self–and that is essentially what coaches do–requires awareness of a number of concepts that may be quite new to an executive coming to a business school for a leadership program. Introducing these new concepts may require a certain degree of psychological preparedness on the part of the participants, or, as a minimum, curiosity and openness to new experiences and new paradigms. The context of a leadership program, which by definition demands looking at oneself, has been shown to be a relatively safe environment psychologically in which executives can start to get attuned to their inner world.[7]

Very early on, we describe to our participants specific situations where understanding the new concepts may be critical to their functioning in a coaching role, and relevant to their overall effectiveness as business executives and human beings. In Chapter One, we introduced some of the core concepts from the psychodynamic tradition, such as transference and counter-transference, psychological defense mechanisms, boundaries and working on the boundaries, and identification and projective identification. The following example from the practice of one of the authors illustrates how such an understanding can be critical in not only running coaching assignments successfully, but being effective in daily interactions with others.

MAKING SENSE OF THE SITUATION USING A PSYCHODYNAMIC APPROACH: A COACH'S STORY

I was coaching a senior executive in a large European company. I had known him for quite some time, because I had worked with him in his previous job, and he had asked me to continue to coach him in his new position. He had just been appointed as CEO of a company. At our third meeting, he began to talk to me about some issues he was confronting in his new role. I began to have questions in my mind about why I was meeting with him, whether I could really help him, and whether I had perhaps oversold myself. In other words, I started to have questions about my own competence. This slowly developed into what can basically be described as a panic attack. This was in the middle of our meeting and the situation is still very clear in my mind: I was sitting in a large office with a big boardroom table; he was at the end of the table with me at the side, so we were sitting close together. Because of my previous work with him we had a good relationship and knew each other professionally quite well.

While he was talking and, as I found, I was pretending to listen, I was absolutely flooded with a feeling of not understanding a thing he was saying, and a feeling of complete incompetence. The feeling grew until it reached a pitch where I no longer knew why I was there, or what the point of my being there was. I felt that I brought no value, that I was an impostor, more like a charlatan rather than a competent coach. I had the thought that if this guy found out how little I really understood about what he was talking about, I would be fired immediately. It was an overwhelming feeling: I even developed a plan of escape based on my saying that I needed to go to the bathroom and running away. I would leave my briefcase and everything behind. I was actually trying to figure out how to get my car keys and my wallet out of the briefcase so I could escape. And the fantasy went as far as imagining that if I left, I would never call him again, never send him any invoices for what I had done, and that I would just write it off as a bad experience. The fantasy was so intense that it was extremely difficult to contain it. In fact, I could hardly pretend to be focusing on him and his words because of my preoccupation with my escape.

At some point the psychodynamic perspective kicked in and I started to think, "Wait a minute, I don't normally feel like this, in fact, I've never felt like this in my life. What does this say about what's happening either with me, with this guy, or with the situation?" I can't say whether this internal dialog went on for three seconds, five minutes, or half an hour. I have no idea. I finally got to the point where I had enough integration, enough perspective, and enough understanding to be able to externalize it, to think, "Maybe it's not me, may be it's the situation." After I regained my composure, I was able to offer my hypothesis to my client. I very cautiously said to my client, "As I listen to you at times, I wonder if you don't feel like an impostor? Or that you are not sure why you are here?"

My client leaned forward, and he looked at me, and said, "That's amazing ... Let me tell you how I feel; let me show you something." He took out two business cards. One was his, and the other was from the CEO he was replacing. He was supposed to be working with the previous CEO during a six-month transition period. The previous CEO's card still said "CEO," but my client's card didn't, even though now he had the title and was doing the job. After about ten minutes he said, "Wait a minute. We are on something that is too important." We were probably 45 minutes or so into what was planned as a maximum two-hour session, and he asked, "What's your afternoon like?" I told him that I was available. He called his assistant and cancelled all his other appointments. Although I don't normally do this, we spent four and a half hours in that coaching session, exploring his feelings of being an impostor, which were reinforced by the system, and his feelings that he might not be up to the job, which probably led to his agreeing not to have the title "CEO" on his card and accepting a six-month "transition period."

Discussing stories like this in the executive classroom shows participants the value of going below the surface and looking at their own feelings and behavior. The paralyzing thoughts the coach had about being an impostor developed while the client was talking to him, with the client's conversation and the coach's internal thoughts operating in parallel. One of the critical learning points for the participants provided by this story is that developing an observing ego is an essential element for being successful in coaching. This story helps bring home to participants how important the clinical approach and an understanding of psychodynamic concepts are in coaching situations. We then discuss (without attempting to turn people into psychodynamic theorists or practitioners) how psychodynamics help them fine-tune their own observing ego and develop a capacity to be in the moment, in the situation with their client, and also to observe what is happening in a detached way–the essential qualities of a coach.

This story is a very good example of using an observing ego in coaching practice, as the participants hear that the client did not know what was going on inside the coach during the meeting. We tell the participants that the coach later followed up with the executive and found out that the latter had had no idea about the internal turmoil in his coach. This raises the opportunity for further discussion of issues such as containing one's own feelings and emotions, another critical concept where coaches can learn a lot from the psychodynamic tradition. When this level of discussion is reached, the participants start to understand why the self is the primary instrument in coaching interventions, and therefore simply applying off-the-shelf coaching tools does not make much sense.

The clinical perspective and the psychodynamic tradition give us a way of understanding what is going on, particularly things beneath the surface that can be explored by the individual and the coach. This lens provides the opportunity for both coach and client to bring to the surface and discuss the otherwise unexploited and hidden issues. Executives learning coaching in our programs come to understand that, at the very least, someone using coaching methods has to be able to ask "Why am I feeling this way? Does it say something about me?" This is where the coach's own self-awareness comes into play. In the situation described above, the difficulty encountered by the coach might have had nothing to do with the client, but rather with the coach himself. Hypothetically, the coach might have "oversold" himself, might in some ways have manipulated his own insecurities, or even his own fears that he was a fake (the "impostor syndrome").[8] Participants come to realize that the only way to challenge such a hypothesis is to know about psychodynamic processes, have experience of looking inside one's own self, and to have developed a certain degree of self-awareness and self-understanding.

We strongly believe that a heavy dose of learning about self, deepening one's understanding of self, should be part and parcel of developing as a coach or as a coaching executive. Business schools and other executive education providers now make self-awareness an increasingly important piece of leadership development interventions and coaching skills programs. Increased self-awareness can be partly achieved by building small group coaching or individual coaching interventions into the programs. Such interventions have to be reinforced through in-class discussions of coaching competencies and one's own experience of being coached. We also build self-reflection sessions in most of our leadership or coaching courses. The goal of the self-reflection exercises is to have people to stop and "get off the dance floor and onto the balcony."[9] By this, we do not mean some kind of an intellectual perspective, but more a position from which to look into the inner workings of one's mind and emotions, one's inner theater.

Learning self-reflection and deepening self-knowledge can start with simply taking time to think about oneself and one's functioning as an executive. In fact, thinking about self in an executive role may be a relatively easy start for someone who wants to reflect on his or her life as a whole, not just at work. In our programs, we deliberately create time and space for people to go through some semi-structured thinking and reflection process, uninterrupted by external intrusions. For example, some of the basic questions we ask executives to reflect on during our programs include:

- When were you at your best as a leader?
- When were you at your worst as a leader?
- When in the last three months at work did you find yourself so involved, and so focused, and so engaged, that time seemed to be irrelevant?
- When did you get that sense of flow where you really enjoyed what you were doing? What was it?
- Conversely, when didn't you have it? When did you hate every moment of what you had to do? And what were those tasks?

Very often we hear that the program is the first time in many years that people have had a moment to think about themselves. Discussing strengths and weaknesses is usually an integral part of any type of coaching intervention. These questions are as ideal entries to thinking and talking about strengths and weaknesses in a slightly broader way than if a coaching client was just asked, "Tell me about your strengths." As we often discover in coaching situations, strengths do not necessarily mean things that coaching clients do well. They can also mean things that they like doing. Conversely, weaknesses do not necessarily mean things that someone cannot do; they can also be things that the person does not like doing. Using these questions to reflect, and subsequently discussing them with a coach, faculty member, or fellow participant, usually gives individuals further insights into their own functioning. It also helps them to understand how someone being coached might feel, and how the coaching executive could make it easier for the coaching client to start discussing his or her own situation.

There are various ways to help executives work on self-reflection. Paradoxically, our experience shows that improving one's listening skills is one of the most helpful aids to self-reflection.

The ability to actively listen to what others are trying to convey is another critical competence for coaches and leaders. By teaching managers to listen as coaches, we also help them develop the capacity to challenge *themselves* in terms of how they think, behave, and impact on others through feedback loops. We help executives ask themselves questions such as, "Why am I doing this? Why am I not doing that? What does it mean? What kind of an impact am I having on the other party in this discussion?"

INCREASING SELF-UNDERSTANDING THROUGH LEARNING TO LISTEN TO OTHERS

One example of how self-reflection can be taught while simultaneously developing listening skills is our modified version of a listening exercise recommended for coaching training.[10] In this exercise, we first remind participants about listening and listening skills. We particularly want them to be aware of the "deep listening," that is, attuning not just to the words and nonverbal communication of the speaker but to the kind of reaction that they are having to the speaker, their counter-transference feelings, as well as their own thoughts and fantasies that they having during the exchange (this kind of listening was explained in depth in Chapter Twelve). We then pair people up and tell them that each of them has ten minutes to explore an issue, with their fellow participant acting as a coach. Participants have to think about a problem or an issue that is bothering them. The issue can be related to their work or private life, and we explain that it has to be something that they would like to understand, something that they don't seem to be able to get their head around.

We instruct the participants to take turns listening to each other. We tell them that the task of the listener is only to ask questions that take the speaker further or deeper into his or her understanding of the issue, or to open up ways for other perspectives. Listeners are forbidden to make any recommendations or suggestions, and they are even forbidden to guide by asking leading questions, as much as humanly possible. The listener's only goal is to listen and to ask questions that make the speaker more effective in dealing with his or her issue.

The amazing thing after this exercise is that most people are really surprised by how much they have learned in such a short amount of time. Both the speakers and the listeners claim that they have learned not only about the issues faced by them and other executives, but also about their own feelings and thoughts.

The learning for the speaker in this exercise comes from being listened to differently. A participant in an executive MBA class once said, "I really don't want to do this exercise. The issue that I have identified is the thing that I have talked about to almost everybody I know, and I am not getting anywhere with this. I'll do the exercise, but it's a waste of time." The response from the professor was, "Look, I can't promise it will help, but try it." The participant came back after the exercise totally blown away. He said, "This is amazing, because I have talked to so many people about this before. And here, in just ten minutes, because this exercise partner of mine gave me no advice or suggestions, I have understood the issue, where I had been unable to get my head around it by talking to scores of other people over the last week."

The vast majority of executives are astonished when they experience what it is like to have somebody who listens and asks questions that get *them* to think, that force *them* to change the way *they* look at things that offer new lenses for examining the issue at hand. The participants' next revelation is that actually they often *do have* the answer or a way to deal with the issue at hand, either in their mind or in their preconscious. Last but not least, they are amazed at how much one can achieve in just ten minutes.

The learning for the listener is often about themselves, and their own feelings, emotions, and behaviors that arise during the conversation. First, people in the listening role are surprised at how hard it is to listen to others. Most of the executives struggle with their urge immediately to make recommendations or suggest solutions. They find it extremely difficult to ask the type of questions that take the person further into his or her understanding of the issue at hand. They also learn how long ten minutes feels for a listener. Many participants report that they found it very difficult to hold to the rule of not giving suggestions for a full ten minutes. One executive reported how unbelievably long ten minutes seemed when he was forced into the role of "just listening."

While learning to listen, we want people to become aware not only of what they are thinking as their partner is telling their story, but also of what they are feeling, and how they are reacting, to bring the observing ego into the picture. We enhance the exercise in a second round by putting participants in coaching triangles, where, in addition to the speaker and listener, we add an observer. The role of the observer is to monitor what both parties are doing and saying, to notice the body language of the coach and coaching client, and to think about what they might be feeling. The observer notices and later reports to the partners whether they seemed to be bored, angry, anxious, excited, or frustrated during the conversation. The idea is to help executives begin to attune to how they are feeling, and how what they are feeling may be related to what is going on in the discussion. This makes the exercise an excellent opportunity to work on empathy, another coaching quality. Because the participants swap roles, they find themselves in several different positions, each requiring different ways of observing oneself or being able to put oneself in someone else's shoes.

We always add the caveat "maybe" to whatever is reported by speakers, coaches, and observers. The reason is that what is reported may not be the reality. We always remind participants that what they notice may be something linked to what is going on inside the observer, rather than what is going on outside. Teaching people to apply the "maybe" helps them avoid jumping to conclusions and passing judgments, another critical element in developing coaching abilities. It also helps them develop a hypothesis-testing approach that they can use later in coaching interventions.

By running the listening exercise this way, we not only teach executives to become better listeners, but we also create an opportunity for managers and leaders to stop for a moment and say, "Interesting that I am feeling that way. What might this say about me, the other person involved, or the situation?" For a short period of time, we create a reflective space that we hope the participants will internalize and take into their leadership and coaching practices.

When developing powers of reflection, or enhancing one's leadership competence with coaching skills, it is important to appreciate that coaching does not always mean an hour-long session, or a series of sessions. Coaching results can be achieved in five minutes, but those five minutes have to be focused, attuned, and reflective. The exercises described here allow participants to experience first hand the significant impact that they, in a coaching role, can have on other people. This is another moment of revelation for the participants, particularly those who were adamant that they wanted to be given coaching instruments as early as possible. These exercises help participants to recognize that it is not the particular set of tools or script of questions that makes a difference, but rather the coach's involvement and ability to attune to what is happening inside the other person, and themselves. Learning a script, a model, or a tool that suits one's coaching style then becomes significantly easier.

Teaching executives to coach by starting with the use of self as an instrument requires creativity and courage. Our search for new teaching methods has been prompted by our research, consulting, and coaching experience. We often see people in different types of organizations who claim that they want to (and can) be a coach to others in their organization, but coaching clients, psychologically or physically, run away from them. We also see people who are asked or "strongly encouraged" to become coaches to other employees, but are scared to death by the prospect of dealing with other people at a rather personal level, or helping them be more successful. Both categories are usually familiar with the techniques and approaches popularized through training courses and airport business books, but which are hardly useful in reality for coaching. Worse still, people are sometimes forced into claiming to be a coach to match their organization's competencies model; they simply dress their usual style or behavior in coaching terminology.

An example of the latter occurred during our consulting and teaching activity with a global organization that is actively working on integrating coaching into their *modus operandi*. This organization has a large pool of trained senior coaches positioned globally. All of them are expected to be coaches to other people in the organization when the new coaching way of working becomes the norm. When we asked them to tell us what they do as coaches, their typical response could be summarized as: "It's very clear. People come to us with questions about what to do and we give them answers." These people deal with the very major issue of substantial change in the way people work (and even think) at the surface, without really going into the ideas, hopes, anxieties, expectations, emotions, and other factors that influence people's behavior when it comes to working in a new, and often revolutionary, way.

Providing expert advice can hardly be called coaching. When those senior coaches manage to move just a little bit in the direction of awareness and appreciation of what is going on below the surface, they suddenly have a new perspective on why certain initiatives work and others fall flat, regardless of their content and analytical merit. Obviously, both the psychodynamic and the systems approaches give these senior coaches a chance to look beyond individual resistance to change and begin to understand what may deserve looking at within the organization's culture or processes.

As these senior coaches have to facilitate change in the way the company operates, and change naturally causes discomfort and resistance, it is critical for them, as for anybody in a coaching or leadership job, to understand psychological defenses and defense mechanisms. We discuss with them the role of defenses in helping people process their internal experiences in a way that allows them to understand and tolerate these experiences emotionally, manage the anxieties, make sense of their life, and express meaning of life. We reiterate that defenses help human beings to function in a world that is not always psychologically benign. However, they may become a real roadblock on the way to change and transformation.

In teaching managers about defenses, we try to help them become attuned to their own defense mechanisms and avoid the trap of shifting into unconstructive behavior. If the coach or leader is aware of those signals in themselves, along with some of the common signals in verbal or nonverbal expressions that indicate defensiveness in others, they will be able to respond in a constructive way, before it is too late and the other person has become blocked in their defensive behavioral pattern. In this regard we are fond of telling our participants that the "golden rule" with regard to defensiveness is "strike when the iron is cold." A frontal attack on defensiveness only results in increased defensive behavior and, ultimately, a breakdown in communication.

We spend time looking into how people recognize when they are becoming defensive. From that, we can move to what we can learn about the other person and their defensive reactions. A discussion about defenses involves program participants sharing examples of defensive behavior that they have observed. We succeed if participants also learn to recognize their own defensive behavior, and then can act on that recognition. Teaching about defensive behavior involves using some rather challenging teaching methodologies. We use cases – but these are not traditional case studies about something happening to someone, somewhere: they are real life cases of people present in the auditorium. By getting into the hot seat and being a protagonist in their own case, participants gain first-hand experience of being given a chance to explore the issues they face at work or, sometimes, beyond work.

Another method that helps executives learn about coaching is 360-degree feedback (described in Chapter Five). We couple this feedback with group coaching sessions where participants learn to benefit not just from a coach or discussion facilitator, but also from the inputs of a collective coaching mind and heart made up of fellow participants. By involving participants in group coaching[11] and, in longer programs, inter-modular telephone conference calls to discuss how participants are progressing in the particular situations they have presented to the group, we try to create a kind of para-supervision coaching environment. In this environment, participants learn more about exploring their own feedback results; work challenges; and associated thinking, feelings, and behaviors with the help of others. To continue the process, we encourage participants to cherish and develop the relationships that they establish in the program for future para-supervision or peer-coaching opportunities.[12]

Developing the relationships starts when they begin to learn that coaching skills in a group of their peers is, in our opinion, a critical challenge faced by executives wishing to learn and use coaching in their work, HR and learning and development practitioners, and providers of executive education. The intensive work that people do while learning to use self as a critical coaching instrument often leads to a change in views on self, others, one's organization, and one's leadership role. In order to make this work in terms of a profound positive impact on the organization or coaching clients, the change needs to be internalized.

In psychological literature, internalization is seen as a way of turning psychological change into an enduring and functioning part of human personality, and results in greater flexibility in dealing with new internal states or interpersonal situations.[13] In change-oriented literature, internalization has been conceptualized to occur when people accept influence from a change in situation, environment, or people, because the content of this change, and the ideas and actions behind it, are seen as intrinsically rewarding, congruent with one's value system, and useful to meeting one's needs.[14]

One of the ways to achieve internalization is to allow participants to stage several experiments in using new coaching and leadership behavior approaches, and then evaluating the results, with the help of para-supervision created within the executive program. This is possible if the leadership or coaching program is not a one-off event but a series of modules spread over time. A multi-modular program gives participants the chance to see what works and what does not, and to get support in their experimentation from program faculty, fellow participants and, it is hoped, their own organizations.

It is not easy for modern executives to become effective coaches. Each coaching interaction brings with it multiple possibilities for inter- and intrapersonal dynamics, so the coaching executive has to be prepared to act again and again as a sort of psychological detective (something that this book argues for in many chapters), investigating their own reactions to what the coaching client is dealing with. When this work is done, when the self is engaged and open to work with the coaching client, any of the available coaching instruments can be used to supplement the use of self as the primary coaching tool.

NOTES

1. Brounstein, M. (2000). *Coaching and Mentoring for Dummies*. New York: Wiley.
2. Landsberg, M. (1997). *The Tao of Coaching*. London: Harper Collins Business; Whitmore, J. (2002). *Coaching for Performance*, 3rd Ed. London: Nicholas Brealey.

3. For example, Valerio, A.-M., and Lee, R. (2005). *Executive Coaching: A Guide for the HR Professional*. San Francisco, CA: Pfeiffer; McAdam, S. (2005). *Executive Coaching: How to Choose, Use, and Maximize Value for Yourself and Your Team*. London: Thorogood Publishing Ltd.; Peltier, B. (2001). *The Psychology of Executive Coaching*. New York: Brunner-Routledge; Landsberg, M. (1997); Kilburg, R. (2002). *Executive Coaching: Developing Managerial Wisdom in a World of Chaos*. Washington, DC: American Psychological Association.
4. Peltier, B. (2001).
5. Ibid.
6. Ibid.
7. Kets de Vries, M., and Korotov, K. (2006). "Creating Identity Laboratories to Enable Executive Change and Transformation." INSEAD Working Paper 2006/36/EFE.
8. Kets de Vries, M. (2005a). "The Dangers of Feeling like a Fake," *Harvard Business Review*, September, pp. 108–120.
9. Heifetz, R.A. (1998). *Leadership without Easy Answers*. Cambridge, MA: Harvard University Press.
10. Starr, J. (2002). *The Coaching Manual: The Definitive Guide to the Processes, Principles, and Skills of Executive Coaching*. New York: Prentice Hall.
11. Kets de Vries, M. (2005)."Leadership Group Coaching in Action: The Zen of Creating High Performance Teams," *Academy of Management Executive*, 19 (1): 61–76.
12. Korotov, K. (2006). "Peer Coaching in Executive Education Programs." *ESMT Technical Note 2006-09*.
13. Rutan, S., and Stone, W. (2001). *Psychodynamic Group Pscyhotherapy*. New York and London: The Guilford Press.
14. Kelman, H. (1958). "Compliance, Identification, and Internalization: Three Processes of Attitude Change." *The Journal of Conflict Resolution*, 2 (1): 51–60; Bunker, B., and DeLisle, J. (1991). "Individual Change in Organizational Settings." In: Curtis, R., and Stricker, R. (Eds.) *How People Change: Inside and Outside Therapy*. New York and London: Plenum Press, pp. 129–155.

PART FIVE: COACHING IN ORGANIZATIONS

15

COACHING: A CHAIRMAN'S POINT OF VIEW

STANISLAV SHEKSHNIA

INTRODUCTION

When I was offered the position of nonexecutive chairman of the board of Siberian Coal and Energy (SUEK)–the largest Russian coal and power generation company (and the eighth largest coal producer in the world), with mining facilities in seven regions from the Russian Far East to Krasnoyarsk, 45,000 employees, and exports to 20 countries–I felt I had plenty of relevant experience to draw on. In the past I had been a CEO, and executive chairman, and had sat on the boards of a number of joint ventures and public companies as the representative of the investors. The task of leading a newly created board with a majority of independent nonexecutive directors at a privately owned corporation that had the ambition to become a world-class energy company seemed challenging, but manageable.

It took two months and two board meetings for me to realize that my previous experience bore little resemblance to what I was trying to do. Even though some of the activities seemed, on the surface, to be the same as previous assignments, the fundamentals were quite different–I was not the ultimate decision maker. Looking for similar experiences, I made a surprising discovery–the job of nonexecutive chairman resembled that of an executive coach, especially the type of group coaching format developed by the INSEAD Global Leadership Centre (IGLC). After realizing this similarity, I consciously and consistently applied the coaching philosophy and IGLC's specific tools to my work at SUEK. Taking this approach not only helped me personally, but I also believe it helped build an effective and efficient board, an effort now recognized by the company's major shareholders, management,

275

the board itself, and international rating agency Standard and Poor's. This chapter describes my experience of applying coaching methodology to managing a board of directors, and some of the lessons learned which I believe to be more widely applicable than to just one person and one company case.

CHALLENGES OF A NONEXECUTIVE CHAIRMAN

To give an idea what I was up against, I need to present some background about SUEK. The company was created by two young Russian entrepreneurs through a series of acquisitions and swaps of coal-producing and power-generating assets, and when I joined in 2004, it was three years old. Tightly controlled by its founders, it went through an initial restructuring phase, but still looked like a rough amalgamation of different companies rather than one unified enterprise. There were over 150 legal entities within SUEK at that time. The shareholders wanted to make the company a world-class operation and believed that the best way to go about this would be to introduce modern corporate governance, including having an independent board of directors. I was appointed nonexecutive chairman, and in November 2004, chaired a first "nonofficial" meeting of the board, followed by 24 official meetings since then.

It did not take long to realize how challenging the whole board idea was–to have a very diverse group of people, meeting only once a month to make collective decisions that would have a direct impact on thousands of people, apart from putting billions of dollars' worth of assets in play. Our first two meetings were not very productive, to put it mildly. We spent over eight hours in the room each time, but could not reach a decision on any of the important items, which were consequently pushed forward to the next meeting. The situation was quite frustrating. I tried most of the intervention techniques I had learned in previous board meetings, such as defining (and repeating) the rules of discussion at the very beginning and monitoring them, allocating more time to important items on the agenda, limiting management presentations to five slides, and so on.

By the end of the second board meeting, it was clear that most of our challenges were of a psychological nature. Of course, like every other board chairman I faced traditional issues such as uneven preparation by the directors, the balance between management presentations and discussions, and the quality and timing of the topics. These issues turned out to be of secondary importance and easy to manage when the fundamental psychological issues were dealt with.

DIFFERENT WORLDVIEWS AND MODELS OF SUCCESS

The first SUEK board consisted of ten members. Among them were the two founders of the company, who were not yet 35 years old, but had built and owned three other multibillion businesses along with SUEK; an ex-CEO of the first publicly traded Russian power generation company (a Siberian gentleman in his early seventies); a leading Russian academic authority on coal (a fit Muscovite in his early sixties); a Russian female banker from an international investment bank (a charming lady with a Chicago MBA and 14 years of career experience); the CFO of a publicly traded Russian company; an ex-European Bank for Reconstruction and Development (EBRD) officer; SUEK's CEO (a former successful banker in his early thirties); his first deputy (a career mining engineer in his fifties); and the chairman. That great diversity of people was potentially the greatest strength of the board, but at the beginning it was a major challenge.

Not only did the majority of the directors have little previous board experience, and therefore very different ideas about what they were expected to do, but they were all very successful professionals in their respective fields. As it is often the case with successful people, they felt they had discovered a magic formula for success that worked everywhere, all the time. For example, one of the directors believed strongly that the best way to get results was to stretch people, which made it very difficult for him to accept a standard budgeting approach. Another board member was a strong proponent of management by committee, and pushed this idea forcefully whenever the opportunity came up. As is also common with successful people, many of the directors tended to ignore information that contradicted their preconceptions and actively sought data that supported their ideas. Thus at the beginning, I often observed a dialog of the deaf.

The challenge was to break through the armor of the initial success syndrome and to create an atmosphere where others could be heard. To do that, I had to deal with another important factor—the presence of narcissistic personalities.

A QUESTION OF NARCISSISM

Not surprisingly, many of the directors considered being on the board as a confirmation of their success and a boost to their self-esteem. I was surprised, however, at the degree to which these professional and mature people let their narcissistic disposi-tions drive their behavior at the meetings. One of the directors could not let even the most insignificant item be closed with-out saying something. Another always waited for an important discussion to come to an end before making his last remark. I watched classic psychological defensive mechanisms float-ing in the boardroom, such as interrupting an opponent to state one's position a second or even a third time, nonverbal irritation, and even traditional Russian yelling. To make the board more productive, this pattern of behavior had to change. I needed to create a new, safe space where people felt comfort-able and their sense of self-esteem was not under threat.

Fear and withdrawal

The abrasive, narcissistic behavior from some of the directors created another negative phenomenon—other directors became afraid to express their own points of view. At the second board meeting I noticed that some members preferred to withdraw and became passive spectators, which, of course, did not help the process. I had to bring them back mentally by reducing their level of anxiety.

Meaning

The twin challenges of narcissism from some and withdrawal by others became very clear after the second meeting was over, when two directors approached me with the same

278

questions: "What are these meetings for? To please the owners? To fulfill stock exchange requirements for future listing?" After the initial excitement at being selected to the board had faded, and having discovered that being a director involved real work, these successful and busy people started to search for meaning to justify their efforts. Even though the directors were paid quite well, for most of them the money they received was marginal to their income from other sources. We had to find a purpose beyond money and personal prestige to get them excited.

Confrontation with management

Although two key executives were members of the board, from the first meeting onwards they formed a group within the group. The two were always aligned in their position and supported each other. This strategy and the other directors' search for their own identity within the company created a tangible antagonism between executive and nonexecutive board members, which sometimes led to arguments for the sake of arguing and criticism for the sake of criticizing. The confrontations deepened as time went on and the board risked becoming dysfunctional.

These profound psychological challenges had a direct impact on my duties as chairman, such as setting the agenda for meetings, ensuring directors' preparation, managing the discussions and decision making, and supervising the follow-up. In fact, to a large extent they defined the content of my job.

CHIEF FACILITATOR

When accepting SUEK's offer, I had a pretty good picture of what the chairman's job comprised and how I could contribute to the development of the company. The chairman shares with other board members the roles of "owner" (treating the company as if it were his or her property; building an organization that will prosper in the long term, beyond his or her tenure; selecting executives; allocating resources; and so on) and "strategist" (interpreting the world and company environment, anticipating and initiating changes, understanding value creation process, defining business strategy, and so on). But the chairman also plays the roles of "mentor" (providing feedback to the CEO and key executives, facilitating their development, and sharing social capital, for example) and "facilitator" (creating a productive working environment for the group, leading discussions, encouraging contributions of individual members, controlling agendas and time). Taking into account SUEK's desire to become an effective and efficient enterprise and my previous business experience, I felt that my major contribution would come from strategic and organizational insights, along with first-hand knowledge of managing organizational transformations and developing senior executives.

The real picture revealed different priorities. To make the board functional, I needed to assume the role of chief facilitator and devote the lion's share of my time to that role, sacrificing the other roles to a certain extent. I defined my principle goal as creating a working environment in which every director could contribute productively to a collective effort that would be more than the sum of its parts. To achieve this goal, I had to deal with psychological and somewhat irrational issues, and consequently my experience as a CEO and chairman was of much less relevance than my three years' work as executive coach at IGLC and with private clients. I had to look into my coaching toolbox to find solutions to the board problems.

Over the next 18 months I used various coaching instruments to performing the chairman's job, including various types of feedback exercises, active listening, 360-degree assessment tools, and personal development plans. However, it was primarily the coaching philosophy, emphasizing the coaching client's central and the coach's supporting roles, holding ongoing conversations about important issues, focusing on gradual improvement with a limited number of priorities, building personal trust, and creating transitional space that helped me to play the role of chief facilitator productively. Below are some of the major milestones passed as the new SUEK board became an effective and efficient governing body.

Building trust

Having worked with highly successful entrepreneurs and senior executives as a coach and consultant, I knew that I could only have an impact if we could establish what I call a "working alliance"–a relationship in which the other party had confidence in me regarding whatever issue we were working on, whether it was governance reform in the company or the development of that person's mentoring skills. Working alliance is narrower than trust *per se*, since it is limited to a particular area, but it takes less time and fewer ingredients to build. In general, a trustful relationship emerges when the other side becomes perceived as nonthreatening to the executive's social and professional status, when the other person is perceived as being knowledgeable about the area and genuinely interested in positive outcomes from the relationship.

After the first board meeting, I went to see all the directors and asked each of them the same set of questions: "How did I do as a chairman? What did I do well? What did I do poorly? How could I improve?" Most were surprised to see the chairman seeking feedback, but all responded positively and in turn asked about their own performance. Very important conversations were begun and gradually extended to other significant issues, such as, "What is the mission of the board? How do we relate to management and shareholders? What does it take to be a good director? How do we develop the necessary skills?" Immediately I had nine individual conversations going, each of them different, although covering similar issues.

At the next meeting I followed the same blueprint: I asked for feedback, listened and probed, provided encouraging, but specific, feedback to each of the members, then moved on to talking about myself, my motivation and expectations, and then closed by discussing my vision for the board. I spent a good deal of time explaining myself, convincing them that there was no hidden agenda, that I did not take instructions from the founders, but respected their points of view as I respected the views of other directors; that my sole ambition was to make the board and the new system of corporate governance work and take the company to new heights; and that I saw a two-year time limit to fulfilling this task. This kind of openness melted some ice and some (although not all) directors responded with very frank talk about themselves.

Consecutive conversations took different formats, reflecting the individual characteristics of each director, their working styles, their "success formula," and their fears and concerns. I spent a lot of time listening to one of the founders, who needed to think aloud and tried to be very factual and precise in dialogs with his partner. With some directors, my meetings sometimes turned into tutoring sessions on best practices in corporate governance from my side, and on coal production methods or power generation technologies from theirs. Whatever the format and specific issues discussed, we always touched upon the fundamentals: the board's mission, how it could be made to work, and what each director's, contribution should be.

After three months of intensive conversations (3 to 6 one-on-one meetings with each of the directors), I achieved some tangible results. First and foremost, I managed to build a working alliance with almost all the directors. I became perceived as a non-threatening figure with relevant knowledge and good intentions, which gave me huge leverage in conducting board meetings and undertaking some other steps, which I will describe later.

Second, I developed some understanding of my colleagues, of how they operated and related to the outside world–each one's "success formula." I also obtained some insight into their inner theaters, their unconscious motivation, how they perceived me, and what they expected from the chairman. This knowledge allowed me to adjust my style of running board meetings in very specific ways, such as providing a short summary of each position after a discussion finished and before the decision was made, and removing a corporate secretary from the seat on my left (perceived as a threat to their status by some directors). I also knew how to deal with each director–who needed encouragement, who should be stopped, and who needed to be asked clarifying questions in order to make their point. The discussions became more focused. The members of the board clearly appreciated this change in working and gave credit to the chairman. It reinforced the working alliance and enhanced my ability to manage the personal egos of the directors when they threatened the productivity of the board.

Having established an initial relationship with individual board members, I started to expand to larger groups. In addition to committee meetings, I organized a number of informal gatherings with three or four directors. Although each time we had a theme, the discussions always extended into other areas, encompassing the issues of company vision, the board's identity and mission, operating principles, etc. The meetings gradually transitioned the initial chairman-director working alliances into larger groups and helped the boardroom process. These discussions were also instrumental in defining and applying behavior norms, which later became part of the board culture, such as respect for another person's opinion, frankness, critique of views rather than the people who express them, and informality. Such norms are easier to establish and reinforce in a small group/loose agenda format than in the more formal board setting.

Finally, individual sessions with directors prepared them for a very important element in my board-building program – the assessment of the board and its members. Receiving and giving feedback and acting on it is rarely a part of board culture, even in developed economies. In Russia, with corporate governance still in its infancy and an old tradition of indirect talk, such a process is virtually unknown. My requests for feedback after each meeting accustomed the directors to the idea that feedback is not something threatening, but potentially interesting and useful. It cleared the path to fully fledged assessment/feedback exercises. But before doing such assessments we had to agree on what we were striving for.

Defining the board's mission

Three formal board meetings, and a number of one-on-one and small group conversations, prepared the ground for a large-scale discussion on what the board's role should be, how to measure its effectiveness and efficiency, what contributions the directors should make, and what competencies they needed to possess. The discussion turned out to be very intense, constructive, and productive in terms of specific outcomes. It demonstrated that some level of trust had emerged. Every director participated passionately and constructively, people kept their narcissistic disposition under control for most of the time, and a mutually satisfying closure was achieved. The discussion also confirmed that the executive directors were preoccupied with their managerial duties and had little interest in their directors' work.

The board defined a long-term vision for SUEK (to become a world-class Russian energy company), and specific targets to support this vision in the areas of employee health, safety and environmental protection, labor and capital productivity, innovation, and community relations. We also formulated a three-year vision for SUEK to become the uncontested leader of the Russian coal industry. The modern system of corporate governance was to become the principle instrument in achieving both short- and long-term visions. The board was to be a core element of the system and its chief ideologist, architect, and guarantor by performing five functions:

1. selecting, evaluating, and deciding on remuneration of the top executives (CEO and members of the management board), along with succession planning;
2. defining company vision, goals, and strategic priorities, including long-term vision and strategy, 3–5 year strategic plans, annual budgets and following up on their implementation;
3. approving material projects such as investments, divestitures, mergers, and acquisitions;
4. defining organizational social architecture–values, structural principles, key procedures and processes; and
5. monitoring the major risks.

The management was to ensure the implementation and staffing of the system.

We agreed that for the next 12 to 16 months, the company needed an engaged board, which should focus (according to the IGLC's coaching philosophy of keeping the number of priorities low) on three areas: improvement of the governance system, management of the management (improving quality and performance of the top executive team through assessment, feedback, remuneration, and selection), and the development of business strategy for the next five years.

Based on previous discussions outside the boardroom, the board formulated two specific, high-stretch goals to measure the company and its progress–to move one point up in Standard and Poor's ten-point scale valuation of the corporate governance within a year, and to achieve recognition for corporate governance excellence in the Russian mining industry. To make sure this would not happen at the cost of declining performance, we set a goal of creating positive economic value added (EVA) for the enterprise.

When the board concluded that topic of discussion, I pointed out that we were about to do something that had not yet been done in Russia–a private company building a system of corporate governance according to tough international standards; the owners delegating the running of the company to independent directors without keeping even negative control on the board; and turning a young fragmented enterprise into a world-class operation. We set the bar very high and the stakes were pretty serious. If we (the board) failed, the company and its owners would suffer not only financial losses, but also lose face in the public eye. The independent directors would seriously damage their reputation. It would reinforce the opinion of those who were skeptical about sound corporate governance. Most importantly, however, we as professionals would feel bad about our inability to make our vision a reality. At this point, the nature of the interchanges between the directors led me to believe that we, as a group, were ready to reach our goal. This turned out to be only partially true: although we shared our beliefs in what needed to be done, the personal styles of the directors required more monitoring.

As a second step, we discussed what was required from the board as a whole and from each individual director to make the vision happen, i.e., how to be productive. The discussion was lively and constructive due to the clearly defined tasks and criteria, their importance, and earlier conversations on the subject. Repeatedly, directors evoked the various themes that I had hoped for, including respect for others' opinions, effectiveness in expressing points of view and understanding others, cooperation, creativity, specificity, the value of informal interactions outside the boardroom, thorough preparation, the need to improve communication skills and deepen knowledge of corporate governance, strategy, finance and accounting, mining, power generation, etc. This particular conversation allowed me to do what I had failed to do at the first board meeting: put into place a set of behavioral rules for the board (see Appendix One) that would serve as a blueprint for our board culture. Most importantly, however, it gave me the opportunity to implement another important decision: to conduct a fully fledged assessment and feedback exercise.

Assessing performance and developing action plans

From the results of our discussion about the board's mission and operating principles, we designed assessment/feedback processes and developed assessment forms for the board as a whole, the chairman, and the directors (see Appendix Two). The process was simple: each director received an envelope with blank forms for assessing the board, the chairman, and each of the directors, including himself or herself. An HR expert collected the completed forms and presented the aggregated results to the HR committee. Subsequently, as the chairman (and I was also in charge of the HR committee) I presented a summary of the results, the HR expert's assessment, and the HR committee's recommendations to the board. In follow-up one-on-one meetings, I shared their personal profiles with each director, provided explanatory comments, answered their questions, and discussed (if the director wished) potential actions to close any gaps.

To reduce the level of anxiety, I had emphasized the benign nature of the exercise in my pre-assessment communication, both written and verbal. Assessment needed to be seen as a way to help the board collectively, and each director individually, to improve. I assured everyone that the outcomes would not be used for any purposes other than development and repeated many times that we were conducting an "experimental" evaluation. Knowing how hard it is to implement 360-degree feedback with senior executives (particularly in Russia), I was not very optimistic about outcomes from the first exercise, although I was convinced we had to start doing assessments to create a culture of feedback, reflection, and continuous improvement.

The results exceeded my expectations. We received the forms back from all but one director. The results formed a good foundation for a series of very interesting and important discussions in the boardroom and the offices of the directors (following the coaching philosophy, I tried to visit them rather than invite them to my office). The first assessment/feedback exercise provided four main outcomes:

- In general, there was a positive assessment of the board and each individual director. My emphasis on presenting the overall picture to the board reassured its members, boosted their self-confidence, and lowered their defense mechanisms.
- Following the assessment, and going much deeper and further than the forms intended, we developed a shared vision of what we as a group were good at, and where we were merely average, where we had to take immediate action to improve, and what required long-term efforts. By openly discussing the *status quo* and ways to improve, the group and its individual members committed to improve themselves. The idea of self-improvement was taken up, became part of the board culture, and very soon started to yield results in the form of adjusted behavior.
- This behavior was reinforced at my individual meetings with directors, most of whom committed themselves to specific improvements and asked for support in terms of advice, specific interventions, additional resources, etc. Even more importantly, perhaps, the results of the peer feedback made many directors question their assumption that they had a formula for success and that their formula was the right one. For the majority of them, this was the first time they had gone through this type of exercise and they were sincerely surprised to find out that their peers might see them very differently from how they perceived themselves. That revelation was reinforced at my feedback sessions and helped to make them more open to different opinions and the people who expressed them.
- Presenting the results of my assessment as chairman, I changed tactics and emphasized gaps rather than achievements (in my case these were specifically: my interaction with the CEO and senior management, my industry knowledge, and the strategic focus of the meetings). By openly discussing problems with my performance at the board meeting, and actively seeking advice on how to improve, I made it clear that I not only trusted my peers, but that I also (despite having a reputation as a

developmental expert) valued their nonspecialist opinions. These at times difficult discussions, where I had to pull comments from other directors, played a very important role in reducing their defensiveness further. I showed that discussing one's own shortcomings did not lead to a loss of face.

Although many of the directors were anxious before the assessment/feedback took place, and I was skeptical, the bottom line was a general acceptance of the instrument, and a commitment to improve, both individually and as a group. The exercise has since become a six-monthly event and has been expanded to include the board committees, their chairmen, and the corporate secretary. The exercise is no longer optional and the results are taken into account when evaluating each director for reelection. It has become the norm to discuss collective and individual performance openly and candidly, and I believe this has a tremendous impact on the effectiveness of the board.

One unexpected result of the board assessment and the subsequent discussion was a decision to discontinue the participation of the executive directors on the board. In their ratings and comments, the directors emphasized that the CEO and his deputy used their board membership to promote narrowly defined management interests, did not engage in generating new ideas but defended their prefabricated solutions at all costs, and often acted as a block to creative discussions. Although from the corporate governance point of view there were some benefits of having executives on the board, the group dynamics view required decisive action. With this background, and taking into account the board's mission and priorities, the amount of work that should have been done both by directors and executives, and the latter's lack of board experience, the board made the decision to fully separate oversight and executive bodies, a move that was endorsed by the shareholders. This move provoked a high level of discontent on the management side and required some crisis management intervention from the founders and the chairman, but in the medium term proved to be a wise decision. It allowed the CEO to concentrate on operational challenges, increased the level of candor at board meetings, and in the end reduced the level of antagonism between directors and executives when the former received further confirmation of their "superior" status.

ACTION IN THE BOARDROOM – AND OUTSIDE IT

Four months in, the SUEK board had the fundamental building blocks of an effective governance body in place: a diverse group of professionals, an atmosphere of trust, a shared vision and a set of success criteria that gave meaning to the group, three top priorities for the year, operating principles, formalized expectations for directors (profiles), and an evaluation and remuneration system. After investing a lot of time and energy into creating those elements, I could now concentrate on behaving like a traditional chairman – setting agendas for board meetings, ensuring preparation, leading discussions, managing decision making, and ensuring follow-up. Although those functions required many approaches and skills outside the coaching domain – updating the company charter, the board and committees statutes, developing corporate standards, setting internal audit and follow-up systems, managing external advisers and support staff – the coaching philosophy, and the specific tools that came with it, helped me enormously in playing this more traditional role.

In planning the board meetings for the year and a detailed agenda for each one, I never looked at the board as a decision-making machine that would work at whatever speed the situation required, but used an approach developed through observation and analysis of our first meeting. In one day, the board could comprehensively discuss and reach consensus on one large-scale issue, intelligently approve well-prepared decisions on three to five items that did not require further discussion, comprehend information on one to two new subjects that did not require decision, and approve from five to seven less important decisions in a semi-automatic mode. Based on this principle and keeping in mind the three priorities, I set the agenda for the meetings, instructed the chairs of the various committees to prepare board decisions, and instructed the management to organize materials and their presentations. If some pressing matters, usually of procedural and legalistic nature, could not fit into the agenda, we used meetings *in absentia*. The board's productivity improved after six months and the rule was modified – two large-scale issues per meeting.

As with any working system, the quality of input is very important for the quality of output. After a couple of meetings, we had formalized requirements for materials submitted to directors in advance and management presentations to the board. However, that procedure only began to work after a number of informal coaching-style individual meetings with the CEO and a few other key executives took place. During those meetings, I asked the executives to try to put themselves into the shoes of the directors and understand the latters' needs, expectations, and level of sophistication. I also encouraged informal feedback from other members of the board. Although we achieved some progress quite quickly, the issue of materials reemerged constantly as the board moved on to improving its productivity, requiring permanent attention from the CEO and myself and periodic adjustment to the formal procedure, regarded as an important part of the overall philosophy of continuous improvement rather than another directors' request designed to irritate management.

Leading board discussions – my main responsibility as chairman – became much easier after we had gone through the assessment and initial one-to-one meetings. These helped me to understand each director's thinking and discussion styles, motivational themes, and expectations vis-à-vis the board. That knowledge allowed me to adjust my style, which made a big difference to the quality of our discussions.

Seeing the principle goal of my role as chairman as achieving quality group decisions, I concentrated on ensuring that all members contributed the maximum of their knowledge. Some directors had to be helped with questions or words of encouragement, and others had to be silenced, allowing more time for slower thinkers, etc. Although initially some were frustrated by what they felt was a sluggish process, they later began to appreciate individual differences and the need to respect them in order to produce collective decisions.

Although the board did not make all its decisions by consensus, I felt that to have credibility all major decisions had to be supported by each director, so did everything necessary to achieve group consensus – extending discussion time, breaking the meeting up for small groups consultations, pushing the issue to the next meeting, and discussing it privately with each director. We invested significant time in building consensus on major issues, such as the five-year strategic plan, CEO compensation and key performance indicators, and the scope and structure of the internal audit, but eventually produced decisions every director fully supported. Building consensus on important issues became a key element of the board's culture. At the same time, I often used voting to resolve ego-driven deadlock on issues of secondary importance.

As facilitator, I consciously reduced my personal participation in the decision-building process, and often did not express my own views, in the same way as a facilitator does not express his or her own views during group coaching work. However, whenever I felt there was a threat to one of the board's operating principles, I used the authority of the chair to deal with it. There were occasions when I felt that I as chairman had to speak up strongly, for instance when one of the directors was trying to push through his favorite idea even though it had already been rejected by the board, or when two board members turned the discussion on a minor point into an endless dialog. Those rare, but painful, cases reminded me how important it was for the chairman to practice what he or she preaches, since the chairman is, or should be, looked up to by other directors, executives, and support staff. Even small variances can have significant consequences, as was the case when I half-jokingly, but publicly, criticized one director for always trying to have the last word, thus breaking the rule of criticizing opinions not people. Immediately some of the other directors jumped in with personal criticism and the meeting became dysfunctional for some time.

That episode reinforced my view that the chairman is the chief guardian of the board's rules and norms, its culture. In fact, I regard the emergence of a productive culture as the major achievement of SUEK's board. The rules are simple, clear, and ingrained in the minds and hearts of directors. They allow for effective and efficient group work with minimal guidance or supervision. The culture we have built also makes the chairman's role easier and allows him to do less facilitation work and spend more time as strategist and organizational architect–the roles I had in mind when I joined SUEK.

A CHAIRMAN'S REFLECTIONS ON COACHING

The coaching philosophy and instrumentation were critical aids to building and leading a board of directors under very demanding conditions. They allowed me to deal effectively with psychological challenges that could have turned the board sessions into a nightmare, and to organize productive collective work. The directors have not become less narcissistic or egotistic since my interventions, but have moved on to a new level of self-awareness, discovering new and productive ways to express their narcissism and fulfill their needs, and forming a solid foundation for the board's process.

Coaching by itself would not have made me into an effective chairman of the board. General business acumen; knowledge of strategy, HR, operations, and safety; first-hand executive experience; and the status of having been an ex-CEO were extremely important. The situation at SUEK, with its freshly minted board made up of relatively inexperienced directors, was atypical and required a higher than usual level of involvement in the human side. However, after looking back at the SUEK adventure and comparing it with some fellow chairmen's experiences, I have come to believe that coaching skills are a necessary element of every chairman's skills set. Most chairmen develop these skills through trial and error in the boardroom, but they would be better-off using professional help.

While I discovered that coaching was extremely useful in helping me function as an effective chairman, the SUEK board experience also enriched my views on coaching itself. I would like to share three insights on executive and group coaching that derive from this experience.

Executive coaching

I reconsidered my view on building a relationship with a coaching client (entrepreneur or senior executive). The goal should not be to develop an atmosphere of complete trust between the parties involved, but to establish a working relationship covering one aspect of the client's life–self-improvement in certain areas where the coach possesses professional expertise. The coach should play a leading role in establishing this working relationship, invest significant time at the very beginning of the relationship, and open up rather than let the coaching client take the lead and then adjust to his or her behavior. Opening up, sharing information about personal strengths and weaknesses, and especially asking for feedback after each meeting will help to set the tone and create a working relationship quickly. Having said that, I certainly do not advocate a one-size-fits-all algorithm—individual specifics should be reflected in how the trust is built and developed.

My second insight is about judging versus nonjudging in working with senior people. Previously, I emphasized the process of self-discovery, helping the coaching client to arrive at important conclusions on his or her own while the coach keeps his views to himself. Although the above approach remains for me the essence of the coaching process, I believe that in working with time-pressed, rather narcissistic executives, it helps if the coach has strong opinions on the important issues of the coaching partnership, such as the coaching client's strengths and weaknesses, developmental priorities, progress made, solutions to specific challenges, etc. The coach should openly express and defend them, of course, without turning the relationship into a class on public argument. Such an approach will reinforce the working trust, strengthen the coach's reputation, and help the client to improve.

The third idea is about breaking up the relationship relatively soon if productive dialog does not emerge. If after two to three months of intensive relationship building, the client does not listen to the coach, breaks the agreed norms or does not alter his or her behavior, given the kind of feedback he or she has received, the coach should say "Enough," and close the show. Things will not improve, and the relationship will waste the coach's energy and time, not to mention the client's money. At SUEK, we procrastinated in terminating one director who stubbornly refused to alter his behavior in spite of consistent feedback from the other board members, and wasted time and money on an intractable situation. The coach should not make such mistakes and should make the decision to leave quickly.

Group coaching

As with individuals, I now believe that coaches acting as a group facilitator should be more proactive in building the atmosphere of trust in the group and should assume the role of active culture builder rather than careful facilitator. Creating such an atmosphere–emphasizing the need for the prevention of hidden agendas, demonstrating professional credibility, opening up, speaking about one's weaknesses, seeking feedback–will help to foster a safe space for discussion.

This safe space will become one of the most important instruments of the coaching session, and the coach should preserve and reinforce it by personally exemplifying established rules and principles, interrupting dysfunctional behaviors, restating the norms, and so on.

The facilitator should deal with each group member individually, while making sure that the universally agreed working principles are observed by everyone. Investing time in learning about the participants' backgrounds, competencies, and profiles, but most importantly their information processing and discussion styles, pays off handsomely. Such a customized approach to organizing group feedback sessions increases their effectiveness, and the participants' satisfaction and motivation to improve. It also raises their appreciation of the coach and again reinforces working trust.

I cannot claim authorship for the approaches to coaching presented at the end of this article: I have heard these discussed by other people many times before. However, my experience as chairman awakened them from my coaching memory and made them operational, producing results for the clients and satisfaction for myself.

APPENDIX ONE

BOARD RULES

- We come to the board meetings well prepared.
- We operate under an astronomic concept of time (one hour = sixty minutes = 3,600 seconds) and respect agenda and deadlines.

- We respect and encourage diversity of opinions. We discuss and criticize ideas, not the people who express them.
- We speak one after another, requesting the floor by turning our name tag on its side.
- We use questions actively to help the speaker present his point of view, to receive additional information, and to deepen our understanding. We do not use questions to present personal opinions on the subject, to criticize those of the speaker, or to bring up another subject.
- We stand for the decisions the board has made no matter what our personal position was, promote them, and ensure their implementation.
- We strive to be better with every meeting; we help one another to grow; we use all the resources available to improve our knowledge, skills and quality of interaction.

APPENDIX TWO

BOARD'S EVALUATION FORM

Using the following criteria evaluate the board's performance during the last period

	Requires improvement	Acceptable	Good	Outstanding	Comments
Special knowledge of the board as collective body					
1. Business strategy					
2. Corporate finance and investments					
3. Corporate governance					
4. Industry					
Items on the agenda					
1. Strategic value for the business					
2. Fit with the mission and role of the board					
Decision-making process					
3. Quality of decisions made					
4. Efficiency of the decision-making process					

Interaction between directors			
5. Effectiveness and efficiency			
6. Candor			
7. Cooperation			
Interaction with key board stakeholders			
8. Interaction with shareholders			
9. Interaction with CEO and management board			
10. Interaction with corporate secretary and support staff			

DIRECTOR'S EVALUATION FORM

Using the following criteria evaluate the director's performance during the last period

	Requires improvement	Acceptable	Good	Sets example for others	Comments
Special knowledge					
1. Business strategy					
2. Corporate finance and investments					
3. Corporate governance					
4. Industry					
Contribution of the board					
5. Generates original and constructive ideas					
6. Convincingly presents one's arguments					
7. Preparedness					
8. Assumes leadership in bringing and resolving principle for the company issues					

9. Subordinates personal ego to the interests of the company					
10. Actively participates in board meetings					
Business communication					
11. Listens actively and attentively					
12. Initiates and supports constructive discussions					
13. Actively interacts with other directors outside formal meetings					

CHAIRMAN'S EVALUATION FORM

Using the following criteria evaluate the chairman's performance during the last period

	Requires improvement	Acceptable	Good	Outstanding	Comments
1. Ensures strategic focus of the meetings					
2. Provides directors with adequate information					
3. Conducts productive board meetings					
4. Creates working atmosphere in the boardroom					
5. Ensures fair and effective decision-making process during the meetings					
6. Ensures every director's participation in discussions and decision making					
7. Interacts with directors outside the boardroom					
8. Organizes the board's interaction with the company shareholders					

9. Interacts with CEO and senior managers				
10. Ensures effective support to the board from corporate secretary and other staff				
11. Promotes principles and practices of modern corporate governance in the company				

16

CRACKING THE CODE OF CHANGE: HOW ONE ORGANIZATION TRANSFORMED ITSELF THROUGH TRANSFORMATION OF ITS PEOPLE

CORNELIE VAN WEES

In this chapter, I explore how my company created a leadership development culture that was critical for a successful organizational transformation. My personal experiences highlight the link between organizational development, and personal development and growth.

INTERPOLIS: THE STORY

Interpolis is a Netherlands-based insurance company with many decades of history and very strong roots in the agricultural community. It started out as a cooperative, mutual insurance company for farmers, with solidarity between its members as the driving force behind its existence. Solidarity is impossible without trust, and the latter remains an important success factor for the organization. In 1991, Interpolis was acquired by Rabobank. In 1994, a major turnaround operation, named "Firm & Secure," was initiated to revive the once-successful company. Massive reorganization, many layoffs, and a different strategic focus were some of the results of the turnaround process. The change was in many ways disruptive and painful, but it was necessary for survival, and the transformation was successful.

By the end of the 20th century, Interpolis had grown into a fully fledged, top league insurance company. In 2001, just weeks before I joined the company, contracts for two major mergers were signed. With these signatures, Interpolis more than doubled in size and made significant new additions to its products and services.

At the end of 2005, Interpolis was sold to Eureko for a 37% stake in Eureko. Eureko is the holding company, and Dutch operating company Achmea was merged with Interpolis. Together, Achmea and Interpolis are now a market leader in all segments of life and nonlife insurance, pensions, and related products.

FIRM & SECURE (1994–1998)

Rabobank had made several attempts to merge Interpolis with another major player in the insurance market, and failure to do so led to rapid deterioration in the company's results. A strategy consultancy conducted a thorough analysis and recommended drastic change. In a nutshell, Interpolis had to change its identity from being an insurer to being an entrepreneur.

Change was launched with an all-encompassing turnaround project called "Firm & Secure," which was then executed with an almost military discipline. The project had a multidimensional approach from the very start. First, core processes were redesigned to improve cost levels by 30–50%, together with a 100% improvement in market share. The cost of damage settlements had to be lowered by 10%. In parallel, all corporate services had to come up with an Activity Value Analysis, with the intention of reducing costs by 50%.

Second, the organizational structure was carefully examined. Divisions became business units that had full responsibility to "create, make, and sell" their products. Very small staff units were kept to support the business, and the number of hierarchical layers was cut.

Third, a tailor-made "social plan" was developed, as 700 jobs were to vanish. Together with the trade unions and the Workers' Council, a powerful body in the Netherlands, it was determined that there would be no forced layoffs. Instead, the company planned to reassign people, offer lump sum compensation for voluntary redundancies, or propose early retirement. A separate legal entity was set up to help and support the people affected in this process.

Interpolis returned to profitability by the mid-1990s. With the restructuring well underway, it was time for a new vision and mission statement that would reflect the changed spirit of the organization, and tangible signs of the new corporate identity, such as a new logo. "Firm & Secure" was no longer to be a project but rather to become a movement, a new way of living. This meant transforming not only the external and internal images of the company, but also changing the attitudes and behaviors of the employees.[1] Structures, processes, technology, and skills and behavior were to change to define a new culture for the organization. The new Interpolis was to have only one strategic focus: the customer.

THE CUSTOMER COMES FIRST

Putting customers first in business processes meant looking at what customers really expected from an insurance company, and reviewing the range of products and services delivered. Before the transformation, Interpolis matched the rather negative perception that people had of traditional insurance companies: being slow and bureaucratic; having the devil indeed in the details; never doing what was promised; going to great lengths to delay payment for damage, if paying at all; making huge profits; etc. In short: the reputation of the industry as a whole was (and, in general, still is) deplorable.

Through internal efforts to solicit customers' suggestions for improvements, it became clear that customers had a clear set of expectations: "do as you promise, understand my situation, be clear about what my situation is, give me insight into my situation, provide me with solutions when things go wrong." But to put these points into practice meant a complete shift in culture at Interpolis.

Product innovation and operational excellence were key to getting things moving, resulting in simplified and standardized products, processes, and solutions for customers. Insurance policies were now sent to customers in a matter of days instead of months. Employees were trained in communicating clearly with their customers, and measures were introduced to make sure that the communication really *was* clear, for example, outgoing and internal mail was checked and rated for clear language and legibility. A rule was introduced that phone calls had to be answered within 15 seconds and that e-mails had to be answered within 24 hours. The employees were charged with finding solutions to customers' problems instead of simply sending them money. Responsibility for decision making in the primary customer contact was put at the lowest possible level, i.e., the person who dealt directly with the customer. Overall, Interpolis became a significantly decentralized company, with financial responsibility devolved to the business units.

With the downsizing and restructuring well in hand, the CEO decided to have offices and functions concentrated in one building, and a new office building was commissioned. Half-way through construction, Interpolis started to make profits again and business was booming. New people were hired, expansion plans were laid out, and the executive board realized that the company would simply not fit into the new, and only, building.

The CEO happened to bump into an interior designer who had a totally new view on work and the working environment, encompassing the concepts of flexible offices and teleworking. With him, the CEO started talking about the office as a place to meet and work in a flexible way, both in terms of hours and locations, and about encouraging people to work from home. The result was a new office building that could accommodate 30% more people than it was originally designed for. Although being able to fit more people into the building was not the highest priority, it was a wonderful side effect of the concept. New architectural arrangements suggested totally new concepts for work-life balance, office interiors, information and communication technology (ICT) structure, and HR and leadership development.

Nobody in the new building had their own permanent office or desk, so the flexible office became a reality for everybody, up to the highest-ranking officers. Today more than half of the staff, including board members, work from home one or more days a week. Social cohesion and team atmosphere is created and facilitated in the office, where people meet when they need to work together. The rest of the work is done from where it is most convenient: in the office, at home, or on the road. The development and refinement of the concept is still ongoing, with new insights and technical features constantly being woven into the way people work.

Trust became the key concept in how people worked with one another and how they related to Interpolis's customers. Trust was essential because one of the goals of the change effort was freedom for employees to make their own decisions and have full responsibility for their customers and results.

Not all individuals are comfortable with the weight of responsibility of this way of working, and a very strict selection process was introduced for new hires. As in any other company, a series of interviews explore competencies and previous work history. But once it was decided that a candidate qualified based on their competencies, an in-house assessment was carried out, during which the assessors looked at how genuine, open, responsible, and customer-driven the person really was. About 20% of candidates are now routinely turned down in this final stage of the selection process.

CULTURE

What happened in the organization was almost in line with textbook approaches to managing change.[2] The sense of urgency was expressed, a guiding coalition was formed rapidly, and the clear and simple strategy was openly communicated over and over again at different levels throughout the organization: *we are here for our customers.*

Although some of the proposals were difficult, employees soon understood that it was a "change or die" situation. The organization succeeded in getting the new behaviors adopted by rapidly changing the structures and processes, and then supporting changes in employee behavior. Gradually, new, shared basic assumptions of "how things are done around here" spread through current employees and newcomers who were now being selected on the basis of both professionalism and trustworthiness. Thus a new culture was developed.

An interesting question, obviously, is why the turnaround at Interpolis was so successful, while so many other change efforts, arguably also done according to well-known recipes, fail to deliver results. The answer is actually quite simple: in this particular transformation process, the CEO, an honest and outspoken individual with a very convincing story, was present, engaged, and involved throughout. What is particularly important is that the CEO himself believed in the transformation story, and, even more importantly, *he was the story himself.*

THE ROLE AND IMPORTANCE OF LEADERSHIP

Managing by values

Let's take a closer look at the Interpolis values, beliefs, and (declared) norms and see how they influence decision making, sharing of information, and accountability. What is the "contract" that defines how employees work with one another and their customers? Why does it seem to work so well?

Interpolis's core values describe the way everyone deals with interacts in decision making, working, sharing, communicating, openness, and accountability. They are the "contract" the people abide by: the four Vs. The four Vs translate into English as: Trust (Vertrouwen), Responsibility (Verantwoordelijkheid), Freedom (Vrijheid), and Cohesion (Verbondenheid). Interpolis's core values have not been "invented" or "engineered." Most have been lived implicitly throughout the organization for many years, although some were probably dormant. The CEO simply made the core values explicit and started actively referring to them when making decisions. Top management was expected to revitalize the values and constantly prove that they were being lived in the organization.

By putting trust in people, giving them the freedom and responsibility to do what was in the customers' best interest and allowing employees to work where and when they liked, a lot of enthusiasm and energy were created. People are quite capable of understanding what it takes to put their customers first. Interpolis supported this with clear, achievable targets for all employees, for which they became accountable.

Leadership and management had the courage to steer according to the values and allow their employees to live those values productively; to let decisions develop, and to have people follow on the basis of conviction and belief, and not "because the boss says so." Such efforts resulted in a balancing act for leaders and managers, creating tension between cohesion and autonomy, between uniformity and tailor-made solutions, and between performing and caring.

PERSPECTIVES OF THE CEO

So incredibly much has happened since 1994, when Firm & Secure started as a movement in the organization. ... Firm & Secure was a program of total business redesign: Interpolis put the customer first, the products were simplified, systems were integrated with Rabobank, costs were cut at least 30%, and decentralization was key. The changes were very extreme. A giant playing field was created.

CEO Interpolis, 2002–2005

In 2001 Interpolis started correcting the balance between freedom and responsibility. The company's management drew some very visible white lines on the giant playing field, reasoning that knowing where the lines are helps you to play a better match.

The balance between caring and performing, and autonomy and synergy had to be restored on several levels. For example, the extreme decentralization prohibited a coordinated business approach, so the organization needed to create incentives for people to work together. Interpolis started working, very consistently, on the concept of "inside–outside," meaning whatever you promise to your customers, you have to make it happen internally (by promoting internal openness and clear working concepts). The company linked policies on communications, ICT, HR and leadership development, and the physical workspace to the working concept. Curiously, knowing where the boundaries were gave people more freedom to move.

Is our way of dealing with challenges unique? Well, you need certain requirements to make it all come together in a company. One: the CEO and executive board must really embrace it; the management should lead by example and be vigorous in showing that this is the only way to work. Two: you really need the consistency of "inside–outside" principle. And three: you need to be consistent over the years; people have to see that this is not a one-off, not the "flavor of the month" type of thing. If you add it all up you create a flywheel. If I had to do it all over again, I would do much the same. I would still take the management board with me in the movement. Maybe I would create a small group, a guiding coalition that shares and leads by example. I sometimes wonder: could we have made the changes of the last years quicker? I realize that some things really need time, but there is always a risk attached that you struggle along and lose momentum.

CEO Interpolis, 2002–2005

At Interpolis, we strongly believe in coaching as a leadership style that results in better performance. There are two sorts of coaching: one, you coach somebody to become more effective as a person by working on the "who" that person is and "how" he or she can best make a contribution; and two, you coach somebody in actually doing his or her work better. To manage the transitions within the company, Interpolis needed leaders and managers that could be coaches to their teams and individuals. The company needed people that could make change happen, people that realized that change is not only about the nuts and bolts but also, and primarily, about the people that have to make it happen every day.

The developmental investment was seen as first and foremost in the *person*, not just in his or her knowledge and competencies. Interpolis is clearly not a traditional company. Much is left to the discretion of managers without the support of traditional management instruments. There is a cost in adopting such a style of management–managers may feel lonely, anxious, and even scared. To manage and lead others in such an environment, executives need a lot of support. Traditionally, organizations offer support to managers through training or educational courses. However, Interpolis needed an untraditional type of program. Executives in the organization would have to make a personal change at a rather deep level, dealing with, and responding to, the different ways they saw reality.

In response to the challenge of bringing in coaching as a leadership style, the organization, helped by clinically oriented consultants, set up a series of team-based coaching interventions. Interpolis started with managers in the Open Leadership program and subsequently rolled out an Open Team set of programs that were designed for all teams in the company. This created an unstoppable coaching movement in the company that now permeates both our language and the way people in the company deal with each other.

In 2001 Interpolis doubled in size through a couple of mergers. The focus was the customer, but there also was a need to build cohesion in the new group of people formed. A new tower was added to the head office, and new leadership came into play. And so there was a real need to make the personal and implicit way of dealing with one another into a more explicit and even a "registered," explicit way, so it could be replicated in the company. We started to describe the "culture artifacts" and to talk about them in our communication, and we described them in our HR policies. We made them visible and tangible in abolishing time clocks, cafeteria cashiers, and private offices with doors. We opened up our electronic calendars for one another. This was all a starting point to formalizing our new way of leading the company. While most important things for the customers had been organized, it was now the time to focus on leading people internally.

A former HR Director

The consultants helping Interpolis to build its Open Leadership program showed the managers that leading others starts with themselves. Change, and involving other people in change, only works if it comes from within, from the personal side. But the personal side has to be emancipated, and this feeling of being free is very different from a bureaucracy where you simply have to know and apply the rules. In practice, it means starting by understanding yourself, then understanding the team, and finally, understanding the company.

This change has to start with the managers, with their view of themselves: one has to learn to be open to oneself in order to learn to be able to be open to others. That has to do with emotional intelligence and awareness, and it starts an understanding of the impact one has on others.

Consultant, Open Leadership program

With the Open Leadership program, a common understanding started to develop between managers. The program helped them develop a deeper level of trust toward one another. As one participant recalled, "We all delved into the richness of people. That is fun and very useful. Importantly, understanding self, others, and teams is not about a particular technique, but rather about being real and authentic."

From the consultants' interviews with managers, two central themes emerged. The first was about synergy versus autonomy: Interpolis wanted to be one company without taking away the autonomy of the individual parts. The second was the issue of caring versus performing: Interpolis wanted to be a caring employer, but at the same time it had to deliver results. With these dilemmas, the company had to find an optimal mix rather than a weak compromise. How do you do justice to values that are seemingly in conflict with one another? This question served as a starting point for the Open Leadership program.

Leaders are critical to the success or failure of any change process, as they bring about change or hinder it through their person. As was mentioned in Chapter One, the involvement of the leader's personality, emotions, fantasies, other aspects of his or her inner theater, and their capacity to connect to others are of vital importance to any change process. This was absolutely the case with the change needed at Interpolis.

FROM CEO TO TEAM LEADER

The dilemmas identified earmarked some typical themes in the company and were addressed in a specially tailored program, where each manager had the opportunity to look at himself/herself as a leader, and to work with and learn from other managers. The program was designed in two modules totaling three days, working in small groups of eight to ten people. Everyone with management responsibilities, from the CEO to team leaders, participated in heterogeneous groups. Before the first module, everyone had to complete a 360-degree feedback process to obtain data to be used in the program.

The first program module lasted two days. The aim was to create a shared context in which to work together, and to work at the personal level, toward opening up to oneself, in order to be more receptive to change. In this workshop, sharing one's personal story, listening to one another, and practicing coaching skills were the central themes. The coaching was usually linked to a real example from the daily routine of a manager. In the safe environment created for the workshop, the participants got to know one another and could experiment with openness in a team environment. The group sessions were all about listening, telling, sharing, and helping one another.

These conversations offered a great opportunity to practice listening and coaching skills. In these sessions real contact was made and trust was established. It created cohesion between the participants and allowed for the development of a shared context and language. A social contract emerged to discuss with one another in a safe, contained environment any kinds of issues that had to do with the dilemma of caring and performing. The 360-degree feedback and debriefing helped people to open up more easily. They came to realize that they were the "main dish," so to speak, during these sessions. Participants really worked hard to look deeply into themselves, their personal values, and their key tasks at work.

Consultant

The issues of personal values and drivers were especially crucial. Our values and drivers are determined by our personal life and development. Talking about these created an abundance of reflection points for all participants. The program was not therapy. There was always a strong correlation with day-to-day work: how do you deal with things that occur at work and why do you react like you do? What does this say about you as a manager? After the module, participants were asked to write a reflection paper and also to share their experiences at home and with their colleagues and teams.

The second module of the program discussed the connection with daily practice and experiments that participants carried out after the first module: what happened, what did you learn, what did you encounter? It was the start of deep introspection within the group, where the goal was to look at interactions in the group and *not* organizational change per se.

I don't want to pretend that three days is enough for real and lasting personal change, but Interpolis has developed this code amongst its managers to reflect on their own and others' behavior. And that has a more permanent effect. For many people these workshops marked a starting point for personal development. And that impacted the organization in the long run.

Consultant

The Open Team program was designed to get employees below managerial level involved in the organizational change process. The bridge between Open Leadership and Open Team, however, could only be provided through managers who had completed the Open Leadership program.

Open Team was not aimed at the individuals in a team, but at the performance of the team as a whole.

> Open Team is less personal than Open Leadership, and it is more about the organization. The build up is to work with your own team, which really changes the dynamics in it. In turn, the change in the way the teams work has its impact on the organization. If you would want to close the loop after Open Leadership and Open Team, I would propose to do Open Team in cross-functional teams.
>
> *Consultant*

The Open Leadership and Open Team movements confirmed and made the core values of Interpolis, Trust, Freedom, Responsibility, and Cohesion, visible once again. The movement brought back a much-needed balance, giving teams and the people within them both the freedom to be successful and the strong results orientation necessary for growth. We all started to look at our work in a different way. We began asking why we did things the way we did. We posed the "why" question more and more, reflected on what we were doing, resulting in different and deeper conversations than just a couple of years before.

LESSONS FOR OTHER ORGANIZATIONS

> What Interpolis has done is quite unique. There was an important critical success factor for the whole intervention. It was that the executive board committed themselves so strongly to this movement and that they were the forerunners in participating in the program and that they made the importance of the movement concrete and visible through their behavior, decisions, policies, and so on. The behavior of the executive team was also aligned with the corporate values of openness and trust, orientation toward the customers, trusting people within the company, and creating the conditions for new ways of working. The top management's behavior consistently showed that it was all about the people that make up the company. That is very special.
>
> *Consultant*

So what are the most important lessons leaders can learn from the experience at Interpolis? These are as follows:

- Take the time to reflect with key executives. Develop a vision on leadership, people, and organization.

- When implementing the vision, do it well: invest in quality, professionalism, and carefulness.
- Make sure that the leadership stays on course; leadership must see the change as a part of the vision and not as something cosmetic.
- Remember that the leader must be authentic.
- Create a safe environment in which to discuss personal effectiveness with your employees, without losing the edge when you talk about performance.
- Try to make as many people as possible "accomplices" when you discuss new directions or new values. Share your views with as many groups as possible.
- Be enthusiastic, have fun for yourself, and create a good atmosphere for others.
- Invest in management development to put the right people in the right positions.
- Create a delicate balance between encouraging creativity and applying the brakes.
- Leadership should act from trust, and guide in an invisible manner.

The head of HR at Interpolis adds:

- Always ask why, and always make the link to the business focus.
- Make sure that your vision is aligned and consistent with your leadership behaviors, company culture, HR policies and procedures, management development efforts, and internal communications.
- Adhere to the three Cs: be Consistent, be Congruent, and accept the Consequences.

A PERSONAL JOURNEY: ALICE IN WONDERLAND

I've had days at Interpolis when I've wondered whether it was all for real. How did offering such a high level of trust work? It seemed very risky initially, but financial results improved, customer satisfaction grew, and productivity went up by at least 15% after we started working anywhere and anytime. And even

314

the level of "forgetting" to pay for lunch at the now cashier-less cafeterias was below 0.5% and improving.

It was also pretty scary at times. My job as a leader at Interpolis was by no means easier than it was before and required different skills than I had expected when I joined the organization. There was no handbook for managers on how things were done. There were no traditional status symbols to show how important you were. I didn't necessarily see my team most of the day: we were in meetings, or working in different parts of the building or from home. And I was not supposed to provide all the answers to the questions and be the expert; I had to coach people to find the answers by themselves rather than direct them. I was expected to be vulnerable, trusting, open, and attuned. My targets were both on results *and* fair process, inspiration and motivation. It was exciting, but daunting. And it required a lot of personal effort. But if you asked me if I would ever want to work in a traditional work environment again, I would wholeheartedly say: no way!

My own Open Leadership

My story is also the story of many others. It was the starting point of a new way of talking and relating to other people. Informal interview sessions started up, managers started to discuss the issues they had in their teams and with one another, openness became the norm. Managers learned to pick up signals from themselves and others, and dare to be vulnerable. They had to learn not only to listen (a huge task in itself), but also to do something based on the signals and let others know about it, or, if they didn't know what to do, acknowledge that they did not have an answer. Furthermore, they had to be attuned to themselves and others and be committed to self, others, and the organization.

Experimenting with learning about the self in the Open Leadership exercises made me realize that I wanted and needed to learn more if I was to really change myself and be part of the changes Interpolis needed to make. The INSEAD program Consulting and Coaching for Change (CCC) was just what I needed. During a year of introspection and reflection, I gained far greater awareness and understanding of the issues in my own development, and where they came from. The pieces of the puzzle fell in place. I realized that my personal development could impact the organizational development of Interpolis, albeit in a small way.

Closing the loop

There are similarities in managing (successful) change in large organizations and the change I tried to achieve in myself. The year of CCC had a miraculous synchronicity between personal learning points, and what I wanted to achieve at work and what Interpolis as a whole was trying to do in its development.

I discovered how the different facets of personal and work reality are linked, noting how they take a different form in different settings. I realized that in order to make the necessary changes in myself, I needed to take a multidimensional approach. I also needed to consider how Interpolis could benefit from the awareness, learning and perhaps even the changes in me. And with the experience I built up, I was able to address issues with the people I coached and the team I led.

Small steps

Research on organizational culture tells us that the accumulation of small consistent changes in individual behavior throughout an organization can bring about significant organizational change. And that is what programs like Open Leadership and Open Team were designed to do: no shock and awe, but small steps undertaken by many people simultaneously that would change behaviors and attitudes, reinforce our values, and ultimately influence our culture.

Psychological pain of one sort or another is a prerequisite for personal change. If I change one thing, as a wife, mother, daughter, friend, boss or colleague, something or someone else will then be affected too. But it isn't enough to just stir things up. If you really want things to change in a sustainable way, you have to work on the different drivers of behavior simultaneously; you have to take a multifaceted approach. The clinical approach, as used in Open Leadership, helped me recognize issues that I needed to address in myself, my team, and in Interpolis as a whole. As for change management, I now look at it from different levels: what happens above the surface and what goes on below the surface. And if I look at the coaching exercises that I practiced during my year on the INSEAD program, I realize that I have become much more aware of what I can do on an individual level as well as on the company level. I now eagerly engage in coaching conversations with colleagues and team members, not only because I enjoy talking to people about their personal development, but also as a way to influence the personal development of the individual, which will then influence the development of the organization.

Coaching as a leadership style

Despite all the different definitions of coaching popping up in literature, I tend to agree with what I heard from faculty and participants during my CCC program: coaching is nothing more or less than a meaningful discussion, where you pay attention to the context, contract, risks, and time. There are boundaries that you always have to bear in mind when coaching: one, it is coaching, not therapy; two, your task is to help the client focus their thinking and problem-solving energy; three, beware, you cannot change another person, only they can change their behavior; four, if the problem is a severe psychological issue or the client is distressed, refer the client to a mental health professional; five, and this relates to four, know your own limits in coaching situations.

So how do we at Interpolis teach our executives to coach beyond Open Leadership and Open Team? The answer is, we don't! Instead, we do everything to ensure that good coaching questions are formulated. A couple of years ago, as a spin-off from Open Leadership, an in-depth program was developed to assess current and new top and senior executives. This program aimed to get a complete profile of the executive through in-depth interviews, 360-degree assessment and tests, analysis of references from other people, and the writing of a reflection paper. A report was compiled from all the information, describing how the executive scored on the *what* (strategic, business and conceptual competencies), the *who* (personality and chemistry with the group), and the *how* (the way the executive coaches, influences, develops, inspires, and confronts, for example). Based on this report, a committee discussed future career steps and development needs with each executive. The executive then had the information needed to formulate a good coaching question and understand the underlying development points that would have to be addressed.

Coaching leadership has become the leadership style at Interpolis, through the corporate culture change and the help of the Open Leadership and Open Team program. The interventions were a form of group coaching, which can be instrumental in creating high-performance individuals, teams, and organizations.[3] As the consultant working with Interpolis said, "What was so powerful about OL was that every participant shared his or her life story and received feedback from the group. And the power of feedback is to see and test how sincere and open someone really is." In an intervention like Open Leadership, you have to create an atmosphere and a social contract that allows participants to give and receive feedback. Team coaching can be so much more effective than individual coaching, especially if applied throughout the organization. People learn from one another and create a flywheel effect that is transformational for the whole organization. To paraphrase a well-known saying, if one person says you are a donkey, you can ignore the comment. But if three people say you are a donkey, you'd better buy yourself a saddle.

All managers went through the same program and engaged in the team coaching experience. But it didn't stop at that. With the social contract we shared with one another, the shared language and codes, people started individual coaching conversations with their colleagues and with their team members to promote personal development and to change things in the teams.

The changes at Interpolis mark a unique example of how intertwined leadership and personal and organizational development can help bring business success. Interpolis is perhaps a good example of an *authentizotic* organization[4] (a concept that will be explored in the conclusion of this book). These are the kinds of organizations that help their employees maintain an effective balance between personal and organizational life. Very few organizations nowadays create an environment in which employees have enough trust in their colleagues and in the company to be real and authentic. Interpolis worked hard on being an exception.

NOTES

1. Vast & Zeker-project, 1994–1998, as described by Roel Ferwerda, "Gevoel en Verstand," 2004.
2. Kotter, J. (1995). "Leading Change: Why Transformation Efforts Fail," *Harvard Business Review*, 73(2): 59–67.
3. Kets de Vries, M. (2005). "Leadership Group Coaching in Action," *Academy of Management Executive*, 19(1): 61–76.
4. Kets de Vries, M. (2001). *Struggling with the Demon*. Madison, CT: Psychosocial Press, pp. 302–303; Kets de Vries, M. (2000). *The Happiness Equation*. London: Vermilion, pp. 94–95.

17

THE CASE FOR NOT INTERPRETING UNCONSCIOUS MENTAL LIFE IN CONSULTING TO ORGANIZATIONS

ABRAHAM ZALEZNIK[1]

A NOTE FROM THE EDITORS

In reading this revised version of a journal article that appeared years ago, it is important to keep in mind that it was written well before executive coaching entered the imagination, let alone common practice, of organizational leaders. However, we found it important to include a chapter written by one of the founders of the clinical orientation to management (to whom we have dedicated this book). After devoting most of this book to an exploration of the clinical approach, we thought it useful here to remind the reader to pay attention to the dangers implicit in dealing with unconscious phenomena.

Zaleznik reiterates that we as coaches should do no harm, and he also advises us to be careful in making unconscious processes conscious. While we may recognize specific unconscious patterns, that doesn't mean that we have to express our observations to a coaching client. Often, it is much wiser to keep these observations to ourselves. As a general rule, he argues (as an advocate of ego psychology*), it is advisable in consulting or coaching work to start at the surface and not to engage in "wild analysis." These caveats have been touched upon in other chapters in this book, but we felt it would be appropriate to let Abraham Zaleznik have the last word.

---

* Ego psychology refers to all areas of study and clinical application that place a major emphasis on the developing structures and processes that are the domain of the ego (i.e., memory, language, judgment, decision making, and other reality-oriented functions) and less on unconscious conflict or drives.

FIRST, DO NO HARM

A distinctive feature of all psychoanalytically oriented therapies is their attempt to bring unconscious mental conflict to
consciousness. Does this apply in organizational consultation?
I argue that, unlike clinical psychoanalysis, more harm than
good occurs when consultants attempt to interpret unconscious
material to clients in organizations. The main use of psychoanalytic psychology in consulting work is for observation and
understanding on the part of the consultant.

A consultant to organizations with an orientation derived
from psychoanalysis reported the following case example from
his practice:

> A woman started a mental health clinic in a poor neighborhood. She
> enlisted volunteers and as the clinic provided valuable services, it grew
> in size. After a time, it received grants and soon took on the characteris-
> tics of a bureaucratic organization. The entrepreneurial woman acting as
> CEO of the now expanded and formalized mental health clinic became
> unhappy. She was a fish out of water, and the consultant advised her
> to quit her job and start a new storefront clinic in a different neighbor-
> hood. She took the consultant's advice and benefited personally from
> the return to the conditions she seemed to prefer.

In explaining the favorable outcome, the consultant wrote, "We
can assume that the CEO's wish for grandiosity represented an
attempt to capture the self-object relations that may have been
unavailable in childhood." He continued by stating not only
that the woman was afflicted by her ostensible grandiosity, but
also that she suffered from narcissistic injury and that she had
regressed to a paranoid position.[2]

It is not at all clear whether the consultant shared his interpretations about grandiosity, childhood deprivations in self-object
relations, and narcissistic injury with his client. Whether he did
or not, I am immediately tempted to reread Freud's paper on
wild psychoanalysis. In my experience, a consultant to organizations cannot obtain the kind of information that permits
assumptions and conclusions like this, which derive from experience with deeply regressed patients who have been working
assiduously in psychoanalysis. It takes a long time for such

material to emerge and unless the client is manifestly psychotic, organizational practice does not facilitate such regression. But another possibility comes to mind: perhaps the consultant is indeed practicing wild psychoanalysis. If this is the case, I would judge the consultant's behavior irresponsible and in violation of the time-honored principle, "Do no harm."

The harm that comes from interpreting unconscious conflicts and motives outside the very controlled psychoanalytic situation is twofold: first, these interpretations tend to engender new defensive positions of a regressed nature; and second, the subject of these interpretations (the very technical language used in the previous illustration being a good example) will not have the foggiest idea what the consultant is talking about and consequently will become emotionally confused, especially if the consultant has achieved some authority in the eyes of the client. The net effect would be to diminish the capacity of the client to function in a situation in which unmet responsibilities have grave consequences for many people.

"WILD" PSYCHOANALYSIS

The potential abuse of psychoanalysis was the subject of Freud's paper *"Wild" Psychoanalysis*. Freud was concerned primarily with the deleterious effect, on both the patient and psychoanalysis itself, of offering interpretations and advice to a patient based upon limited observation that may be combined with superficial knowledge of psychoanalytic theory and practice. A distraught lady, recently divorced, came to Freud because her physician had told her that her anxiety was a result of frustrated sexual urges. She turned to Freud for a corroborative opinion because her physician had also told her that in order to gain relief from her anxiety she would have to follow one of three courses of action: first, return to her divorced husband and resume a sexual life; second, find herself a lover; third, masturbate and satisfy herself. The advice only aggravated her anxiety because she had no intention of returning to her former husband and because she had a strong moral aversion to the second and third recommendations, a fact that her physician had neglected to take into account. As Freud pointed out, she would not have needed the physician's advice had her conscience permitted her to do what she herself would have understood as the obvious.

The burden of Freud's short paper on wild psychoanalysis emphasized the part resistances, or what he later called "defenses," play in illness. To interpret one aspect of the unconscious, such as thwarted sexual urges, while neglecting defenses and moral standards, only heightens the resistances to influence no matter how correct the surmise regarding impulses may be. But even the cleverest surmises are often only conjectures that at best portray incomplete understanding of mental conflict. The woman who consulted Freud for a second opinion may well have been totally cold sexually as a result of her defenses and may not have experienced heightened sexual urges following her divorce. Freud wrote:

> If knowledge about the unconscious were as important for the patient as people inexperienced in psychoanalysis imagine, listening to lectures or reading books would be enough to cure him. Such measures, however, have as much influence on the symptoms of nervous illness as a distribution of menu-cards in a time of famine has upon hunger. The analogy goes even further than its immediate application: for informing the patient of his unconscious regularly results in an intensification of the conflict in him and an exacerbation of his troubles.[3]

As I shall demonstrate in this chapter, the consequences of making "deep" interpretations as an aspect of consulting with organizations are even graver than "wild" psychoanalytic interpretations in the pure clinical situation. Perhaps of more significance are the effects of *thinking* along "wild" psychoanalytic lines, whether put in words or not, on the practice of consulting. My conjecture is that somehow the clients will feel misunderstood, if not demeaned, by the implicit infantilization contained in so-called deep interpretations of the unconscious.

THE ORIGINS OF CONSULTATION TO ORGANIZATIONS

The origins of psychoanalytic consultations are generally attributed to the Tavistock Institute of Human Relations. The Tavistock has traditionally followed the theories of Melanie Klein in individual psychoanalysis and Wilfred Bion in group psychology.

In addition, the Tavistock has been attracted to systems theory to advance understanding of organizations. As described in Chapters Three and Four of this book, systems theory defines an organization in relation to an environment. Boundaries separate the organization from its environment. Internally, the organization is structured into roles and tasks necessary to deal with environmental issues. Often the impediments to dealing with environmental issues relate to problems in defining boundaries, although following Bion, the internal psychological state of the organization (degrees of regression and defenses against anxiety) may act as impediments to relating to the environment, ultimately threatening the survival of the organization.

Theoretically, the unconscious conflicts that arise and persist in organizational life should be major impediments to performance of the tasks necessary to assure survival in the environment. If it were possible to remove the impediments to rationality that derive from unconscious conflict in group and organizational relationships, then presumably energy could be spent in performing in roles and accomplishing tasks.

This theoretical model is a direct derivative of Bion's exposition in his book *Experiences in Groups*.[4] In group psychotherapy it is the stated purpose of the group to look for the interlocking effects of individual pathology and pathology manifested in group behavior. Thus, Bion's basic assumption that groups represent the pathologies derived from their individual pathology. Once the basic assumption modalities are dissolved, presumably by interpretation, a modality called the *work group* takes over and performs useful tasks furthering the group's purpose.

In organizational life, calling in outside consultants is an accepted practice. Consultants offer a wide range of expert services. At one end of the spectrum are the services of scientific management that attempt to establish practices, organizational roles, and procedures designed to heighten productivity. No psychological practices are applied at this end of the spectrum. The consultant performs according to his or her expert knowledge, is compensated, and leaves.

Psychoanalytically oriented consultation to organizations lies at the opposite end of the spectrum in terms of its finiteness, definition, and clarity in the expert services offered. What is the psychoanalyst/consultant's expertise in organizational practice?

The Bion model proposes a fairly concise and clear picture as to what this expertise is all about. It proposes to establish a therapeutic procedure to dissolve unconscious conflict and to move the organization into a work modality, patterns of behavior that will succeed in environmental transactions.

Such practice exists, or has been applied, in cases where the culture of the organization is identified as the site of the pathology that prevents rational and effective action from occurring. I participated in such consultative practice during the middle and late 1950s when I joined a group from the National Training Laboratories (NTL) to conduct training sessions with two very large organizations: one an international not-for-profit organization and the other an international oil company. At the time, the NTL consultation was not based on the Bion model. Rather it drew on the work of Kurt Lewin and his research on the effects of democratic group leadership on the culture of the group and the well-being of its members. Nevertheless, there were many similarities in the procedure followed in the NTL and the Bion group relations activities, including the use of the "leaderless" group to set in motion psychological forces that individuals in the group, along with the "leader/trainer," can interpret for the benefit of group members. The end point of this procedure is to establish in the minds of members a model of human relationships, surrounded as it were by authority, to alter expectations, assumptions, and practices in organizations. In general, the aim is to move from authoritarian, bureaucratic, and hierarchical relationships to democratic, sensitive, personal relationships guided by full communication.

I found this activity frequently fraught with unstated intentions and even unforeseen consequences. It seemed to me that the group activity could be as coercive as any authoritarian atmosphere I have encountered. The psychological force derives from substituting the leader and his or her intentions for the individual's superego, at least for a time. If an individual refuses to allow this substitution to occur either by force of ego, or by a highly regressed position in which conflict with authority is reactivated, group pressure is exerted to cause conformity in belief and behavior. Suggestion plays a large part in this not-so-subtle diversion of orientation while individuals learn to adapt to the circumstances of this new group behavior to achieve a degree of personal comfort in a highly charged group environment. Another thing to consider is the psychological fallout when authority figures in the organization legitimize this kind of group relations training. Participants are not free to refuse to attend and, indeed, may face severe sanctions if they do not attend and appear to participate willingly and fully.

To illustrate the extent of coercion and potential for regression, in the oil company experience there was at least one instance of suicide following the training and a number of reported instances of depression. In order to permit the program to continue, a corporate physician attended subsequent programs as an observer. I have not seen data to suggest that any benefits, in the form of the desired cultural changes and behavioral practices in the organization, were achieved by this intervention. But apart from demonstrable effects, it is clear that the organization is defined as the "patient," and that the intended therapeutic effect is the alteration of the authority structure through the resolution of unconscious dependencies, which could be a function of massive defenses against anxiety. The anxiety appears (or reappears) upon instituting the leaderless group as the central feature of the therapeutic intervention through group relations training.

In order for such therapeutic work to occur, it requires a setting in which a group can examine its own process, with the help of the consultant, and deal with the basic assumption modalities that prevent effective work from being performed. It is easy to visualize this setting in group psychotherapy, from which Bion derived his theory of group psychology. It is more difficult to envision how this setting can be established and what the operative effects of producing and interpreting data are.

Let us use as an example of a business consultation, drawn from my own consulting practice.

A large, family-owned manufacturing company was in the throes of a management succession problem. There were significant conflicts between and within the generations running this profitable enterprise.

The older generation believed the younger had not taken responsibility for the direction of the business; was not showing initiative in operations, let alone policy and planning; and despaired over whether fresh leadership would ever be forthcoming from this group. The younger generation (their average age was 40) believed the older generation had stifled them as individuals, trampled on their initiatives, and were intent on keeping them relatively powerless in this organization.

Among the older generation, there were abundant rivalries and conflicts. The most powerful individual in this older group wanted nothing to do with succession planning, opposed using an outside consultant, and in general went his own way in performing his executive duties. He was a talented man, who conceived new product ideas and mobilized engineers and production people to carry them through to fruition, usually not involving members of either generation. He was a powerful loner with a reputation for brilliance as well as harshness. He had become a shadowy presence in this succession problem and refused to enter into the deliberations. My observation of the situation led me to the conclusion that there was a code in this family that permitted any individual to take initiatives so long as he had the drive, enthusiasm, and courage to assume leadership. Thus, one of the junior members of the younger generation withdrew from his peer group and started a new division. He lobbied the older generation for support, which he received without difficulty, and launched his new venture successfully. The response of his peers was to ignore him and the significance of his behavior, which violated their belief that they were capable of great achievement if only the older generation would free them from the constraints of their dominance and control.

It seemed to me that the belief systems of both generations were neither unconscious nor, which amounts to the same conclusion, repressed. Using the venerable, but still valuable, topological model, perhaps these beliefs existed in the system preconscious and were easily accessible to consciousness.

In any case, I decided to deal with the substance of the succession and organizational problems without attempting to uncover what lay behind the beliefs of the two generations. It is possible that probing for unconscious material might have revealed a great deal about sibling rivalry, displaced oedipal conflicts, and homosexual anxiety. If so, there was undoubtedly much to defend against in this aggregation of unconscious material. I chose neither to explore this possibility nor to interpret what could only have been intuitions on my part. Instead, I wrote a report addressed to members of both generations in which I described their beliefs and showed how these beliefs had created the standoff in the conflicts between and within generations. I continued my report with a number of recommendations, including the naming of a chairman of the board from the younger generation, the naming of a president from the younger generation, and steps that would enable them to reconstitute the board of directors to assure accountability to and responsibility on the part of both directors and operating executives.

I submitted my report and met with the two generations. The "real leader" refused to attend the meeting and expressed despair that my report would spell the end of the family business. It is interesting that his claim for family unity and harmony ignored his part in exacerbating conflict and disarray. The wife of one of the second generation appeared at the meeting and was asked to attend and participate. When asked for my opinion, I said she should not be allowed to attend, that the issues belonged to the executives who were there.

I was greeted with hostility from many members of the second generation, but not all. None of the older generation joined in this attack on me. It was clear that my report had confronted a dominant belief that all executives in each generation were equal. They were paid the same, and enjoyed the same benefits and perquisites of executive rank. My report stated explicitly that there were significant differences in ability, and, indeed, my recommendations reflected these differences.

After substantial discussion, the group excused me from the meeting and continued with their deliberations. Representatives were delegated to report back to me on their conclusions. First, they agreed to destroy all copies of my report, and second they agreed to do nothing to alter the organization structure. A little more than a year later, various senior and junior members reported to me that they had accepted and implemented all of my recommendations. Several senior and junior members called me to express their appreciation for my contribution, claiming that they would not have been able to face the realities of succession without my work.

Let us assume for purposes of discussion that my recommendations were substantively sound and were beneficial for the company. Would there have been an alternative way to reach this end point, assuming that the group was prevented from dealing with reality because it existed in one or several of the basic assumption modalities instead of a work modality? This is not a trivial question, and it evokes another. Would a Bionesque group leader have been able to interpret unconscious material, remove repressions, lift defenses, and guide the group to a work modality that would have developed realistic solutions, without the disaffections that were a legacy of my consultation? Perhaps there would have been even better solutions than the ones I proposed if a work group, free from psychological struggles, had been operative.

Consideration of these questions brings me to another of Freud's important papers in which he considers analogous issues applied to psychoanalysis: *Analysis, Terminable and Interminable*. As with many of Freud's other works, *Analysis* requires a historical perspective. The paper was published in 1937. Freud was 81, suffering from cancer of the jaw and from the defection of one of his best and favorite pupils, Otto Rank.

Rank experimented with a brief therapeutic procedure that would uncover the birth trauma, thereby removing the source of all neurotic conflict. In the opening part of *Analysis Terminable and Interminable*, Freud wryly remarked about Rank's treatment:

> We have not heard much about what the implementation of Rank's plan has done for cases of sickness. Probably not more than if the fire-brigade, called to deal with a house that had been set on fire by an overturned oil-lamp, contented themselves with removing the lamp from the room in which the blaze had started. No doubt a considerable shortening of the brigade's activities would be affected by this means.[5]

The general tenor of this paper suggests that the determination of analysis and the concept of a cure are elusive. The decision to terminate reflects the analyst's and the patient's agreement that the progress is substantial (reflected, for example, in the amelioration of major psychological symptoms and the reduction of the anxiety level), but that it is possible, depending on circumstances, that the patient will seek further treatment at a later date. The idea of cure is an alteration of the ego so that the structure of defenses is less costly, the superego does not dominate the ego, and the individual is capable of acting in the service of pleasure as well as reality. In Freud's words, "The business of the analysis is to secure the best possible psychological conditions for the functions of the ego; with that it has discharged its task."[6]

Freud was driven to write this paper not only by questions concerning shortening the length of analyses, but also by the suggestion that future neurotic disturbances could be prevented by stimulating latent conflicts and dealing with them as part of the analysis to prevent their future eruption. In considering a preventive or prophylaxic analysis, Freud became even more cautious than his aversion to therapeutic zeal would explain.

Another of his students, the gifted analyst Sandor Ferenczi, reproached Freud for having neglected to uncover the negative transference and to analyze it during the brief analysis Freud undertook with Ferenczi to deal with some disturbances in relation to women and male rivals. For years after this treatment, Ferenczi was able to maintain a good marriage and be a valuable teacher to men who could easily have been perceived as rivals. Later, Ferenczi felt hostile to Freud and reproached him for neglecting the negative transference.

The questions Freud posed in *Analysis* were expressly directed to clinical psychoanalysis but offer food for thought to those who seek to apply psychoanalytic psychology to consultation in organizations. There is a principle in psychoanalytic technique that directs the analyst's attention to interpretation from the surface. Instead of plunging into deep interpretations, observe what conflicts and defenses are in play, so to speak, and direct interpretations to them. The aim is to alter the defenses and permit regression to occur at a rate that is tolerable to the patient, thereby deepening the analysis to expose conflicts that are being repressed while activating symptoms, including anxiety. This same principle avoids stimulating conflicts by maneuvers and manipulations on the analyst's part. The rule of abstinence implies no active measures to deprive, withhold, or otherwise frustrate the patient in order to bring about conflict.

In consultations that draw on principles of group therapy, the relationship between conflict present and conflict induced by the procedure is murky at best. When the consultant convenes a group and then withdraws into the leaderless group situation, regression will occur at a rapid pace. Predictably, anxiety levels will mount rapidly and defenses will be activated, including the types of defenses that are group determined as explained in Bion's *Experiences in Groups*. Bion's theory, which is derived from Klein, is a conflict-defense model of group psychology. But Bion believes that what Freudians would consider primitive defenses appear regularly in groups, leading him to comment, "The apparent difference between group psychology and individual psychology is an illusion produced by the fact that the group brings into prominence phenomena that appear alien to an observer unaccustomed to using the group." Bion explains what he means in a footnote: "It is also a matter of historical development; there are aspects of group behavior which appear strange unless there is some understanding of Klein's work on the psychoses. See particularly papers on symbol formation and schizoid mechanisms."[7]

Bion draws certain differences between his theories of group psychology and those of Freud, particularly as Freud developed them in *Group Psychology and the Analysis of the Ego*.[8] For Freud, group psychology was a derivative of the followers' common identification with the leader. The incorporation of the image of the leader results in a common representation in the ego of the followers. This commonly held representation becomes the basis of group cohesion. Bion states:

> It is clear that between the theories advanced by Freud and those I have sketched out here there is a gap. It may appear to be more considerable than it is because of my deliberate use of a new terminology with which to clothe the apparatus of mechanisms that I think I have detected. It will be necessary to test this by looking at the group more from the standpoint of the individual. But before I do this, I shall sum up by saying that Freud sees the group as a repetition of part-object relationships. It follows from this that groups would, in Freud's view, approximate to neurotic patterns of behavior, whereas in my view they would approximate to the patters of psychotic behavior.[9]

Bion may be correct in connecting group behavior to underlying psychotic patterns. But the correctness of this view may be a function of the observer and what the observer does to produce the psychotic effect. In a wonderfully ambiguous statement that seems to anchor itself at once in the observation of groups made up of "patients," of "sick" groups of any kind, and

331

even of all groups, Bion clearly forces the issue that is central to this paper. He states:

> This does not mean that I consider my descriptions apply only to sick groups. On the contrary, I very much doubt if any real therapy could result unless these psychotic patterns were laid bare with no matter what group. In some groups their existence is easily discernible; in others, work has to be done before they become manifest. These groups resemble the analytic patient who appears much more ill after many months of analysis that he did before he had had any analysis at all.[10]

Let's put aside consideration of the methods of conducting group psychotherapy. Assume for the purposes of this chapter that group psychotherapy is a procedure that takes place with a number of individual patients who enter the group as part of their personal therapy. Assume also that we can exclude from consideration all group procedures, whether conducted in small groups or large assemblies, where the purpose is cultural change or education through experiential training methods. Let's focus on consultation, which consists of a client engaging a professional to apply some expertise in the solution of the client's problem for which the client pays an agreed-upon fee. What are the conditions that call for the interpretation of unconscious material as part or all of the work of consultation? What is the nature of the consultant's expertise that is the foundation for such work? What are the data that lead to interpretations, and what are the sources of the data?

EXAMPLES OF ORGANIZATIONAL CONSULTATION

Psychoanalysts consulting in organizations should begin their work with a good sense of presenting problems and behave as clinicians do: observe and investigate before drawing conclusions about the underlying pathology and its potential cures.

A young CEO of a business he had inherited from his father called me to ask for consultation. On the telephone he described the source of his referral and then said, "I need a consultant to work on team building in my organization." I told him that team building was not an activity I focused on but that if he cared to describe the problems he and others were experiencing,

I would be glad to meet him and see if I could be of assistance. He agreed to meet. During the meeting, he complained of the inability of two senior executives to work together and cooperate. Cooperation was essential because he had undertaken some outside work that he thought would be of long-range benefit to the corporation. While engaged in this outside activity, he needed a close alliance between these two senior executives. Instead, they appeared to be at odds with each other and relatively uncommunicative with their boss when he appeared in the offices. The CEO then went on to describe the nature of his outside activity and his history in taking over the business from his father. The way he described the current situation and the history suggested that he did not, or could not, make clear to the senior executives the reasons behind his decision to undertake the outside activities. It seemed likely that the CEO had created a leaderless group that set in motion the rivalry between the two senior executives.

Listening to his account of his problems and the history, it became reasonably clear to me that I was faced with a dilemma not of my own making. If I agreed to appear as a consultant and start interviews and other meetings with the two senior executives and the other people in the organization, then I would be in compliance with the CEO's decision to remove himself from the business. It appeared to me as though the CEO wanted his executives to accommodate themselves to his absence, whereas the legitimacy of his absence was questionable. Indeed, I felt that he was running away from his responsibilities. There were many hints about what was behind his apparent abdication, including resentment toward his father for leaving and transferring the business to his son, who felt unprepared for the responsibility. It seemed as though the CEO had repeated actively (leaving the business) what he had endured passively (automatically taking over responsibilities from his father that he experienced as abandonment).

I believed it would be damaging to the CEO if he brought a consultant into the organization. It would reinforce the impression of the CEO's reluctance to take responsibility and fix his image as an absentee leader.

After listening carefully, I asked the CEO what he thought he would do in life if he did not have to run this particular business.

He described with considerable enthusiasm and energy the sort of business he would like to run—which sounded to me very much like the one he had taken over from his father. I told him so. He thought over carefully what I had said and then said that my observation was correct. He really liked the business, had many ideas for its development, but felt ill-prepared for the responsibility. I then said I thought it would be damaging for him to bring me in as a consultant and have me work with senior executives and others to try to bring about cooperative relationships. I said, I thought this was his job, but I recognized that he felt he was not ready for that degree of responsibility. I recommended that he stop his outside activity, return full time to the business, and take psychotherapy to enable him to learn more about his feelings of uncertainty and reluctance to act as chief executive and owner. I offered to refer him to a colleague, who would be prepared to work with him on his conflicts in assuming the leadership of the business. I said that he should think it over and then let me know what he thought of my recommendations. He called me a few days later to say that he and his wife thought my advice was sound, and he asked for a referral. I made the referral. He called months later to report to me that his work was going well, although he had delayed coming back into the business. He found the psychotherapy helpful and he seemed more able and willing to exercise authority in the organization, with some positive results.

As a clinician, I have come to expect of myself the capacity to observe and understand the sort of dynamics affecting situations like this brief case study. My main orientation in consulting with organizations is derived from psychoanalytic ego psychology. Presenting problems vary, as one would expect; therefore it is wise to differentiate among the types of problems presented and the approach to the work with organizations. Given my Weltanschauung, I avoid programmatic activity to bring about cultural changes. I also avoid ideologically driven activity such as efforts to democratize organizations and to increase participation. These activities may be justified by the intent of increasing organizational effectiveness and making work sites more humanistic. However, they go beyond the clinician's abilities to perform, and may even cause harm by the practice of therapeutic zeal in the service of utopian ideals. So far as I have been able to determine, it is possible to solve problems that in the end benefit organizations and people, while still falling short of what might be deemed the best. The clinician's creed is often to seek the good while avoiding the best.

In my experience, it is important to work from the surface, to differentiate problems, and to work in the simplest way possible. The relationship with clients begins with their need for help, not necessarily on their terms, as the example above indicates, but with proper regard for the difficulties they face as they see the situation.

Apart from their acknowledged need for help, the most important foundation for a sound consulting relationship is the client's sense of being understood. Why should anyone seek professional help from an individual with no obvious, clear cut qualifications to provide it?

A corporate chairman and major shareholder called me on the telephone late one Friday afternoon. He wanted my help with a problem that he considered an emergency. With his usual enthusiasm, he had called a meeting of his senior executives, who all reported to the corporation's president and chief operating officer. The chairman had invited the president at the same time that he had asked the other senior executives to come to the meeting. The agenda for this meeting was to consider a product innovation that held promise for the corporation's sales and marketing program. The idea had come to the chairman late in the day, and he could barely hide his impatience in presenting this idea to his management group, including the president.

The meeting took place, but the president did not attend. After the meeting, on the same Friday that I received the call, the president stormed into the chairman's office and accused him of subverting his authority by calling a meeting of people who reported directly to him. The president was so angered at what he considered an abuse of sound organizational principles that he tendered his resignation. The chairman was surprised and upset. He apologized to his president and asked him to take the weekend as a cooling-off period, with the hope that they could re-establish a good working relationship. The president agreed, but left the office. The chairman called him later at home and repeated his apology, his desire for a cooling-off period, and the withdrawal of the president's resignation.

During our telephone conversation, it seemed clear to me that the chairman was reacting largely out of a sense of guilt. In my judgment, it did not seem that the chairman had acted either to subvert the president's authority or to embarrass him. I thought he was probably acting spontaneously out of his excitement over the possibilities of this product innovation. I told him that while I was not sure I understood what was going on, I did not believe that the chairman's action should have been taken as an egregious affront to the president's authority.

The chairman seemed relieved when I said that. He asked me to come to the corporate office as soon as possible to investigate the situation and to offer advice. He said he wanted to call the president to let him know that I would be available for consultation. I agreed and we set a date for my visit.

I conducted individual interviews with the chairman and the president. The results of the interviews with the president are of immediate interest here. He complained bitterly of the chairman's actions, repeating his accusation that organizational principles had been violated. He felt that the chairman should sell his stock in the company and get out, hinting that he and one other executive might be willing to arrange for a leveraged buyout. Spontaneously, he recounted his personal history to show me that he had been accustomed to exercising authority. He had outstripped his older siblings in achievement and had developed a close relationship with his father. The president wanted me to know that his father had become dependent upon him for financial security since he had arranged for a joint investment, excluding his siblings, with some responsibility given to the father in managing the investment, but only under the direction and with the consent of this son.

In his interview with me, the chairman helped me understand why he reacted with guilt upon hearing the president's accusations. The chairman had entered his father's business, which was rather staid and without major prospects for growth. The son began some product development that found a ready market. He had established a platform for business expansion. The father acquiesced to these developments and soon found himself in a financially comfortable situation, but with the realization that his son had assumed the leadership of the business.

I thought the histories of these two men interlocked in a most interesting way. My judgment was that probably the president's accusations had reverberated against unconscious oedipal conflicts in both men, with the more serious immediate stirring of guilt feeling on the part of the chairman. I also concluded that the prognosis for the two men developing a solid working relationship that took account of the real power structure in this business was poor. I did not communicate my thoughts about the potential effects of unresolved oedipal conflicts but instead took the position that the chairman's actions did not present a violation of organizational principles, and that the president took too rigid a stance on the nature of his authority. I explained that the president should have gone to the meeting and should have taken a relaxed position on how authority was distributed between him and the chairman. I also reported my pessimistic prognosis.

After a period of time, the chairman worked out a severance agreement with the president. The chairman asked me to assist him in the selection of a new president and COO. The selection was successfully accomplished and the corporation continued on a path of growth through internal product development and throughout carefully selected acquisitions.

One could reasonably wonder about the movement from dependency to transference in my relationship to the chairman. The dependency was short-lived, driven as it was by guilt feelings. I did not encourage transference reactions simply because I avoided issues having to do with repressed material and underlying anxieties. A psychoanalyst acting as a consultant to organizations has to take a stance in relation to psychic structure. Overwhelmingly, in my judgment, it must be reality that dictates. To follow a path that leads from (perhaps legitimate) dependency to an intense transference relationship as a means of exposing and interpreting unconscious conflict–with all the possible regression that propels one down this path–is to court disaster. I am mindful of the fact that in organizations many people depend upon the financial success of the enterprise for their well-being. Nothing pains me more than to see people face the dire consequences of economic failure. People in positions of power have a responsibility. The aim of the psychoanalytically informed consultation is to help them meet these responsibilities, and to be autonomous. Working from the surface, it is possible to overcome conflicts with rational advice that supports the reality principle to the fullest.

One sometimes observes the spontaneous outbreak of transference in the structure of authority relations. These outbreaks occur through the effects of regression that has taken place as individuals continue to act out disturbances. For example, in one organization where I was called in for consultation, it appeared to me that projective identification was present as a natural consequence of regression well under way. This morbid situation is all too frequently found in family businesses in the relationship between father and son. In this case, after careful observation through interviews, I persuaded the father to enter individual psychotherapy. The results proved to be beneficial. What I had observed was the stress the father endured as a result of his inappropriate idealization of *his* father. He was creating roles for his sons and other subordinates equivalent to the roles of "good son" and "bad son." In turn, he acted out the images of the idealized and the hated father. His behavior and the behavior he elicited were causing severe problems in business and personal relationships.

I succeeded in convincing him to enter therapy by describing in simple language his consistent, but highly charged, behavior and how this behavior served to pull the rug from under the most well-meaning suggestions of his subordinates and family members. Follow-up several years after the consultation indicated a very positive outcome, for which I credit fully the psychotherapy.

A client enlists a consultant with certain positive expectations. These expectations may always contain elements of transference, but they also should be driven by rational motives. It is sensible to engage professionals to help solve problems. Consultants should build on these positive expectations as part of their being a "leader" in the solution of problems. The chief executive of a company came to me for consultation. His complaint was that he felt uncertain about his subordinates' views of him, particularly because the company was facing severe financial problems as a result of losses generated in one division.

It struck me at the time that his first complaint referred to his subordinates' views of him rather than the financial problem, but I said nothing. I also observed during my first meeting with him that he had certain characteristics that I had come to associate with excessive use of alcohol (slurred speech, florid face, and difficulties in remembering), but I did not make any comment or ask him questions about drinking.

He opened the second meeting with me by describing his concerns that he was drinking too much. He told me how much he was drinking, and it was clear to me that it was excessive. I asked him when had he last seen a doctor and urged him to have a physical examination. I also suggested that a valuable way for him to determine the effects of his drinking was for him to stop and see what differenccs he noticed. He agreed to take my advice and I began individual interviews with key executives. I also examined financial information: it was clear there was a crisis. This appeared as a classic case of a nonfunctioning CEO.

I did not take too long a time in completing my interviews and observations. In a written report, I presented a description of the critical condition of the company and recommendations, which included liquidating the division generating losses, restructuring the key management group in order to restore integrity in the authority structure, and consolidating various activities once the liquidation had taken place.

We had several meetings to discuss the report. In subsequent follow-up meetings, it was clear that the CEO had taken my advice and felt that the company and he personally were moving in a favorable direction. Interestingly, he had confided to a close friend that he had sought me out for consultation: the comment came back to me that this close friend was enthusiastic about the initial outcome of the consultation and, later, that it was successful.

Although we could conclude that this client had focused his dependency on to me and, as a result, that I had accomplished a "transference cure," we should also explore the effectiveness of old-fashioned age-old giving advice, in both a personal and professional context.

One of the great pleasures psychoanalysis can offer is the overcoming of confusion by clarity. To discover that a seemingly new phenomenon, like consulting, is historically rooted in some venerable aspects of human relations should be a cause for celebration, because it is an antidote to mystification. It helps from time to time to take a commonsensical view of one's activity. This view may help institute delay when the temptation to interpret the unconscious becomes overwhelming.

Although I am content to position what I have described as the application of ego psychology to organizational consultation within the realm of giving advice, I do not want to appear disingenuous. There is a value-added feature to this kind of psychoanalytic consultation, beyond the giving of advice. I hinted at one aspect of this value-added effect, which is the ability to listen and observe carefully so that the client feels understood.

Another aspect of what ego psychology adds to the practice of consultation is the ability to size up situations, to understand the forces at work as well as to provide an explanation for the relationship between these forces and the presenting problems.

What may be unclear is how one moves from observation and explanation to action. I have argued strongly (and I hope convincingly) that acting on the interpretation of unconscious material is ineffective, if not harmful. The main reasons for this conclusion are, first, that the consultant does not know what unconscious forces are at work and cannot find out in the kinds of relationships established in the organization. Hunches, intuitions, and guesses are not good enough. Second, even if the consultant "knows" about the unconscious in its situational effects, communicating this knowledge runs considerable risks in propelling people along a regressive path. In addition, they will probably be confused, upset, and unable to attend to where the consultation is going. Finally, the clients will come to some preconscious preoccupation with the consultant's intent, because interpretations often appear as bludgeons designed to enhance one's power at the expense of another's.

Having stated all this, it is fair to ask what the connections are between observation and active intervention, following the guidelines of psychoanalytic ego psychology. I know from my experience that this type of consultation involves temporarily assuming responsibility and leadership. The willingness of people to respond positively to this leadership depends upon the degree to which it makes sense to the participants, particularly to those who have considerable power. I have found that despite heated conflict and irrationality, whatever grains of rationality exist create possibilities for altering structures and changing attitudes and perceptions.

I once presented one of my consultation cases to a psychoanalytic study group of which I have been a member for more than 35 years. This group was interested in my uses of psychoanalytic psychology in consultation and they listened willingly to my case presentation. At the conclusion of the meeting, one of my colleagues pointed out to me her perceptions of the actions I took in the consultation. She likened me to a stonemason. This reminded me of an experience I had had with a skilled stonemason and it clarified for me what she meant.

Years ago, I had gone to an older man's house to help him with his gardening. He was preparing a new plot in which he hoped to plant new varieties of vegetables. He was an avid, knowledgeable, and experienced gardener. The job became a very different prospect when we realized there were many rocks to be removed. We lifted some but soon encountered what could only be described as a boulder. We had neither the strength nor the equipment to move it. What could we do? My older friend suggested we clear the earth around the boulder. He then extracted a hammer and chisel from his toolbox. He approached the boulder carefully and eyed it attentively. He placed the chisel at a chosen position on the boulder and almost delicately tapped the chisel with his hammer. The boulder broke into pieces. He repeated this procedure until he had reduced the immovable object to pieces that we could handle.

I believe the analogy is apt. There are certain faults in the structure of human conflict that can be reduced to manageable pieces. Some consultants act as stonemasons, particularly those who work as mediators in resolving conflict. As consultants, psychoanalysts have much to learn from stonemasons about creating human understanding of the conflicts that beset people as they go about their work, while not abandoning the wisdom of common sense.

NOTES

1. This chapter is a revised version of a paper first published in *Psychiatry* (vol. 58, 1995), which appears here with permission of the author.
2. Czander, W.M. (1993). *The Psychodynamics of Work and Organizations: Theory and Applications*. London: Guilford Press.
3. Freud, S. (1910). *Wild Psychoanalysis*. Standard Edition. London: Hogarth Press, p. 225.
4. Bion, W.R. (1961). *Experience in Groups*. New York: Basic Books.
5. Freud, S. (1937). *Analysis terminable and interminable*. Standard Edition. London: Hogarth Press, pp. 216–217.
6. Ibid., p. 250.
7. Bion, W.R. (1961), p. 169.
8. Freud, S. (1921). *Group Psychology and the Analysis of the Ego*. Standard Edition. London: Hogarth Press.
9. Bion, W.R. (1961), pp. 180–181.
10. Ibid., p. 81.

CONCLUSION: TOWARD AUTHENTIZOTIC ORGANIZATIONS

MANFRED F. R. KETS DE VRIES

Far in the sea, to the west of Spain
there is a land we call Cokaygne.
Under God's heaven no other land
has such wealth and goodness to hand.
Though Paradise be merry and bright,
Cokaygne is yet a fairer sight.

—*The Land of Cokaygne*
Middle English Text

DREAMING OF COCKAIGNE

All Dutch and Flemish people have heard of Luilekkerland ("land of milk and honey"). This imaginary country is portrayed in many anecdotes and paintings. One of the most famous–*The Land of Cockaigne* (1567)–was executed by the Flemish artist Pieter Bruegel the Elder. Influenced by his illustrious compatriot Hieronymus Bosch, in this painting Bruegel achieved a creative synthesis of Bosch's demonic symbolism with his own personal vision of human folly and depravity, providing a profound and elemental insight into humankind and its relationship to the world of nature. The painting shows a Renaissance notion of Utopia, in the form of three recumbent figures, seemingly exhausted after having stuffed themselves on a splendid meal. These figures–a knight, a peasant, and a burgher–whose forms radiate outward from the centre of the picture–produce a sensation of dislocation in the spectator, suggesting that this painting may have been intended as a critical commentary on life in the real world at that time.

343

Renowned through legend, oral history, and art, Cockaigne became the most pervasive collective dream of medieval times, an earthly paradise to counter the suffering and frustration of daily existence, allaying anxieties about an increasingly elusive heavenly paradise. It was a peasant's dream, offering respite from backbreaking labor and the daily struggle for scarce food. In this mythical country, which could only be reached by eating one's way through a huge mountain of pudding so tall that it reached the sky, the inhabitants lived in candy houses, their dwellings surrounded by fences of sausages. The trees flowered with sweet, buttered buns. Cooked suckling pigs wandered the streets. The clouds were baked chickens swimming in a delicious sauce. From the heavens fell fabulous French wine. Horses, instead of depositing manure, left the dwellers of this Utopia with stuffed eggs, and donkeys dropped figs. When the inhabitants of Cockaigne opened their mouths, perfectly roasted chickens flew into them. In short, Cockaigne was filled with all the things that people lacked in those days. It was a fantasy land, where extreme luxury, ease, and physical comforts and pleasures were always immediately to hand.

Although utopian longing belongs by definition to the realm of dreams and imagination, it does have a bearing on the real world. Cockaigne–if we take these descriptions at face value–is the place where we should go if we want to be happy simply as human beings, and not supernatural or mythical creatures. It is a place where people feel at their best. In other words, the land of Cockaigne is desirable because it is derived from reality. It could, just possibly, exist–after all, many people have eaten, or at least smelled, a roast chicken. Cockaigne is there just outside our grasp. Because we can *almost* see and taste this Utopia, it enriches our lives with hope and optimism.

The allegory of Cockaigne is useful when applied to the 21st century world of work. It provides an interesting framework in which to ask: what circumstances are needed to make people feel at their best at work? What conditions are required to elicit extraordinary efforts from them? How can we help them gain a sense of hope and optimism in the workplace?

Working as executive educators, coaches, and consultants in organizational settings, we often tackle these questions. For example, we ask our clients: "Imagine a workplace Utopia. It can be different from any organization you may have known until now. What would such a place look like?" Unfortunately, most people do not come up with creative answers. They tend to define the ideal workplace in terms of their current organization. For most of them, the ideal is no more than an incremental improvement of the real. Apparently, people have difficulty imagining organizational architectures that extend very far past the boundaries of the familiar. Why is it that more creative alternatives, as symbolized by the dream of Cockaigne, do not come to mind?

BEING AUTHENTIC

What stifles the creative process when considering alternative ways of making the workplace more attractive? One explanation may be that, for a large group of people, work has traditionally not been perceived as a pleasurable activity. The Old Testament injunction–"By the sweat of your brow you will eat your bread"–highlights the fact that for many, work has associations of pain and suffering. For others, a spirit of delayed gratification means that their goal is material rewards from hard work, even if they kill themselves to get them. Some people are so stressed by working in organizations that they make alternative choices. Many people at lower organizational levels have no choice at all but to submit to the daily grind. But life in organizations does not have to be this way. We can have dreams of Cockaigne in an organizational setting.

In a number of other writings we have introduced the notion of the authentizotic organization.[1] The term authentizotic is derived from two Greek words: *authenteekos* and *zoteekos*. The first part of the word means "authentic," in the broadest sense of the word, signifying something that conforms to fact and is therefore worthy of trust and reliance. In authentizotic organizations people feel alive; people feel at their best and are prepared to make an extraordinary effort. The second part of the term, *zoteekos*, means "vital to life." In an organizational context, this describes the way in which people are invigorated by their work. People in these organizations feel a sense of balance and completeness because their human need for exploration, closely associated with cognition and learning, is met. Authentizotic organizations allow self-assertion in the workplace and produce a sense of self-efficacy and competency, autonomy, initiative, creativity, entrepreneurship, and industry. And although authentizotic organizations only contribute partially to the human happiness equation, their importance should not be discounted.

In present-day society (with a very different, more educated workforce), traditional, autocratic, and hierarchical modes of leadership need to yield to an alternative way of working–one based on values, teamwork, and community. In authentizotic organizations, people are able to enhance their personal growth and development while improving the level of caring and quality both inside and outside their organization. Organizations may make grandiose statements about being great places to work, but slogans are not enough. The challenge for us and our leadership education and coaching clients is to make these statements a reality.

Authentizotic organizations are places where leadership walks the talk. Leaders in these kinds of organizations are authentic; they set an example. As organizational architects, through their vision, mission, culture, and structure, they provide a compelling connective quality. Moreover, leaders in authentizotic organizations do not manage for the short run. On the contrary, they think far beyond day-to-day realities. While they engage in a delicate balancing act between long-term vision and day-to-day operational thinking, they create organizations that last.

Authenticity is defined by *Webster's Dictionary* as "worthy of acceptance or belief as conforming to or based on fact ... not false or imitation ... true to one's own personality, spirit, or character." Being authentic means being genuine, not behaving like a hypocrite. Integrity and trust are implicit elements of this definition.

What do leaders have to do to attain authenticity? What kind of behavior and actions are needed? As our description of the authentizotic organization suggests, this means the opposite of putting up a mask, assuming a false self, or being detached and unreachable. Authentic behavior also implies openness to vulnerability. A leader's public and private persona cannot be at odds; rhetoric and corporate actions must be aligned, and there must be consistency between words and deeds. The actions of these leaders must be meaningful, not based on empty slogans.

Most people can figure out quickly whether a leader's words are authentic or just a simple parroting of the party line. Employees see through empty rhetoric; they know when a leader is truly passionate about a specific issue. And it is this need for congruence between inner and outer reality that makes authentic leadership such a rarity. A truly authentic leader goes beyond the often unavoidable, sometimes unpleasant business realities, and communicates both realities and possibilities in a context of uncompromising honesty.

Although leadership is about results, and although great leadership has the potential to excite people to extraordinary levels of achievement, we need to keep in mind that it is not only about performance, it is very much about values and meaning. Like everyone else, the values of the authentic leader are shaped by personal beliefs, developed, as we have discussed in this book, through the modeling of caregivers, study, introspection, and consultation with others during their lives. These values define an individual's "true north," the deep sense of the right thing to do and guide leaders in creating meaning for their people.

In authentizotic organizations, leaders encourage decentralized, flexible structures with clear lines of communication and values. Authentic leaders know they cannot operate in a vacuum, so people are empowered and given a voice. These leaders work to convince others, rather than coerce compliance. They do not see their employees as cogs in a machine, or as easily replaceable assets. On the contrary, they know that leadership is relational, and that without followers, there can be no leaders.

Authentic leaders establish trusting relationships with people throughout the organization as well as in their personal lives. They recognize that enduring relationships are built on connectedness and a shared purpose of working together toward a common goal. They realize that every person has a life story and wants to share that story with others. And as our teaching, coaching, and consulting experience has convinced us (and has been exemplified throughout this book), it is through the sharing of life stories that we make sense of others. It is the way to develop trust and intimacy. The rewards of this kind of relationship, both tangible and intangible, will be longlasting.

To create authentizotic organizations, leaders must be able to tell a compelling story about the fundamental purpose of the organization, and disseminate with great conviction what the organization is trying to accomplish. Without a clearly articulated purpose, meaning is elusive. And as we have said before, people have a great need for meaning in their working and personal lives.

Furthermore, as they are aware of people's continuing need to explore and experience the world, authentic leaders are talented at providing learning opportunities for their employees, encouraging personal development and self-expression. Authentic leaders believe in the power of collaboration, trust, foresight, listening, and the ethical use of power. In addition, their idea of leadership is not of a great man or woman spouting instructions–they believe in "distributed leadership," i.e., that leaders need to be present at all levels of the organization. And by giving their people the opportunity to fly, to get the best out of them, they create a true community.

Ernest Shackleton, the early 20th century explorer, provides an excellent example of authentic leadership. During his famous expedition to the Antarctic in 1914, he was faced with a terrifying, potentially deadly situation. Unexpectedly, his ship, *Endurance*, was captured by pack ice. During the extended period of constant danger and privation that followed, Shackleton never lost his courage but remained positive and decisive, a state of mind that was of great comfort to his crew. A strong believer in teamwork, he ignored the predominant class system of the time and made everybody pitch in, whatever his place in the pecking order, himself setting the example. Shackleton's mantra of unity and show of humanity turned out to be infectious and helped his men bear the most frightful experiences.

Thanks to Shackleton's authentic leadership style, the 27-man crew of *Endurance* managed to flee the stranded ship to Elephant Island (an ice-covered, mountainous island off the coast of Antarctica) in three small boats. Leaving most of his men on the island, Shackleton and four others succeeded in reaching the southern coast of South Georgia (2,000 kilometers east of Tierra del Fuego) in one of these small boats. From there, Shackleton organized a rescue operation, which included a 1,200 kilometer journey in open boats across the winter Antarctic seas, to bring home the remaining men. It took two years, but Shackleton's sense of responsibility toward his men never wavered. He earned the respect of his crew by being a leader who put his crew's well-being, both mental and physical, above all else. Shackleton embodied the kind of leadership that transcends the common top-down hierarchical and narcissistic style, in favor of collaboration, trust, empathy, and the ethical use of power. As a direct result, although they suffered incredible hardship, all of Shackleton's men survived.

Shackleton understood from the start that trust is earned, not commandeered. He knew that when treated fairly and given hope, people have a great desire to do the right thing and make things better if they can. He also knew that allowing people latitude is the essence of motivation. His previous Antarctic expeditions had taught him that empowerment is not a mere tactic; it is the only way to be sure that people will do their best work. Furthermore, he recognized that people have a great capacity to learn and need to test their new knowledge. Responsibility, not dependency, helped his men to rally, and challenges served them better than boredom. He set the example in working cooperatively toward a shared goal. He also understood the value of communication. He realized that he had to be honest about the decisions he made. He knew that trying to gloss over the gravity of their situation would undermine the morale of his men. He distracted them from the hopelessness of their immediate situation, and instilled confidence in the possibility of one day reaching land, by making sure that each one of them felt important, needed, useful, successful, proud, and respected rather than unimportant, interchangeable, useless, fearful, anonymous, or expendable.

Authentic leaders like Shackleton are rare, however. Many more are attracted not by the opportunity to do something meaningful, but to the power, status, and prestige of leading an organization. Far too many are obsessed by financial rewards. Some of today's CEOs earn 500 times the hourly average wage of their workers. This scale of financial disparity suggests that the efforts of the others in the organization do not count, and that financial success is the prerogative of the boss. Obviously, wage differentials like this do not foster employee confidence or loyalty. The actions and words of these leaders fail to create purpose and meaning. Even worse, these leaders are often isolated at the top, as we mentioned earlier in this book, leaving them at the mercy of their own ego and susceptible to narcissistic pathology.

When leaders are perceived as being inauthentic, trust is undermined. And without trust, people become anxious and fearful. The "containment" role of leadership cannot function. Employees become suspicious; they start to question the leader's motives. These insidious undercurrents sap the energy of any group or organization. The kind of give-and-take and playfulness needed to fuel a creative working environment disappears. The loyalty and camaraderie that provide emotional and spiritual reasons to do one's best die away.

CHALLENGES FOR FACULTY, COACHES, AND CONSULTANTS

In our work as faculty, coaches, and consultants, we have seen far too many organizations that are not particularly healthy, although healthy people are able to work there, at least for a short while. We have seen situations in which toxic, neurotic leaders, over time, make relatively healthy organizations sick.[2] Then there are organizations that are not healthy, but quite attractive to people who are rather unhealthy themselves. On occasion, we see an organization that is basically sound, but the people in it seem to have lost any sense of meaning in their work. And there are many other permutations and combinations.

Throughout this book we have emphasized the responsibility leadership development professionals have to help people grow as individuals, to make them healthier, wiser, and more autonomous. We have also explored how educators and coaches can play an important role in assisting people on a personal transformational journey. In addition, while teaching or coaching, they may help people create enabling environments that will empower them. Furthermore, we have indicated how leadership development professionals can play a pivotal role in building trusting relationships that can become basic platforms for creating commitment and collaboration in organizational life.

A major challenge in leadership education, coaching, and consulting is to help clients deal with the question of authenticity. We need to encourage our clients to discover and operate out of an authentic self, to give them the courage to own up to their mistakes privately and publicly when appropriate, to embolden them to seek input from a diversity of people when involved in problem resolution, and to consider constructive feedback in the spirit of personal growth. We need to demonstrate that when a leader operates out of authenticity, there is less need for defensiveness and greater willingness to take responsibility for one's actions. The client needs to be encouraged to focus on what is or is not working rather than on being right or wrong. Helping clients to develop their emotional intelligence and appreciate different styles and expressions will assist them in their relationships, and the coordination of complex tasks and projects. It will help them expand their sense of well-being and trust in the world around them. If done correctly, it will contribute to a highly creative and highly committed organizational culture.

Simple, powerful truths about how to lead people more effectively, about how to change the nature of work, and about redefining our roles in the workplace have been around for a long time. For decades, management scholars such as Maslow, McGregor, Argyris, Bennis, Zaleznik, and others have consistently described more enlightened ways to lead people and design organizations.[3] In fact, it is curious that despite the consistency of these messages and the ubiquity of these views, leaders continue to "talk" a better game of leadership than they "play." The written word seems to have had only a limited effect. As we have discovered in feedback sessions, all too many leaders are better at making good presentations about their enlightened leadership style than at delivery of the real thing. Time after time we have noted that few challenges are as difficult for a leader as examining their own and others' behavior patterns, and finding better ways to organize for whatever the organization plans to accomplish. But that is exactly what is required.

In our roles as faculty, coaches, and consultants, we have put an enormous amount of energy into helping our clients unlearn many of their past practices. We have made great efforts to present them with compelling reasons for change. We have designed (as many chapters in this book show) a number of highly successful intervention techniques that have helped us anticipate and deal with the resistance that is encountered when

351

the best knowledge available differs from the basic assumptions that support the past successes of our clients.

In the past, organization and leadership development scholars and practitioners focused almost exclusively on external measures of achievement, paying little attention to the inner theater of their clients. They did so at their own peril. Too little thought was given to people's inner capacities of emotional intelligence, intuition, wisdom, and compassion. This has not made for effective, sustainable organizations. Their outlook is a recipe for managing for economic decline.

The approach taken by the contributors to this book has been quite different. We are committed to theory in action and believe strongly that a theory with few practical implications can quickly turn into a sterile exercise. Ivory towers have no place in management. In whatever we do, we like to influence people and organizations positively. We want to create "best places" in which to work. We want organizations to change for the better.

All the contributors to this book have been selected because of their effectiveness as change agents. All have demonstrated practically what needs to be done to get people and organizations to move. All of them would go out on a limb to get the best out of the people they work with. It is in this spirit of moving forward constructively that we hope this book will make a small contribution to helping others learn from experience and from one another.

We would also like to think that this book will contribute to changes in leadership philosophy. We realize that we are standing on the shoulders of giants; that many before us have advocated philosophies of a similar nature concerning the workplace. But this does not mean that we have to give up our dreams. In spite of regressive forces in society, in spite of organizational alienation, we strongly believe that authentic leadership can be an antidote to the toxicity found in too many organizations. It is through authentic leadership that people can find a land of milk and honey in the workplace.

We believe emphatically that when people are happy in their organization, it has a positive effect on the bottom line. Our organizational Cockaigne is not lurking in some Cloud Cuckoo Land. It can be found in the here and now. Authentizotic organizations peopled by authentic leaders are the ones that will last, and be most successful. As educators, coaches, and consultants, we hope that this book will make a small contribution to the building of more effective, more human, and happier organizations.

NOTES

1. Kets de Vries, M.F.R. and Balazs, K. (1999). Creating the "Authentizotic" Organization: Corporate Transformation and its Vicissitudes–A Rejoinder, *Administration & Society*, 21 (2), 275–294; Kets de Vries, M.F.R. (2006). *The Leader on the Couch*. London: Wiley.
2. Kets de Vries, M.F.R. and Miller, D. (1984). *The Neurotic Organization*. San Francisco, CA: Jossey-Bass.
3. Maslow, A. (1954). *Motivation and Personality*. New York: Harper; McGregor, D. (1960). *The Human Side of Enterprise*. New York: McGraw-Hill; Argyris, C. (1960). Understanding Organizational Behavior. Homewood, IL: Dorsey; Bennis, W.G. (1973). *Beyond Bureaucracy*. New York: McGraw-Hill; Bennis, W.G. (1997). *Leaders: The Strategies for taking Charge*. New York: Harper Business; Zaleznik, A. (1966). *Human Dilemmas of Leadership*. New York: Harper Collins.

INDEX